Jan M. G. Kleinpenning
The Brazilian Amazonia in Change I

Biblioteca Luso-Afro-Brasileira | Volume 3

Editorial

The Biblioteca Luso-Afro-Brasileira is a publication series of the Ibero-Amerikanischen Instituts Preußischer Kulturbesitz, in which monographs and collections on literature, culture, language, history, economics and politics from the Portuguese-speaking countries are published. The series is multidisciplinary and open to cross-regional and comparative research. The languages of publication are Portuguese, English and German. All publications in this series are subject to a peer-review process.

Jan M.G. Kleinpenning, born in 1936, is a professor emeritus of human geography of developing countries at the University of Nijmegen, The Netherlands. His research focused on the geography of Brazil, Paraguay, Uruguay and Spain.

Jan M. G. Kleinpenning

The Brazilian Amazonia in Change I

Opening Up and Colonisation in the 1970s

[transcript]

Bibliographic information published by the Deutsche Nationalbibliothek
The Deutsche Nationalbibliothek lists this publication in the Deutsche Nationalbibliografie; detailed bibliographic data are available in the Internet at https://dnb.dnb.de

First published in 2025 by transcript Verlag, Bielefeld

transcript Verlag | Hermannstraße 26 | D-33602 Bielefeld | live@transcript-verlag.de

Cover concept: Maria Arndt, Bielefeld
Cover illustration: Photo by Jan M. G. Kleinpenning
Proofread: Patricia Schulze
Typeset: Patricia Schulze
Printed by Elanders Waiblingen GmbH, Waiblingen
Print-ISBN 978-3-8376-7536-8
PDF-ISBN 978-3-8394-7536-2
https://doi.org/10.14361/9783839475362
ISSN of series: 2752-1990
eISSN of series: 2752-1419

Printed on permanent acid-free text paper.

Contents

Preface 11

Foreword to Volume 1 13

About this book 15

Part 1: The Brazilian Amazon up to the 1970s

The Amazon area up to the rubber period 19
The rubber period 20
Developments in the agricultural sector in the early twentieth century 23
The traditional economy 25
Expansion of mining 25
A weak economy 26
Population size and distribution 27
References 32

Part 2: The Brazilian Amazon in the 1970s. How integration began

Introduction 35

Motives underlying the development policy 39
Economic motives 39
Nationalistic and political motives 47
Concluding remarks 52

Some development measures of the 1970s 55
The establishment of SUDAM 55
Financial incentives 56
The establishment of a free trade zone 57
The Rondon project 58

Increasing research activities ... 59
The extensive opening-up programme ... 60

Provisional evaluation of the effects of some development measures ... 67
The developments in the Manaus free trade zone ... 67
The results of the industrialisation policy ... 73
The expansion of large-scale livestock farming ... 76
The expansion of tropical tree and shrub crops ... 84
The development of forestry ... 85
The developments in the mining sector ... 86
The effect of the development measures discussed above. Summary ... 87
The danger of an increasing dependence on foreign countries ... 89
The criticism of the road building plans ... 90

The colonisation plans and the objections to them ... 93
The origin of the colonisation plans ... 93
The objections to the colonisation plans ... 94
Earlier colonisation activity in the Amazon region: government supervision ... 98
Conclusions: The reaction of the Brazilian government to the criticisms of its colonisation policy ... 102

The progress of the colonisation sponsored by the INCRA ... 105
The zone along the Cuiabá-Santarém highway ... 105
Landownership problems ... 109
Conclusion ... 114

The Altamira I Colonisation Project ... 115
The colonisation process ... 115
A provisional assessment ... 134
Conclusion ... 143

The plans for encouraging medium-sized farms ... 147

The development measures of the period from 1974 to 1976 ... 149
The road building programme ... 149
Development of a modern, large-scale agriculture and forest exploitation ... 149
Development of mining ... 150
The role of large enterprises in the development of the primary sector ... 152
The government contribution to the development of the primary sector ... 152
The revised policy relating to colonisation projects ... 154
Conclusion ... 155

Conclusions. Looking back and looking ahead ... 159
Retrospect ... 159
The advantages for the South East ... 159
The advantages for the North East ... 160

The dangers to the natural environment 164
The dangers for the Indigenous population 166
Conclusion 168

References 169

Part 3: Case studies from the early 1980s

Changes in population size and distribution during the 1970s 183
The development measures after 1960 183
Aim and framework of the analysis 186
Changes in the relative position of the Amazon region within Brazil 187
Explanation of the relatively feeble attractiveness of Amazônia Legal 189
Population increase per state or territory 191
Population changes at the meso- and micro-regional levels 195
Aspects of the urbanisation process 205
Conclusions 209
Statistical sources employed 211
References 211

The development of Altamira, before and after the construction of the Transamazônica 213
Ron Milder

Altamira up to the late 1960s 213
Altamira in 1970 216
Changes due to the construction of the Transamazônica 217
Polamazônia. Large scale and privatisation (1974–1980) 220
The rise of large-scale retail and wholesale trade 226
Transport and services 227
Government policy in the early 1980s 228
Modern extractivism and the alternative energy supply (1980–1984) 231
Altamira's altered functional structure (1980–1985) 233
To conclude 234
References 234

In memory of Orlando Valverde and Hilgard O'Reilly Sternberg,
eminent Brazilian geographers and pioneers in research in the Amazon region.

Preface

In over 50 years, the Brazilian Amazonia has experienced man-made destruction of natural resources and the livelihoods of the Indigenous population. In the 1970s, the Military Government granted private capital almost unlimited access to rain forest areas in the planning region Amazônia Legal with generous financial incentives, after the state-led colonisation of landless people remained unsuccessful. The exploitation of the Amazon's ecosystems for the extraction of mineral resources, large-scale livestock farming and national integration measures was carried out without regard for the Indigenous people and regional socio-ecological vulnerability, contrary to the warnings of scientists and NGOs.

Tropical biodiversity and Indigenous areas were seen as obstacles to economic progress. The government's neglect of sustainable development and the inadequate coordination of state and private projects at federal, regional and local level led to high subsequent costs and robbed the marginalised population of their livelihoods.

Later governments have also implemented administratively inefficient and socio-ecologically damaging mega-programmes (including the Grande Carajás programme and hydropower plants with large reservoirs) with disastrous environmental impacts.

The internationally funded Pilot Programme to conserve the Brazilian tropical rain forests (PPG7) started some significant environmental policy improvements for sustainable development but was not deepened by follow-up programmes. Extensive infrastructure projects (including the Cuiabá–Santarém highway) aimed at a conservative modernisation and attracted southern Brazilian soybean farmers, whose activities also expanded into the humid savannahs in the south-east of the region. The often violent conflicts of interest between the social actors operating on the pioneer front remained unresolved and Indigenous territories, conservation units and protected areas remained at risk.

During the Bolsonaro government, deforestation increased rapidly and environmental institutions were brought to a virtual standstill. Violence and chaos became omnipresent.

Tropical forest ecosystems are a huge CO_2 reservoir. To date, around 20 % of the Brazilian rain forests have been cleared, mostly illegally, and a further 20 % are severely degraded. A socio-ecological transformation process and good local governance are only just beginning to emerge. The elimination of violence, illegality and corruption is still outstanding. The demand from industrialised countries for the supply of cheap raw materials and agricultural commodities is endangering Amazônia Legal without bringing any added value for the majority of its 28 million inhabitants.

The new government of Lula da Silva is facing the great challenge of a fundamental turnaround with the final renunciation of deforestation and the goals of sustainable development and environmental justice in Amazonia.

Large-scale destruction of biodiversity, rising temperatures and instability of precipitation not only pose a threat to the region, but also cause global impacts related to climate change. Over the last two decades, Amazônia Legal has evolved from a CO_2 sink to a source of CO_2 emissions. A deforestation rate of 20–25 % marks a tipping point at which rain forests will turn into non-forest ecosystems (humid savannahs). This "point of no return" could be imminent.

The publication *The Brazilian Amazonia in change* by Jan M.G. Kleinpenning (Professor of Human Geography of Developing Countries at the University of Nijmegen, The Netherlands) and Gerd Kohlhepp (Professor of Economic and Social Geography; formerly Latin American Research Centre at Tübingen University, Germany) is organised in two volumes:

Vol. 1: **Jan M.G. Kleinpenning**: *The Brazilian Amazonia in change I. Opening up and colonisation in the 1970s*

Vol. 2: **Gerd Kohlhepp**: *The Brazilian Amazonia in change II. Five decades of exploitation, deforestation and attempts at sustainable development*

Jan M.G. Kleinpenning and Gerd Kohlhepp

Foreword to Volume 1

When I decided to integrate and republish my texts from the 1970s and early 1980s on developments in the Brazilian Amazon, I realized that there would be an interest not only in how the large-scale opening and exploitation of the area started at the time, but especially in the major changes that Amazonia has gone through to this day. I therefore decided to approach my colleague Gerd Kohlhepp with the question whether he could provide an overview of developments in the past four to five decades. He immediately responded positively and ensured that there was a very complete, very detailed and up-to-date Magnum Opus about the occupation history of Brazilian Amazonia. Volume Two of this book is proof of this, for which I am very grateful.

Several people helped me prepare the manuscript for Volume One, the first part of this book.

My daughter Petra improved the digitized files, gave the bibliography a more professional design and adapted the text, which originally dealt with current affairs, but now intends to offer a historical retrospective.

Robert Symonds corrected the English, at least to the extent necessary, because he translated all my writings on the Amazon from Dutch into English as long ago as the 1970s and early 1980s.

Margot Stoete digitized and embellished the maps and other figures.

Ron Milder helped me write the chapter on the changes the town of Altamira has undergone since the construction of the Transamazon Highway.

I am very grateful to all of them for their help and cooperation.

I also particularly appreciated the immediate willingness of the Ibero-Amerikanisches Institut in Berlin to publish the book and include it in the institute's series of publications. I thank Dr. Peter Birle for his support and I am most grateful to Patricia Schulze for carefully preparing the final manuscript.

Odijk/Harlingen, June 2024 — Jan M. G. Kleinpenning

About this book

It is now – in 2022 – half a century ago that the first section of the Transamazônica was opened. And it was also fifty years ago that a start was made with a rapid and complete economic conquest of the Brazilian North, once the "green hell" and the "demographic vacuum." It is now time to look back at how the process of integration started, to assess the results of later developments and to give a picture of the current situation. In other words, it is time for another book on Amazônia.

Jan Kleinpenning, then Professor of Human Geography of Developing Countries at the University of Nijmegen, The Netherlands, was one of the many scholars who started to concern themselves in the 1970s with the attempts of the Brazilian government to stimulate the development of the Amazon region and to integrate it more closely into the national economy. He carried out field research in the area in 1973 and 1976 and has now adapted the publications which first appeared in the 1970s and integrated them into one document, which forms the content of Part 2 of this book. This re-editing of texts is intended to give a retrospective summary of how the integration and colonisation of the Brazilian Amazon started.

Part 3 of the book contains an adapted version of two case studies from the early 1980s: The first one is a chapter that Jan Kleinpenning wrote on population change in the Amazon region in the period 1970–1980, and the second is a summary of parts of Ron Milder's Master's thesis on the town of Altamira, before and after the building of the Transmazônica. Both studies further illustrate the developments that took place during the initial phase of large scale colonisation of the Amazon area.

Part 1 includes a summary of the development of the Brazilian Amazon up to 1970 and is intended to give a background for the parts of this volume which are concerned with the subsequent period.

In Volume 2 – *Five decades of exploitation, deforestation and attempts at sustainable development*– Gerd Kohlhepp gives a detailed assessment of five decades of state-controlled and private exploitation, deforestation, mega-projects and attempts at sustainable development.

This book has become a sad history of what has happened in the Brazilian North during the past fifty years. It tells how use, misuse, plunder and deforestation have changed the largest tropical rain forest area in the world. Sometimes, sad histories have to be written.

Part 1: The Brazilian Amazon up to the 1970s

The Amazon area up to the rubber period

Under the Treaty of Tordesillas, only the mouth of the Amazon belonged to the territory to which the Portuguese crown could lay a claim. All the territory west of it fell to Spain. The Spaniard Orellanos was the first to explore the river in 1541. However, he did not go further. The Spaniards soon became so preoccupied with the Andean and Pacific coast that they had little or no interest in the Amazon basin, which was difficult to reach from the western side of the continent. The Portuguese, too, initially showed little interest in the dense jungle with its flooding during the rainy season that stretched beyond the mouth of the river. The Indigenous peoples who mainly lived near the rivers depended on hunting, fishing, gathering and practising shifting cultivation. They had reached a relatively low level of civilisation. In any event, states had not been formed and great riches were not to be had. Portugal nevertheless, thanks to a lack of interest on the part of the Spanish, gradually laid an increasingly clear claim to the area. They did not want to lose it to the Netherlands, England or any other European power. A small number of Portuguese from São Luis therefore settled in Belém in 1615 and founded a mission post near this place in 1616.

In the seventeenth and eighteenth centuries, the settlement of immigrants from the Azores was promoted in the vicinity of Belém. After the foundation of Belém, the expeditions to collect cocoa, medicinal plants, macaws, parrots and the like increased, and with them the contacts with the natives. Especially from then on, the latter also experienced the ill effects of infectious diseases and slave hunts.

The attempts of missionaries to further develop the Amazon region with the involvement of the Indigenous population testified to a more constructive approach. In the seventeenth century, the Jesuits managed to gather many Indigenous people along the rivers in mission stations, where they taught them, converted them to Catholicism and led them to a more sedentary existence. Places such as Santarém, Obidos and Manaus owe their origin to the fact that they were once mission posts. The fathers not only encouraged the cultivation of crops for which there were markets in Europe, but also the collection of various forest products. In the mid-eighteenth century, the Jesuit missions exported significant quantities of cocoa, vanilla, cloves, indigo, wood and aromatic resins. The activities of the Jesuits were so successful that Pará managed to acquire a large degree of autonomy within the Portuguese colony.

Missionary activities also had drawbacks, such as a faster spread of infectious diseases and the fact that the Indigenous people could more easily fall into the hands of slave hunters. This last danger became real especially after 1759, when the work of the Jesuits throughout the Portuguese Empire came to an end and the Indigenous peoples had to do without their protection. Many mission stations fell into decay or even completely ceased to exist. In the eighteenth century, more than 100 000 Indigenous people are said to have lived in mission stations in northern Brazil, but in 1825 the total population of the Brazilian Amazon was estimated at less than 40 000 people.

In the second half of the eighteenth century, agriculture was stimulated not only in Maranhão, but also in the area near Belém, to compensate for the declining gold mining in Minas Gerais. The trading company founded by Pombal was also active. Near Belém plantations were established that produced crops such as sugar cane, cocoa, rice, cotton and coffee. At the end of the eighteenth century, no less than 30 000 slaves of African descent were brought in for plantation agriculture. Many died as a result of diseases and ill-treatment. In the longer term, commercial agriculture proved unable to compete with that of the better organised farms elsewhere in the colony. As a result, agricultural activity gradually became increasingly limited to some shifting cultivation, mainly for self-sufficiency, and to a rather irregular gathering economy. In the mid-nineteenth century there were only a limited number of plantations of coffee, tobacco and citrus near the mouth of the Amazon, which did not provide great prosperity for their owners. The island of Marajó opposite Belém was used for cattle breeding. The cattle grazed there on the moist savannas and had to survive in the wet season that flooded part of the island. Elsewhere in the Amazon, savannas were also used for livestock farming during the dry season.

After 1875 new attempts at colonisation were made in the area east of Belém to near the border of Marahão. The main intention was to create a zone of nurturing agriculture and livestock for the city of Belém, which was experiencing a strong population growth thanks to the rise of rubber gathering. In view of this, the construction of a railway to Bragança was started in 1883 and completed in 1908. Most of the state-established colonies did not flourish. Many settlers (partly from abroad) left because the colonies were poorly governed and insufficient guidance was given.

After the severe drought that occurred in Northeastern Brazil in 1915, the area experienced spontaneous colonisation of *nordestinos* who tried to find a more favourable habitat. In the area of Belém–Bragança, they not only found land on which to practice subsistence farming, but also an environment that still showed a certain resemblance to the Northeast (at dry season). The local population growth also stimulated colonisation. As a result, the area between Belém and Bragança became a relatively densely populated zone. In the 1960s, densities of between 15 and 20 per km^2 were to be found. It was then one of the few regions where activity was not limited to collecting forest products, but where arable colonisation had taken place on a relatively large scale in the past. The area had benefited greatly from its proximity to Belém, which had been a collection point for all kinds of Amazon products from its foundation and also functioned as a distribution centre, from where the settlements upstream were supplied. Particularly after 1870, the city saw a sudden growth in its function as a collection and distribution centre as a result of the rubber boom. This created an urban market for the sale of agricultural surpluses.

The rubber period

In the second half of the nineteenth century it seemed as if Northern Brazil would play an important role in the world economy. After the invention of vulcanisation, rubber got more and more applications and the Amazon region turned out to be the only area where the *Hevea brasiliensis* (rubber tree) occurred. Rich extraction areas were mainly located south of the main river and to the west. A monopoly position seemed assured. This was all the more true since Brazil had the advantage that the Amazon was navigable all year round for seagoing vessels as far as Peru and that many tributaries could also be used by shipping.

The growing demand for rubber awakened the entrepreneurial spirit present in many Brazilians. Speculators, in possession of capital, managed to purchase large areas of forest in the Amazon region or acquired the right to exploit the existing rubber trees. Gradually they organised the tapping of rubber trees on an increasingly large scale.

A North American colony

Shortly after the end of the North American Civil War a group of people from the Southern States of the United States, desiring to continue under a regime of slavery, established a settlement not far from Santarém, bringing their slaves and tools with them. In the 1870s this group was visited by a North American traveller who found it filled with pioneer zeal, enthusiastically engaged in clearing the forest and planting cotton and sugar cane. But the place selected for the colony was too remote. Although steamboats sailed the Amazon after 1866, making Santarém a regular port of call, the cost of transporting the small volume of cotton or sugar to distant markets and of importing essential articles, was so great that the North American colony near Santarém was almost entirely cut off from the outside world. No occidental pioneer colony which remains in isolation has been successful in the modern period, whether in the Amazon or elsewhere. Today, only a few impoverished families remain, and these have lost the optimism which is the chief strength of the successful pioneer (James 1969, 840–841).

Labour power was initially a problem. The Indigenous people were few and unwilling or unfit to serve as rubber tappers, and slaves of African descent were difficult to employ in self-employed work in the jungle. Moreover, the import of slaves was already forbidden. That is why the operators mainly tried to recruit their workers from the (*mestizo*) population of the nearby Northeast. When catastrophic droughts occurred there at the end of the 1870s, this recruitment was no longer a difficult matter. Tens of thousands of *nordestinos* moved to the Amazon region to find a new living as rubber tappers. After that, the gradually emerging migration tradition and some new droughts ensured that new workers regularly became available. It is estimated that, in total, about 300 000 *nordestinos* came to the Amazon region in the period 1870–1910. Among them were many residents of Ceará.

The workers did not gain much from collecting. The entire rubber extraction activity was soon completely controlled by landowners, concessionaires and merchants, who made good profits.

The workers led a hard and poor life. After being recruited in one of the towns and committing themselves to rubber tapping for a period of time, they were dropped off along one of the rivers with some food and the necessary equipment. Since the rubber trees in general were widely spread, the extraction became a labour-intensive affair. The collected latex had to be evaporated over wood fires, after which it was collected at regular intervals by the traders. On those occasions the tappers were provided with fresh food and other necessities. They were almost never paid in money; the rubber was taken in exchange for goods. Many *seringueiros* began with debt because they could not pay for the necessities for their initial stay themselves. Most traders abused their position and supplied relatively few items in exchange for significant quantities of latex. Many tappers only got deeper into debt. The copious consumption of liquor caused a lot of financial problems. The tappers had little or no additional resources; most lacked the time and energy to practise some subsistence farming. On balance, the earnings were small, the tappers were deprived of all comfort, and had to contend with diseases and the dangers of the tropical jungle. Many perished; their places were taken by other *nordestinos*.

In the period 1820–1830 Brazil exported less than 50 tons of rubber. In the years 1860–1870 the amount had increased to 4 000 tons and in the years 1908–1910 an average of 38 600 tons per year was exported. Rubber supplied more than a third of the total value in exports at the time, making it an important source of foreign exchange.

After 1910, the golden age quickly came to an end. As early as 1876, Wickham had smuggled rubber seed from Brazil so that rubber plantations could be established in Southeast Asia. These started to produce rubber at a much more favourable price and were much better able to meet the growing demand. While the wild rubber trees yielded on average no more than 1.5–2 kg of rubber per year, the Southeast Asian plantations achieved yields of 5 kg or more, thanks to better tapping methods and better care. The more favourable cost price also arose because the vegetation in the tropical rainforest is heterogeneous in composition. Rubber trees stand among many other trees, leaving one worker in the Amazon region unable to tap more than about 200 trees. On the plantations, on the other hand, only one worker was needed for 500 trees. In densely populated monsoon Asia, a large number of suitable workers was fairly easy to find, while recruitment for the Amazon region was much more difficult. It soon became clear that Brazil's initially strong market position could not be permanent.

In 1910 the plantations of Malacca and Sumatra still produced only 10 % of the rubber, in 1922 it was already 93 %. The Amazon region was eliminated as a significant producer in a short time. The Brazilians had failed to establish plantations. The desire to get rich quickly and easily was paramount and many thought that the Amazon basin was only suitable for a gathering economy. The money earned was mainly spent on consumption (such as for the construction of an opera house) and not for investment in improving the rubber sector and certainly not in diversifying the economy. Even the expansion of agriculture remained very modest. Brazil lost unique development opportunities.

The direct result of the boom was a significant increase in population. In addition to hundreds of thousands of *nordestinos*, Brazilians from other regions moved to the North, and foreigners also settled there. In 1872 the North had 333 000 inhabitants, in 1900 that had increased to about 695 000 and in 1920 to 1.439 million.

Of the towns, Belém and Manaus grew in particular. For the first time, these cities took on real significance and even a cosmopolitan character, becoming abodes of Brazilian and foreign rubber entrepreneurs. The extracted rubber was brought mainly to these two cities and they also became the main distributors of foodstuffs and other necessities. Manaus would exercise this trade function for only part of the North, but Belém for the entire Amazon basin. In 1872 only 62 000 people lived in the entire municipal area of Belém, in 1920 there were already 236 400. The municipality of Manaus saw the population more than triple from 29 300 to 75 700 during the same period. The growth was accompanied by a remarkable modernisation and embellishment. Both cities were among the first to be provided with electricity and early on with public transport. Many public facilities were realised by British companies. Manaus still has a large opera house from that time. The port then had the largest floating quay in the world, at which ocean-going vessels could load and unload all year round.

Rubber extraction did not create an extensive network of roads and railways. The dense vegetation and periodic flooding were a hindrance and the rivers were good communication routes. There were only simple country roads where land transport was necessary to avoid the falls and rapids. Furthermore, small roads led upstream from the points where the tributaries became navigable. The location of the newly emerged settlements was mainly determined by the waterways. They arose, *inter alia*, at the confluence of the rivers and at those points where the rivers became navigable.

Brazil's rubber economy collapsed after World War I. The strong population growth came to an end: large numbers of *nordestinos* no longer came to Amazônia and part of the economically stronger population moved away. In the period 1920–1940, the population of the North increased only from 1.439 million to 1.462 million. Many capable people left for the Southeast. In Acre, which had been heavily dependent on the rubber economy, the population fell from 92 379 in 1920 to 79 768 in 1940.

Those former rubber tappers who did not leave the region were forced to switch to subsistence farming or to collect other products. A number of them moved to the small towns, where employment was limited, so that open and hidden unemployment increased, (larger) slums were created, and the public service apparatus was overloaded because it could not be expanded and modernised sufficiently through a lack of capital. Many small settlements saw their population decline, even entire villages and workers' encampments disappeared.

In the 1920s and 1930s, the Ford car company tried to set up several large rubber plantations to supply its own company. However, the plantations faced several difficulties. The whole experiment was ultimately unsuccessful.

Such rubber as was produced on a few plantations in the 1960s was entirely for the domestic market. In 1970 Brazil produced no more than 35 000 tons of natural rubber, only a few percent of the world total. Pará, Amazonas and Acre supplied about 90 % of Brazil's natural rubber. The country was unable to meet domestic needs in the early 1960s, which is why the Brazilian government decided to plant two million rubber trees in 1973, but we shall enlarge on this elsewhere.

Developments in the agricultural sector in the early twentieth century

During and after the Second World War, the agricultural sector underwent a modest but certainly not insignificant development, thanks to Japanese immigrants. They had settled in the Amazon after 1920 and, in the 1930s, focused on jute and pepper cultivation. After some experimentation, they were so successful with this that cultivation expanded quite quickly. Non-Japanese people also started to focus on production. In the 1960s, jute and pepper were among the most important commercial crops. The value of each of those products exceeded that of the collected rubber.

The pepper culture was concentrated entirely on *terra firme* (non-floodable soils) in the vicinity of Belém and Manaus. However, the area near Belém was by far the most important. About 90 % of the pepper production took place in the state of Pará, where pepper was the main agricultural crop. The Japanese colony of Tomé Açu, which had been founded in the 1920s about 200 km south of Belém and which had become heavily involved in pepper production, especially after the Second World War, supplied no less than two thirds of the Brazilian harvest in the 1960s. Total Brazilian production had increased to 14 522 tons in 1970, while in 1952 it had been only 350 tons. The production not only covered the national need; most of it could even be exported. The success was due mainly to the intensive way in which the Japanese had devoted themselves to cultivation. They obtained high yields. They also started to keep poultry and other animals, so they were not forced to buy expensive fertilizers. All manure was produced in-house. The level of prosperity achieved by the Japanese was considerably higher than that of the average northern Brazilian farmer.

The jute culture was practised entirely on the *várzeas* (periodically flooded grounds). Initially, cultivation was also mainly an activity of the Japanese, but gradually they withdrew and left the fairly heavy work on the flooded fields to Brazilians. However, the Japanese continued to play an important role in the trade and processing of jute. Commercial production became significant only in the 1940s, but by 1970 it had already risen to about 60 000 tons, thanks in part to the government distributing seed and giving cultivation instructions. From 1953 Brazil was able to meet its own needs, and export to other South American countries was also possible. The area west of Manaus was the main production zone, the state of Amazonas supplying about three quarters of the national harvest; the rest came from Pará. Modern factories in the cities along the Amazon (Belém, Santarém and Manaus) processed the fibres.

Japanese settlers also introduced various Asian fruits, showed that it was lucrative to sow pasture grasses on the low *várzea* soils and to use the artificial meadows thus formed for breeding water buffalos. In addition, they started to focus on raising poultry and growing horticultural crops to supply the cities, especially near Belém and Manaus. They also introduced wet rice cultivation on a limited scale and showed that rice grown in that way gives much higher yields than that grown without irrigation. The Japanese numbered less than ten thousand, but all in all they made an important contribution to the development of the agricultural economy. They had also settled along the Belém–Brasília road at the time and managed to build a decent life in the cities.

The Japanese settlers owed their success to the fact that they formed a select group that had greater agricultural knowledge than the average Brazilian settler (mainly from the Northeast), that they applied intensive production methods, received support from the mother country and the Brazilian government, had perseverance, set up cooperatives and were able to establish themselves as independent farmers with Japanese or Brazilian support and thus did not become dependent on landowners. All this could not always be said of the *nordestinos* who spontaneously settled in the Amazon region.

After the Second World War, the cultivation of malva, a weed that sprang up spontaneously on the cleared lands, also started. It turned out to have fibres that are better than those of the jute in several respects. The Belém–Bragança area became the main production area and malva even became one of the main commercial crops there. In this zone there were quite a few depleted plots that turned out to be suitable only for malva cultivation. Production had also expanded southwards along the Belém–Brasília road in the 1960s. The emerging production of synthetic fibres was already a threat to the cultivated ones at that time.

The traditional economy

The production of pepper, jute and malva was an activity of only a small part of the agricultural labour force. In the 1960s, the emphasis was on traditional rural livelihoods. Simple arable farming, extensive livestock farming and the collection of forest products employed 57 % of the labour force.

Arable farming consisted largely of shifting cultivation, was practised on small areas by *caboclos* (*mestizos*) and Indigenous people and was primarily aimed in many cases at self-sufficiency. Corn, manioc, beans and rice were the main crops. The *roças* (cultivations) in most areas formed only small enclaves in the vast jungle. Typically they were used only for two to three years, after which a new piece of land was cleared. The practitioners of shifting cultivation lacked capital and knowledge for more intensive agriculture and did not always feel the need to do so, because large areas of forest were still available for clearing. To the extent that arable farming took place on the *várzeas*, there was often a more permanent use, at least during the period of the year when the water level allowed it. The *várzea* farmers were also generally not very prosperous.

Cattle farming was limited. In the 1960s, no more than 2 % of Brazil's livestock was located in the North. Livestock farming took place largely on the savannas, which were found mainly in the higher parts of the Amazon basin (especially near the border with Venezuela and Guyana). The *campos de várzea* near the rivers were also used for livestock farming, but here the livestock had to be moved to pastures on the *terra firme* during the wet season or to be stabled on large platforms. The island of Marajó has long been an important cattle ranching area. The low parts were flooded during the wet season, so that evacuation was necessary here too. In the 1960s it had already become quite common to use the *várzeas* more for the raising of water buffalos. Livestock farming was generally at a low level. The *fazendeiros* were fairly prosperous; the people tending the livestock, on the other hand, were poor.

The collection of forest products, such as fruits, aromatic plants, rubber, oilseeds and precious hides, was widely practised. The buyers and their trading posts were to be found at the confluence of rivers, at points where they became navigable, and in the towns. Many merchants had acquired a monopoly position and also supplied all kinds of goods. An important part of the collecting and distributing trade was in the hands of Brazilians of Syrian and Lebanese origin. The collectors were poor, simple peasants who depended on the merchants to whom they were often in debt. Collecting was for some the main activity, for others a secondary activity next to arable farming.

Timber exploitation was traditionally also a collecting activity. Tree cutters went in search of suitable trees; planting did not take place. The wood was processed mainly by small companies. This started to change only in the 1950s and 1960s.

Expansion of mining

After the Second World War, not only commercial arable farming expanded, but also mining. Rich deposits of manganese ore had been discovered in the Serra do Navio in Amapá, and their exploitation began in the 1950s. A railway line was built between the inland mines and the Port of Macapá, port facilities were upgraded and energy supplies increased. In 1957 the first shipload of manganese ore left the port of Macapá and, in 1969, the American-Brazilian company that controlled the production exported 1.4 million tons. At that time, manganese ore was the most important export product of the North. A part was destined for the United States. Expanding mining led to significant population growth. In the early 1950s, the municipality of Macapá had only 20 600 inhabitants, by 1970 the population had increased to 98 700 and the city had undergone a remarkable modernisation. However, Macapá had also attracted quite a few rural people for whom no suitable employment was available.

Another post-war development was the rise of tin mining in Rondônia. This was made possible by the construction of a road connection between Porto Velho and São Paulo in 1965. As a result, the ore could be transported in trucks to Volta Redonda, where processing would take place. In 1960 only 49 tons of tinstone were produced in Rondônia. Rubber, Brazil nuts, hides and some vegetable oils were still the main export products at that time, but in 1970 production was estimated at 4 000 tons and tin ore was in first place. In 1967, 97 % of production was done by tin washers, who worked in groups of two to four people and had only simple resources at their disposal. They sold the ore to companies that somewhat concentrated and transported it and also supplied food and other necessities to the washers. Of the approximately 30 000 tin washers in the area in 1968, many had previously been rubber tappers. Tin mining had become so important in a few years that almost half of the population outside the towns of Guajará Mirim and Porto Velho found a living in it. In the period 1960–1970, the population of Rondônia increased from 71 000 to 116 600. The expectation at the end of the 1960s was that production would increase considerably. At that time, the army had started building a road connecting Ariquemes to Guajará Mirim. This would no longer make it necessary to transport a large part of the ore by air to the larger collection centre Ariquemes, but made it possible to transport the ore directly into trucks. At the end of the 1960s, large-scale production started to increase. Several large foreign and Brazilian companies began to show an increasing interest in tin mining, so that several large concessions had already been issued. One problem was that the *garimpeiros* occupied the best grounds. Their existence was threatened. It was expected that the large companies would use modern mechanised extraction methods; they were used only in a few places in the 1950s.

Mining stimulated agricultural activity. Settlers started farming along the Cuiabá-Porto Velho road and milk and poultry production had increased around Rondônia's capital.

A weak economy

In 1970, no more than 11 % of the active population were employed in industry. This was limited to the processing of local raw materials such as jute and to companies that provided basic needs such as foodstuffs. In 1969, the North had only 1.25 % of the Brazilian industrial population and 2.6 % of the number of industrial enterprises. Most of these were small.

In 1965 the vast North contributed only 1.7 % of the national income. According to official estimates, the average *renda interna per capita* in Brazil that year was 298 cruzeiros. In the North, this average was approached only by the territory of Amapá, thanks to manganese mining (270 cruzeiros). In the other areas it was between 116 cruzeiros (Pará) and 193 cruzeiros (Acre).

The level of prosperity was low. 47 % of the active population earned a monthly income of less than 150 cruzeiros. 45 % of the population of five years and older could not read and write. In 66 % of the homes there was no running water or a well available.

Only two cities were really significant and they owed this mainly to their collecting and distribution function. Belém was the most developed and served the entire Amazon basin, including the nearby Belém–Bragança zone, the most populous and most colonised region of the Amazon Basin. Because of their transport and trade function, their infrastructure and their population, both cities had managed to attract the larger part of the northern Brazilian industry.

Until 1970, other parts of the vast country of Brazil had been increasingly more attractive as settlement areas than the Amazon Basin, with its tropical jungle, high average annual temperatures, abundant rainfall, high humidity and danger of disease. It had received little attention over the centuries from private investors, the mother country Portugal and the government of independent Brazil. There was no question of a development policy for the region. The North was just a resource frontier. All federal development activities focused on the Southeast (also referred to as Centro-Sul), as did private initiative. The North attracted mainly poor population from the Northeast.

In 1946, it was decreed that 3 % of federal tax revenues should be used for a period of at least 20 years to promote the progress of the North. However, it was not until 1953 that the Superintendência do Plano de Valorização Econômica da Amazônia (SPVEA) was created to coordinate the intended development activities. By no means every year were the funds earmarked for the North actually set aside, while the funds that did eventually become available partly disappeared through corruption or could otherwise be used only for a limited number of projects, such as the establishment of some jute processing industries, construction of a small petroleum refinery near Manaus and the construction of the road from Brasília to Belém. The socio-economic structure was not transformed by these measures and there was, in fact, no noticeable progress.

In 1966 there was a clear turnaround in the interest of the Brazilian government. Since then, the latter made it increasingly clear that it was serious about opening up the North better, colonising it more intensively, integrating it more into the national economy and thus developing it more. To what extent it has succeeded in this will become apparent in Volume 2.

Population size and distribution

Northern Brazil has often been characterised as a "demographic vacuum." Because of the low range of (high) temperatures, the constant high humidity, the incidence of various tropical diseases, the dense tropical forest and the predominance of soils which rapidly lose their fertility after clearance, Northern Brazil has always been a difficult area of settlement. It would be inaccurate, however, to attribute the fact that this enormous forest region still remained largely uncolonised, until the 1970s, to the generally unfavourable environment of the humid tropics. Other circumstances must also be considered in explanation.

A very important factor is that Brazil proved to be a country where one form of agricultural activity or another could be practised everywhere and that areas in eastern Brazil offered more attractive possibilities than the Amazon Basin. The immigrants accordingly moved mainly to those areas, so that population growth took place predominantly in the East.

It is not without significance in this connection that many Portuguese did not emigrate to Brazil with the intention of earning a livelihood through hard work, but were seeking rather to make a quick and easy fortune, preferably through the mining of precious metals (*imediatismo*). As far as agricultural production was concerned, many quickly came to the conclusion that the Amazon region was suitable only for the gathering of forest products. This conception persisted for a long time and was not unreasonable, but nevertheless acted as brake on the efficient occupation of the region, which consequently remained primarily the domain of the Indigenous population.

Added to this was a great lack of manpower. Portugal had for centuries a very small population, so that it was not able to supply many colonists. It was also opposed to the immigration of foreigners. Moreover, the natural increase of the colonial population was for a long time very low. Consequently, when independence began, the whole of Brazil had a population of no more than about 4 million on a territory with an area falling between that of Australia and Canada.

When millions of migrants set out for the New World in the nineteenth century the migration currents were not directed towards the Amazon region, which was regarded as a "green hell," where it was almost impossible for whites to make a decent living. Hardly any investments were made there. This changed when the Amazon region began to emerge as an important rubber producer after 1870, but the change was short-lived, as we have mentioned.

During the 20th century the population of Brazil has greatly increased and many areas, particularly the North East, have already had to contend with population pressure for a considerable time. Until about 1960, however, the Amazon region was still so undeveloped and inaccessible that the only prospect for many people was an arduous pioneer existence. This frightened off a great many potential colonists; many poor country people preferred to move to the cities in their search for better opportunities.

The tardiness in developing the Amazon region arose partly from the fact that, after the rubber boom, the government had little further interest in the region. Nor did private enterprises show much interest, with the result that almost all government and private investment was made elsewhere. The region had lost its attraction.

In view of this situation, it is not surprising that the "North" had a population of only 332 847 in 1872, i.e. 3.4% of the total Brazilian population, although it accounted for 42.1% of the area of the country. There was a fairly marked increase up to 1920, related mainly to the rise of the rubber gathering economy and the expansion of employment indirectly connected with it. During the period 1872–1920 the population quadrupled, as a result of which the North gradually even came to account for a larger share of the total Brazilian population (Table 1). During the period 1920–1940, however, growth gave way to a marked stagnation.

Table 1. Population Change in North Brazil, 1872–1970

Year	Population		Population growth relative to previous census, in %	
	Absolute	% of total Brazilian population	North Brazil	Brazil
1872	32 847	3.35	–	–
1890	476 370	3.32	43.1	44.3
1900	695 112	3.99	45.9	21.6
1920	1 439 052	4.70	107.0	75.7
1940	1 462 420	3.55	1.6	34.6
1950	1 844 655	3.55	26.1	26.0
1960	2 601 519	3.67	41.0	36.7
1970	3 650 750	3.90	40.3	33.7

Source: Sinopse Estatística 1971.

After 1940 there was again an increase, and at a level not greatly different from the national rate of increase during that period. This increase was related, among other things, to the enhanced interest in the Amazon region during the World War II (for rubber collection), the development of some mining (Amapá), the colonisation activities of Japanese immigrants and – partly because of this successful colonisation – a gradually more favourable perception of the production potential of Amazônia. Last, but not least, there was a further expansion of shifting cultivation arising from a greater natural increase of population. The latter became possible because, at that time, the Amazon region had recovered from the deleterious effects on the age structure of the large-scale exodus which took place after 1920. A further factor was that medical facilities had somewhat improved, causing a further fall in the death rate. It was, in fact, particularly the natural increase which was responsible for the more rapid growth after 1940. Up to 1970 there was no large-scale immigration into Amazônia.

Despite the changes which occurred in the growth pattern after 1940, the North still contained only 3.7%, of the Brazilian population in 1960 and 3.9% in 1970. It was not without reason, therefore, that reference was made to a "demographic vacuum." This description appears all the more appropriate, since the population of the Amazon region at that time was very unevenly distributed. Of the approximately 2.6 million inhabitants in 1960 no less than 1.55 million (59.6%) were concentrated in the state of Pará, while the much larger state of Amazonas, with its approximately 721 000 inhabitants, accounted for only 27.7% of the region's population. Within both states the majority of the inhabitants lived in the vicinity of the main river, the principal, if not the only significant traffic axis. Marked areas of concentration within these zones were the cities of Belém and Manaus, which historically performed an important function as commercial collection and distribution centres and had also succeeded in attracting to themselves a large part of the other tertiary activities. The two cities together, therefore, contained 22.2% of the northern population.

Table 2. Distribution of the North Brazilian population between the different states and territories and the percentage resident in the metropolitan municipalities; 1960 and 1970

State/ Territory	Population			Metropolitan Municipality		Population in Metropolitan Municipality			
	1960	1970 Abs.	1970 %	Name	Area (of State/ Territory)	1960		1970 (sept.)	
					%	Abs.	%	Abs.	%
Pará	1 550 935	2 197 072	60.2	Belém	0.06	402 170	25.9	642 514	29.3
Amazonas	721 215	960 934	26.3	Manaus	0.9	175 343	24.3	314 197	32.7
Acre	160 208	218 006	6.0	Rio Branco	9.4	47 882	29.9	84 845	39.0
Rondônia	70 783	116 620	3.2	Pôrto Velho	24.0	51 049	72.1	88 856	76.2
Amapá	68 889	116 480	3.2	Macapá	20.0	46 905	68.1	87 755	75.3
Roraima	29 489	41 638	1.1	Boa Vista	41.9	26 168	88.7	37 062	89.0
Northern Brazil	2 601 519	3 650 750	100.0	All Municp.	5.9	749 517	28.8	1 255 229	34.4

Source: IBGE, Sinopse Estatística 1970; Sinopse Preliminar do Censo Demográfico 1980.

Special mention should also be made of the north-eastern corner of the state of Pará and, in particular, the area between the cities of Belém and Bragança. Because the occupation process had been largely concentrated here after 1600 and had even been intensified during the second half of the nineteenth century under the influence of the rapid growth of the city of Belém, a considerable intensification of agricultural activities had taken place in the course of time. This zone, including the city of Belém, which is formed roughly by the micro-regions of Salgado (023), Bragantina (024) and Belém (025) and covers 1.6 % of the state of Pará, accommodated no less than 29.2 % of the population of North Brazil in 1970 (See Figs. 4 and 9 in the chapter on Population Change, Part Three).

A similar concentration occurred in the state of Amazonas in the area around Manaus. The statistical meso-region of Manaus, which covers only 13 % of the area of the state, but is incidentally nearly as large as Great Britain, accommodated, with the city of Manaus, nearly 15 % of the population of the North in 1970.[1]

As far as the other states and territories are concerned, it is noteworthy that also in 1960 and 1970 a considerable part of the total population was concentrated in or relatively close to the metropolitan core. This concentration was particularly marked in Rondônia, Amapá and Roraima.

Figure 1 gives a picture of the population distribution in around 1960 and shows clearly that most of the population outside the metropolitan municipalities lived in small towns, villages and hamlets near the waterways which opened up the region.

1 The boundaries of this meso-region correspond with those of the micro-region of Médio Amazonas (Fig. 4, Part Three, Chapter on Population Change).

Figure 1. Population distribution in the Brazilian North about 1960

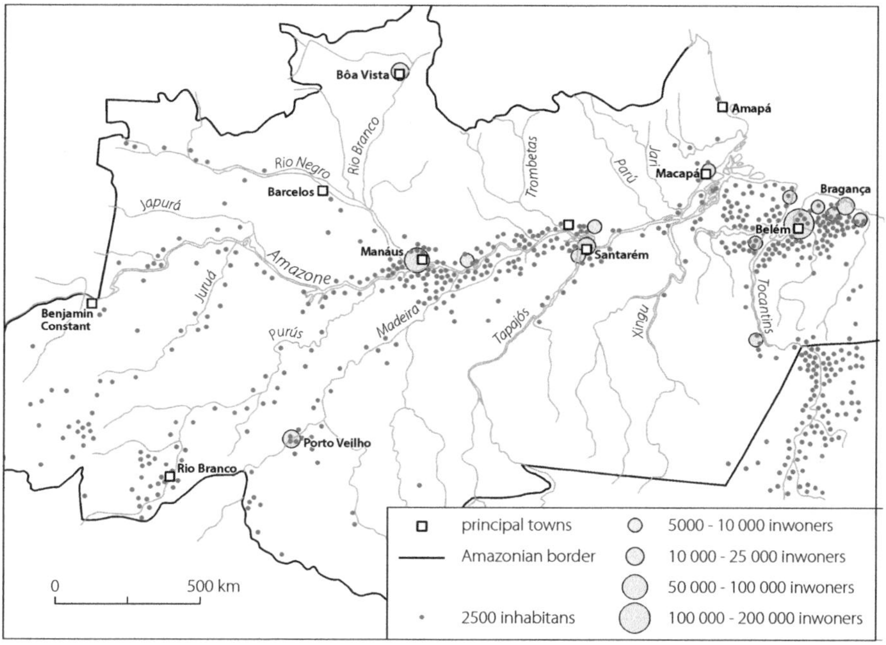

Source: Author's own elaboration.

In the Belém–Bragança zone the rural population densities reached 15–20 inhabitants per square kilometre; near the main river rural densities were in many places 1–5, but elsewhere they often fell to well below one inhabitant per sq km. For the North as a whole the average density in 1960 was only 0.72 per sq km and 1.02 in 1970 (0.09 in 1872) (Fig. 1).

Another impression is obtained if one considers not the North, but Amazônia Legal, the legally defined planning region which is the field of operation of the regional development body created in 1966 and to which many government measures for the benefit of the Amazon region apply. Apart from the North as it is customarily defined (see note 1), Amazônia Legal also includes the part of Goiás lying north of the 13th parallel, the whole of the recently created state of Mato Grosso and the part of Maranhão situated west of the 44th meridian. While North Brazil, with an area of 3.58 million sq km, covers 42.1 % of the total land area of Brazil, Amazônia Legal, with its 4.98 million sq km, occupies no less than 58.5 % of the total area of Brazil. Because the occupation process had already advanced further in North Goiás, Mato Grosso and western Maranhão, these marginal areas had a relatively large population in 1960 (see Part 3). As a consequence of this, Amazônia Legal had a population of 5.16 million in 1960, i.e. nearly twice as many people as the North and 7.3 % of the Brazilian population.

References

Burns, E. Bradford. 1980. *A History of Brazil*. New York: Columbia University Press.

Instituto Brasileiro de Geografia e Estatística (IBGE). 1971. *Sinopse Estatística do Brasil*. Rio de Janeiro: IBGE.

James, Preston E. 1969. *Latin America*. New York: The Odyssey Press.

Kleinpenning, Jan M. G. 1973. *Brazilië*. Roermond: Romen.

Part 2: The Brazilian Amazon in the 1970s. How integration began

Introduction

Extensive livestock farming, the search for gold and other minerals, and the possibility of penetrating far into the interior by way of easily navigable rivers in order to establish military support posts or gather forest products – these were the main reasons for the vast extent of the Portuguese colony of Brazil. The country now has an area of no less than 8.5 million square kilometres and this makes it one of the largest states in the world.

The greater part of the population, however, had been concentrated in the eastern fringe up to the 1970s. In the eight southeastern and southern states, which occupy less than 18 % of the area of the country, lived no less than 62 % of the total population and these states formed the economic centre of gravity of Brazil (Fig. 2). The North East, which is usually defined as consisting of nine states, accommodated about 29 % of the country's population on 18% of the national territory. In the extensive interior areas formed by the "North" and the "West," on the other hand, together accounting for no less than 64 % of the country's area, lived only 8.7 % of the Brazilians. These areas still had little economic importance up to 1970, as appears from the fact that they contributed only 5 % of the gross national product.

Brazilian publications of that time also often contrasted the region Amazônia Legal with that of Centro-Sul. The former comprised part of the "West" as well as the "North" and covered no less than 59 % of the land area, but only 8 % of the Brazilian population lived there and no more than 4 % of the gross national product derived from there. The Centro-Sul region, on the other hand, covered 26 % of the land area, accommodated 67 % of the population and provided 83 % of the GNP (see Fig. 3).[2]

The need to reduce these marked contrasts in development and the uneven distribution of the population had already been felt for some time. The poverty of the North East, in particular, was regarded as a serious problem. The new capital Brasília, built under Kubitschek, and the construction of a number of links with this centre formed the first modest attempts to modify the socio-spatial structure in order to reduce somewhat the dominance of the coastal zone.

2 Figures derived from *Sinopse estatística do Brasil* (1971), Ministério da Agricultura (1972a, 8), and from *Revista Geográfica* (70, June 1969, p. 224).

Figure 2. The administrative divisions of Brazil in the 1970s

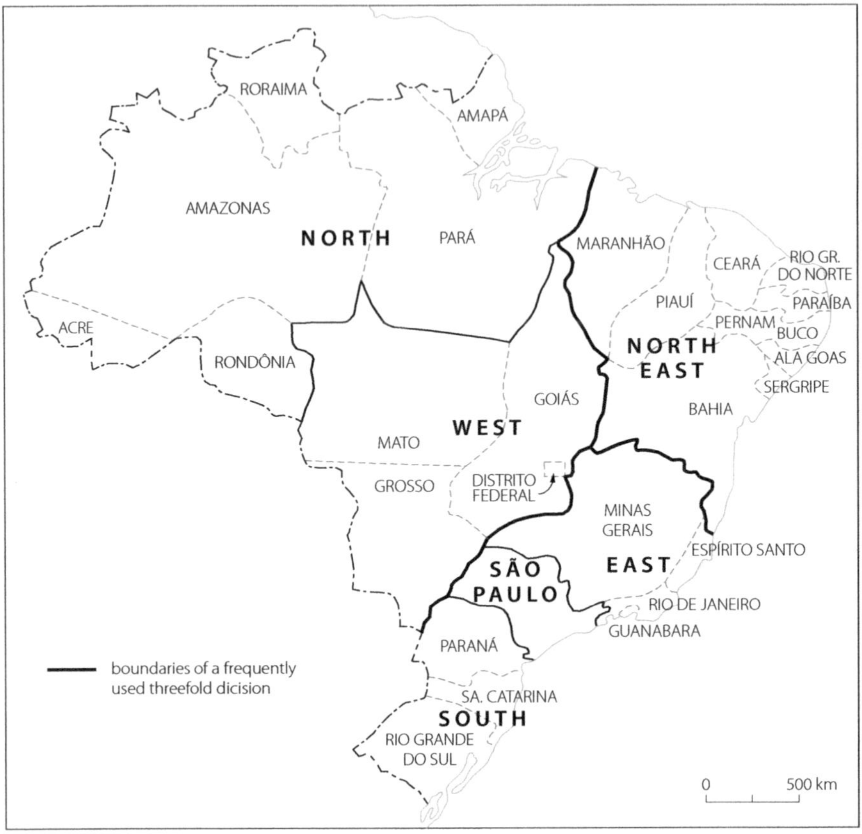

Source: Kleinpenning (1975) (author's own elaboration).

Since then, the problem of regional inequality has not been lost sight of. On the contrary, integration of the different regions by means of further economic and social development, accompanied by a less uneven distribution of the population over the territory, officially became one of the main objectives of the Brazilian regime which came to power in 1964. It even aimed to make such progress in Brazil that the country would, in a few decades, become one of the great developed nations.

Within the framework of this policy, an important share of the attention and activities were concentrated on the vast Amazon region. While this region had enjoyed little or no attention after the decline of the rubber gathering economy, now there was a marked change, particularly after 1970. The government made it increasingly clearly known that it was serious in its intentions to open up the North, colonise and develop it, in order to integrate it more into the national economy and society. This policy of integration was regarded as the logical and necessary continuation of a centuries' long and still incomplete colonisation process. In the past, a more intensive occupation and utilisation of the immense northern territory had lain beyond the capacities of Brazil for a number of reasons, but at the end of the 1960s the country felt equal to the task.

Figure 3. The boundaries of Amazônia Legal, Centro-Sul and Nordeste

Source: Kleinpenning (1975) (author's own elaboration).

From the beginning, the efforts to integrate the Amazon region more into the country and to develop it – a policy known in Brazil as Operação Amazônia – gave rise to criticism and resistance, but the government did not let itself be discouraged by this, especially since the plan also evoked sympathy and enthusiasm among a considerable part of the Brazilian people. Many Brazilians believed that the integration of the Amazon basin was indeed necessary and had even come to regard this integration as one of the principal national tasks for the coming decades. They assumed that not only the Amazon region would benefit from this integration process, but also that the further opening up and development of the North would bring considerable advantages for the rest of the country.

As far as the latter were concerned, people were thinking, for example, of an enlargement of the market for the industries of the Southeast and of a considerable expansion of the production of raw materials.

Amazônia was spoken and written about in Brazil more than before. Natural resources were increasingly mapped and, in other fields too, the development prospects and problems were being, or began to be, investigated. Besides the federal government, the various states started to take a number of measures to encourage development.

The growing interest in the Amazon region was incidentally not limited to Brazil. There had already been a certain international interest in this immeasurable and still scarcely inhabited primeval region for a long time and this interest had clearly gained in strength over the years. In fact, it may be stated that, since the building of Brasília, nothing had so much caught the attention, both nationally and internationally, as the plans for the further opening up and development of the Amazon basin.

This study discusses in detail the various attempts since about 1965 which were to give the Amazon region a more important place within Brazil, while attention is also paid to the underlying motives and to the results achieved up to the early 1980s. Particular attention will be paid to the extent, the nature and the results of the colonisation activities of the Brazilian government. In the early 1970s, colonisation as such was regarded as an extremely important means of realising the aims of integration and development. In particular, colonisation would help to lessen the socio-economic problems of various Brazilian regions and bring about a more balanced population distribution.

The ultimate aim of this analysis of Operação Amazônia is to answer the question whether the effect of the changes sought in the socio-economic structure of the Amazon region in the 1970s were of such a kind that the policy of integration would indeed contribute towards the reduction of under- and uneven development in Brazil.

A more detailed discussion of the motives underlying the attempts to development the North – and the characteristics of the policies after 1970 will follow in Part 2.

Motives underlying the development policy

Economic motives

The idea that the Amazon basin could be further developed and enabled to make an important contribution to the progress of the remainder of the country was based upon the realisation that Northern Brazil is suited not only to the gathering of forest products, as people often used to believe, but also offers many other possibilities. The region possesses great natural wealth, the extent of which was still not precisely known in the 1970s, and which had been exploited hardly or not at all at the time.

Mineral wealth

The continuing geological explorations of the period 1965–1975 revealed that the Amazon region contains iron, bauxite, tin, copper, lead, zinc, aluminium, gold, silver, chromium, manganese, wolfram, haematite, uranium, thorium and ilmenite. Since the detailed mineralogical surveys were still in full swing (with the aid of modern aerial photography techniques) and had not yet been completed over large parts of Amazônia, the figures of the known reserves were subject to constant review. It was already accepted, however, that the then known reserves of iron ore, bauxite, tin and manganese, in particular, considerably exceeded the original expectations. In the Serra dos Carajás, in southern Pará, there were iron ore deposits with an average iron content of 65 % and a total reserve of certainly 8 000 million tons. The principal iron ore region known at the time covered an area of 160 000 hectares and was situated about 150 km southwest of Marabá (SUDAM/Banco da Amazônia 1972, 19; Kohlhepp 1971, 76 f.).[3] This has opened up unimagined export prospects.

Nor were the raw materials lacking for a ceramics and a chemicals industry. Apart from gypsum, limestone, kaolin, rock salt and diamonds, central Amazônia contains extensive underground salt deposits. Diamonds are also to be found (Valverde 1968, 253).

The brown coal deposits were also thought to be very extensive and the Amazon region might even contain the largest reserves in the world. The existence of coal had been confirmed in the eastern part of the Amazon basin (catchment area of the Xingu

3 The estimates of iron reserves in de Serra dos Carájas vary somewhat according to the source and date at which they were made. The statistics given here are derived from an article in a Brazilian newspaper in the early 1970s.

river) (Kearns 1969, 542; Valverde 1968, 254). The water power present in the basin could certainly generate 6 million kilowatts, which was 11 % of the Brazilian hydro-electric potential (Daemon 1969, 350).[4]

There were also indications of the presence of petroleum and natural gas. The existence of important oil and gas fields was suspected, particularly in the neighbourhood of the Peruvian frontier and near the mouth of the Amazon. Experts of Petrobras even believed that the Amazon Basin might contain the greatest oil reserves in South America (Tocantins 1973, 6). Unfortunately, in the early 1970s no-one in Brazil had yet succeeded in tapping them, but the search was continued.

In view of this wealth of resources, people were understandably optimistic about the potentialities of mineral exploitation at the time. It was even believed that the Amazon Basin could become an important exporter of ores and other raw materials and that this would make Brazil less dependent upon coffee for its export trade than it was at the time. The ideas about the potentialities for mineral exploitation had, in fact, been fundamentally altered by the discoveries in the 1960s, since official reports from the early 1950s had still assumed that the Amazon was a region poor in *recursos minerais* (Tocantins 1973, 6).

That the ideas had completely changed was due mainly to the exploration work that had been carried out in the 1960s. At the beginning of the 1970s the investigations into the potentialities for the use of the Amazon region were intensified, as appears, for example, from the RADAM project (*Radar Amazônia*), which was carried out during the period 1972–1974 and had as its aim the mapping of 4.6 million square km with the aid of very advanced remote sensing methods. This project provided valuable data, both for the study of soil and vegetation and for geological and mineralogical investigation (Projeto Radam 1972).

The potentialities of forestry

There were also very great expectations in respect of the possibilities of forest exploitation. The Amazon region possessed the world's greatest complex of tropical forest, with many still little used kinds of timber. Nearly 80 % of the forest reserves of Brazil and one third of the total volume of timber in the world were to be found there in 1970 (Condurú 1973, 7). The total area of forest in the Amazon Basin was estimated at about 750 million hectares, of which about 350 million was situated on Brazilian territory. The volume of timber was estimated at about 70 000 million cubic metres (*Industrialização de madeiras* 1970, 1). If these were to be exploited more intensively than at present, Brazil could become an important exporter of timber. As a result of detailed forestry surveys there was already better knowledge than before of the location of the stands of timber most suitable for exploitation. Research into the practical uses of the different tropical timbers had resulted in an increase in the number of exploited species from 53 to 227 during the period (Presidencia de la Republica/Minsterio do interior 1974, 17).

4 Hydro-electricity was initially generated only in a small station at Paredão (Amapá). This station supplied power mainly to industries established in Macapá and to various large concerns in the territory of Amapá, including Brumasa and Icomi. A second hydro-electric plant was built at Curuá-Una, near Santarém. It was programmed to generate 20 000 kw in 1974.

Until 1970, the exploitation of this enormous timber reserve had been limited mainly to the vicinity of the great rivers. The total production had been relatively small. In 1968 the Amazon region produced less than 12 % of the timber exports from Brazil. In 1965 the region contained only 1.3 % of the number of timber processing and woodworking enterprises in Brazil (Soares 1971, 54; Knowles 1971, 25).

Production was kept low by the poor accessibility and the great distances to the home market, but an additional factor was the circumstance that only 20 or 30 varieties were regarded as being of commercial interest, which was only 5 to 7 % of the timber reserve (Soares 1971, 17). On average there occurred only ten trees per hectare, with a total volume of 45 cubic metres, that could be exploited commercially. Consequently, in 1968, four varieties of timber accounted for 93.4 % of the total export of timber from the North (Knowles 1971, 7; Soares 1971, 63). This situation was mainly the result of the very heterogeneous nature of the tropical rain forest and of the circumstance that, until then, the utilisation potential of only a limited range of trees had been developed.

A number of Brazilian bodies, including the Superintendência do Desenvolvimento da Amazônia (SUDAM), had been examining the possibilities for exploitation of the tropical forest in the late 1960s. Within the framework of these studies, experts considered particularly the problems surrounding the great heterogeneity of the tropical rain forest. They believed that they had found a solution in the establishment of industrial complexes served by large, easily accessible areas of forest and which did not limit their activities to the processing of one or a few kinds of timber, but used a great number for the manufacture of a wide range of products and, in addition, used the waste timber to generate electricity (*Industrialização de madeiras* 1970, 8). Certain varieties of timber proved to be suitable for paper manufacture and the heterogeneity of the forest was also no longer regarded as an insuperable obstacle to the establishment of this industry (*Industrialização de madeiras* 1970, 7).

Apart from the more intensive use of the heterogeneous forest, the forestry experts also considered reafforestation in order to obtain more homogeneous stands of timber. As soon as the exploitation of the forest began to increase, the possibilities for reafforestation would obviously also become more favourable. This applied all the more so since the Brazilian *Código Florestal* had made it obligatory for enterprises using timber as a raw material to carry out replanting (Pandolfo 1972b, 4).

Although the possibilities for the establishment of industrial complexes and planting of more homogeneous stands of trees did not prove very successful in practice, the exploitation of the Amazonian forest could nevertheless be greatly increased. Even if the exploitation methods remained simple and half of the forest were cleared, Brazil would still be able to produce 1000 million cubic metres of timber per annum (Knowles 1971, 63).

Apart from the fact that the timber reserves were enormous, the Amazon region had the advantage of relatively level terrain. The waterways offered some possibilities for transport and Brazil was being increasingly opened up by highways. Another favourable factor was the constantly increasing demand for timber, both in Brazil and abroad. The Amazon region might consequently become one of the major timber producers of the world in the near future (Knowles 1971, 63). According to various experts, forest exploitation by modern methods could become a profitable undertaking in the following decades, which would yield a quick return on investment of capital.[5]

The possibilities for the expansion of tropical tree and shrub crops

Apart from the possibilities for a greater exploitation of the forest, the Amazon region also offered wide possibilities for the production of various tropical tree and shrub crops. The Amazon Basin is climatically suited to the production of numerous agricultural crops. Although the low fertility of the greater proportion of the soils constitutes a less favourable factor, this limitation applies least to trees and shrubs, since they produce humus and provide shade, thereby limiting the washing away of the soil and the burning up of the humus which has been formed. It was also thought that the limited soil fertility could be improved through the application of correctives (lime) and fertilisers.[6]

There were good possibilities for the growing of oil palms, especially since there was potentially a good market for oils and fats, both at home and abroad. Experiments raised the expectation that the oil palm would give higher yields per hectare than in Africa (*A Sudam e a cultura do dendê na Amazônia* n. d., 4).

The cultivation of cocoa also offered prospects, according to the agricultural experts, especially since there was good potential for this product on the international market (Condurú 1973, 25).

It was also considered reasonable to encourage the production of natural rubber. Brazil, the homeland of the rubber tree, was still unable to meet its natural rubber requirements from home production, so that about 16 000 tons (30 %) had to be imported in 1971 (Ministério do Interior 1971b, 39). The demand would rise still further over the years, which made an increase in home production all the more urgent.

Since the Japanese had successfully introduced pepper cultivation in the Amazon region in the 1940s, good prospects were also seen for the further expansion of this crop. The attractive thing about pepper cultivation was that it provided very high incomes per hectare (Kleinpenning 1973, 146).

Lastly, an expansion was also considered possible of the production of tropical fruits, such as pineapples and Brazil nuts, of tropical fibre crops, such as jute and malva, and of various other crops, including soy, both for the home market and for export (Condurú 1973, 25).

The possibilities for more livestock farming

There was also optimism about the possibilities for livestock farming. Millions of hectares of grazing land could still be created, particularly on the southern fringe of Amazônia Legal, where the vegetation is less dense than in the more northerly *selva*. In the somewhat higher region near the frontiers with Venezuela and Guyana savannahs occur, where livestock farming could be considerably expanded if only better outlets could be found.[7] This would enable Brazil to become an important exporter of meat and

---

5 This idea is to be found in various official publications, including *Industrialização de Madeiras* (1970).

6 We would refer here to the detailed soil and climatic analyses in Falesi *et al.* (1972b).

7 Savannahs covered 22 % of the territory of Roraima (Silva 1966).

other animal products. Since the start on the construction of a road between Manaus and Boa Vista had been made, the territory had already begun to attract an increasing interest. In 1960, there were in Roraima in the midst of the tree and grass savannahs 837 *fazendas* with about 167 000 head of cattle. In 1970, there were already 235 000 head of cattle and the number of *fazendas* had increased to 1990. The cattle farmers sold the meat and hides mainly in and via Manaus.[8]

According to a number of experts, much wider possibilities existed for a spectacular expansion of livestock production in the tropical forest zone. Brücher believed that the Amazon Basin provided better opportunities for livestock farming than the Venezuelan and Colombian Llanos, provided modern methods were employed. In his view, livestock farming was a "Wirtschaftsform mit Zukunft" (economic activity with future) for the tropical rain forest, especially if the appropriate breeds of animal were kept (Brücher 1970, 217–225). He considered in this connection the poorer lands of the higher ground, which are not periodically flooded (*terra firme*), the most suited to animals for slaughter (including zebus), while the lower-lying, periodically flooded, *várzeas* would be better suited to the rearing of water buffaloes. These give higher milk yields than the zebus and are better adapted to the terrain of the *várzeas*.[9]

Brücher based his conclusions mainly on observations in the Amazon lowland of Colombia, where pastures had been laid down for cattle grazing at various places on the *terra firme* and good results had been achieved. In South-East Colombia and parts of East Peru cattle farming had even become the principal form of agricultural production.

According to Brücher, favourable factors in the Amazon regions were the fact that the pastures were of good quality at all seasons and the circumstance that water was constantly available at numerous places for the animals. In a region like the Llanos this was by no means always the case. Another positive feature was that the pastures remained productive for years without the application of fertiliser. In the practice of arable farming, by contrast, soil exhaustion already began to occur after a few years. Pastures which were laid down in Colombia in 1935 were still in good condition at the end of the 1960s.

A further reason for the success in the region studied by Brücher was the fact that the cattle population had been improved by the acquisition of zebus and the crossing of various cattle races. Cattle diseases were successfully checked by disinfecting the animals regularly in basins, as well as by eradicating harmful weeds from the pastures and preventing the formation of pools of stagnant water in the vicinity of the pastures (Brücher 1970, 220–222). These measures must be considered necessary preconditions for the practice of modern livestock farming.

The views of Brücher and others led to a fairly fundamental change in the ideas which had long existed concerning the possibilities of livestock farming in the humid tropical environment. Many people, including the geographers P. Gourou and H. Wilhelmy, had long been pessimistic about livestock farming in such conditions. Apart from the occurrence of various harmful cattle diseases and the humid, hot climate,

8 *Opinião*, 20 a 27 de agosto de 1973, p. 4 ("A corrida para Roraima").

9 Brücher pointed out in this connection that it would be desirable to retain a considerable portion of the forest in order to prevent unwanted disturbances to the natural environment. He did not support a one-sided economy, based entirely on livestock farming (Brücher 1970, 225–226).

this pessimism was based on the rapid exhaustion of the soils observed with the practice of arable farming (Gourou 1966, Chapter 6; Brücher 1970, 215 f.).

In Brazil, the Amazon region had long been avoided by the majority of livestock farmers. They preferred other parts of the vast country, not only because of the natural conditions, but also because of the poor accessibility of the Amazon Basin and the great distance to the consumer markets. Consequently, livestock farming remained of modest extent in the Brazilian North. Although livestock farming contributed 21.4% of the regional income in 1966, there were only 2.03 million cattle there in 1968, which was 2.2% of the national total (Pinto 1971, 17; *Amazônia. Estatísticas básicas* 1970, 112).

Livestock farming was restricted mainly to the *campos de várzea*, which become available during the dry season, and to the *campos* (savannahs), which occur at various places (including the Ilha de Marajó). The higher, forested *terra firme* lands were, until recently, mainly used when some of the animals had to be moved to safety from the *campos de várzea* during the rainy season. Pastures were generally not laid down there. The cattle farmers were content to utilise the open areas in the forest.[10]

The demand for meat and other animal products would increase still further in later years (Ramalho 1971, 41). The new views about the use potential of the selva region therefore meant for Brazil that it would be able to develop into a very important meat producer and into one of the greatest meat exporters. In the late 1960s and early 1970s people in Brazil became increasingly conscious of these possibilities. By 1970, they had already realised that export via Peru (Lima) and the ports on the Caribbean coast would greatly increase the market potential, and that export through the east coast ports also had the advantage of a relatively favourable location. Calculated in sailing time, the grazing areas south of Belém were situated five days closer to the European markets than the abattoirs of the Argentinian ports were (Foland 1971, 73).

For the time being, Brazilians were still thinking in terms of rather traditional and, in any event, extensive forms of livestock farming in the most favourably located areas. If they were to change to a more intensive form of farming, however, with regular applications of fertiliser and the growing of special fodder crops, if they were to build an extensive network of cold stores and to use refrigerated lorries for meat transport, production could be increased many times.

The possibilities for the establishment of small arable enterprises

Besides the possibilities for livestock farming, the Amazon region also offered possibilities for establishing small and medium-sized arable holdings for the benefit of arable farmers from other parts of Brazil, with the aim of reducing the rural problems of those regions and absorbing their population increase. This would particularly benefit North-East Brazil, where the situation in the countryside gave the most cause for concern.

Although the SUDENE (Superintendência do Desenvolvimento do Nordeste) had tried to relieve the many economic and social problems of the North East by means of a series of different measures since 1959, the results of its development policy up to the early 1970s were modest. There still existed a great lack of good employment in the North East. The government had meanwhile begun to realise that industrialisa-

10 Described in detail in Wilhelmy (1966).

tion, which had been greatly propagated in the 1960s, had not sufficiently increased the number of jobs and that the attraction of industry would also provide insufficient relief in the future (Kleinpenning 1971a, 279 ff.).

Analyses by the SUDENE from that time showed that, after the execution of the proposed irrigation projects, land reform, colonisation and other agricultural development measures in the North East, there would remain a surplus of about 309 000 families in the primary sector. Since it would probably prove impossible to realise completely all the proposed measures in the short term, it had to be assumed that the surplus would, in fact, be larger. A considerable proportion of the 1.3 million rural families for whom there was insufficient work in the North East would therefore have to look for a living outside the agricultural sector or in other parts of the country.

The Instituto de Planejamento Econômico e Social (IPEA) considered that the most adequate contribution towards the solution of the population problems of the North East would be a considerable expansion of the supervised colonisation of the Amazon Basin, where there was land for millions of farmers (Tavares *et al.* 1972, 122-124). One of the important aims of the then government, therefore, was to push forward the agricultural front in the Amazon Basin in order to integrate the North and to reduce the socio-economic problems of the North East (*Metas e bases para a ação do governo* 1971, 31). The more varied picture of the nature of the soil that had been gained in the preceding years had undoubtedly affected thinking in this field. The North proved to possess not exclusively poor soils, as was previously assumed, but also areas with considerably better land.

Moreover, colonisation was an attractive solution from the financial point of view, for the IPEA had come to the conclusion that supervised colonisation was one of the cheapest means of creating large numbers of jobs in a short time.

The average placement costs in ten Brazilian colonisation projects (which had been realised or were still to be realised) amounted to US$ 2547 per family (1971 Dollars). In most instances the amount lay around US$ 2000 (Tavares *et al.* 1972, 114). Panagides put the costs associated with the creation of one job by means of colonisation at between US$ 1132 and 1944, a sum based on calculations by the IPEA, the United Nations Food and Agricultural Organisation (FAO) and the International Bank for Reconstruction and Development. These were only direct costs and so excluded expenditure on infrastructure (roads) and administration (Panagides and Vande Lage 1973, 21 f.).

According to W. Cline, the costs of creating one job in North East Brazil by means of irrigation schemes amounted, by contrast, to US$ 6768. Patrick even came to a higher estimation: he calculated that the costs of creating one job through the capital-intensive projects furthered and approved by the regional development bodies (SUDAM and SUDENE) reached as much as US$ 32 597 and 16 915, respectively. Lastly, various calculations put the cost of increasing employment in North East Brazil by means of land reform at between US$ 800 and 1844 per job.[11]

The IPEA also concluded on the basis of research in various regions of Brazil that colonists, at least if they received government support, could earn incomes above the minimum wage. Another conclusion reached by the IPEA was that colonisation was an activity which was decidedly justified for the government on financial and economic grounds, since most colonists were able to repay the costs and the interest within a

11 All figures come from Panagides and Vande Lage (1973, 21 f.).

period of 15 years (Tavares *et al.* 1972, 114 f.). These findings will also have been a reason for the IPEA to regard colonisation as an adequate solution.

During the first half of 1970 the North East was struck by severe droughts, followed in certain areas by floods. The weakness of the economy of the North East and the inability of large groups of the population to withstand the consequences of catastrophe were demonstrated even more clearly than they had been in the 1960s. In the view of many people, the events showed once again that the development policy of the preceding decade, pursued by the SUDENE and aimed mainly at industrialisation, had failed.

These events did not induce the Brazilian government to carry out a thorough reform of the agricultural structure. Instead it announced in June 1970 an ambitious programme of national integration (Programa de Integração Nacional). Amazônia would be opened up by means of a few great highways (connecting with those in the neighbouring countries) and guided colonisation projects would provide no less than 100 000 families (if not more) with their own agricultural holdings within five years (and as many as 1 million within ten years). It was believed that this would considerably relieve the problems of the North Eastern countryside.

Concluding remarks

The foregoing makes clear that the integration policy cannot be understood if the economic motives are not taken into account.

Since 1964, economic growth had been one of the major objectives of Brazilian government policy. Because of the limited capacity of the home market, however, the phase of import substitution proved largely to have lost its dynamic at the beginning of the 1960s and it consequently became necessary to develop new strategies in order not to endanger the country's further economic growth and to increase the gross national product. In the late 1960s and early 1970s, the Brazilian government came to regard the development of the Amazon Basin through generous investments increasingly as one of the more attractive means, since the "North" possessed characteristics which made possible a considerable expansion of mining, livestock farming and forestry (Rosenbaum and Tyler 1971, 420). It was mainly these sectors that would be able to make an important contribution to a further growth of the economy of the North (Panagides and Vande Lage 1973, 2). In addition, there were possibilities for extensive colonisation on the basis of family holdings. The circumstances were also by no means unfavourable for an intensification of the fishing industry, the expansion of certain branches of industry and of tourism. Apart from an expansion of production for the home market, the stimulation of these branches of the economy might also lead to a considerable growth of exports, especially since the Amazon region was favourably located relative to the world's major areas of consumption. In view of the demand of various foodstuffs and mineral raw materials, the prospects for this export orientation were very good.

By the late 1960s Brazilians were thinking more positively about the potentialities of Amazônia than a few decades earlier, when much less was known about its natural wealth, when the international markets for raw materials could still be plentifully supplied by regions with more favourable conditions of production, and when the Brazilian population was still much smaller. They were no longer so ready to characterise the region as a "green hell." On the contrary, an atmosphere of optimism clearly prevailed in relation to the Amazon region and, as is often the case in such situations, there was now a tendency greatly to minimise, if not completely forget, the negative aspects of the region, such as the permanently hot and humid climate and the poverty of most of the soils.

Nationalistic and political motives

Growth might naturally also result if investments were to be made elsewhere in the country. It might even be possible to achieve a still greater economic growth, since the more developed parts of Brazil enjoyed more favourable conditions in a number of respects. The government preferred, however, to include the Amazon Basin in its economic growth strategy. In order to understand this, we should realise that it was not guided exclusively by purely economic motives, but also by other motives, including nationalistic and political ones.

National security, imperialistic motives

We may begin by pointing to the fact that the North has a land frontier of about 11 000 kilometres and that, in the opinion of some Brazilians, this frontier was still inadequately safeguarded. There was little or no settlement along this extensive frontier.

Now that – in the 1960s – population pressure was increasing in the Andean countries and these countries wished to devote more attention to the opening up and colonisation of their eastern lowlands, an increasing migration from the Pacific coast region and the Andes highlands to the western Amazon Basin was by no means unlikely, especially if oil should be discovered in a number of places. In Brazil it was considered not impossible that this colonisation could lead to infiltrations, deliberate or otherwise, on to Brazilian territory, which would then form a pretext for neighbouring countries to make territorial claims. Tambs accordingly regarded the road building projects in Brazil in the late 1960s and early 1970s as a reaction to the plans to construct a Carretera Marginal de la Selva east of the Andes – plans of which, incidentally, but had been little realised in the early 1970s (Tambs 1973, 51 f.).

Instead of losing parts of the Amazon Basin to its neighbours, Brazil was obviously much more interested, according to Tambs, in strengthening its sphere of influence in the neighbouring regions, especially since oil had already been discovered there in several places, while Brazil was still searching for it in vain in the Amazon region.[12]

These interests incidentally did not exist in a vacuum, but formed part of the redoubled efforts Brazil had made since 1964 to create an important sphere of influence for itself in the whole of Latin America. It had realised in this connection, that the Amazon Basin could fulfil an important communications function, both through the presence of navigable rivers and through its location within South America, and that an improved opening-up of the region would therefore only facilitate the realisation of its aspirations for hegemony.[13]

12 Tambs did not consider it unlikely that Brazil would try to infiltrate into the bordering regions in order to be able to claim these areas after a passage of time. He referred in this connection to the events leading to the annexation of Acre at the beginning of last century (Tambs 1973, 46).

13 Tambs discussed this communications function in detail in *Geopolitics of the Amazon* (1973).

For the same reason, Brazil also strived to link the roads being constructed in the Amazon Basin as rapidly as possible with those in the neighbouring countries. Brazil was even prepared to finance wholly or partly the missing road sections in the neighbouring countries and made an offer to some of them to do this. Use was actually made of this offer in the construction of a road across Guyana.

As a result of a decree by the presidents of Brazil and Venezuela, the former country would also obtain a connection with the Venezuelan coast. Ultimately a completely asphalted link was even to be constructed between Brasília and Caracas. Provision was further made for a connection of the Brazilian road network with the road from Pucalpa to Lima (Peru), while a link was also planned with La Paz (van der Putten 1973).[14]

Purely economic motives also played a part in all this, since the road network could also be used in the future for the export trade, making possible a better conquest of foreign markets, including those of Central America.

Apart from a degree of concern for the possible consequences of a thrusting colonisation front in the eastern part of the Andean countries, there arose some mistrust of various countries outside Latin America in around 1970.

Some Brazilians did not consider it unlikely that Brazil would be put under pressure in the future through international organisations, such as the United Nations, or more directly, to open up the last great, still largely uninhabited area on earth suited for human occupation to immigration from densely populated countries, such as India and Pakistan, where part of the population was living on the verge of starvation. This immigration potential was raised by the Indian sociologist and demographer, S. Chandrasekhar, among others (Reis 1971, 13 f.).

As far as the developed West was concerned, there was fear of an increasing interest in the natural resources now that various sources of raw materials were becoming exhausted. It had also already been remarked that the Amazon Basin could be of interest because it contained vast quantities of fresh water, or could become the location of environment-polluting industries from Europe and North America.

The influence which foreign countries would be able to gain from the exploitation of the region might even enable them to obtain complete control of the Amazon Basin, aided by certain groups of Brazilians. It was pointed out in this connection that the United States, in particular, possessed great economic and political power and were located close to South America. This country, especially therefore, was regarded as the most "dangerous" (Rosenbaum and Tyler 1971, 427 f.).

In the late 1960s, many Brazilians saw in the plans of the Hudson Institute a very real threat of control over the Amazon region.

In 1966, the Brazilian engineer, Eudes Prades Lopes, launched the idea of constructing a dam in the Amazon near Obidos, which would make possible the generation of 70 million kilowatts of electricity per annum. His plan was passed by the Ministério de Planejamento to the North American Hudson Institute, which studied it and elaborated it further, but in doing so, completely adapted it, in the view of many Brazilians, to North American interests. The possibilities for the production of cheap energy were ignored. Of much greater interest was considered the fact that, by ponding up the river at Obidos or Monte Alegre, a very large part of the Amazon region would be submerged,

14 According to Morais *et al.* only 135 kilometres of the road from Pucalpa to Lima were still missing in around 1970 (1970, 45).

creating an area of water comparable with the Great Lakes of North America. The shipping facilities so created would make possible a cheap and large-scale exploitation of the minerals and forests.

There was immediately fierce opposition to these plans and the director of the Hudson Institute, Dr. H. Kahn, was more than once personally denounced. People were afraid, perhaps not without reason that, with the realisation of these plans, the Amazon region would soon fall completely under foreign influence, particularly that of North America. It was also realised that the creation of the lake would lead to the loss of large quantities of timber and ores. The plan was explained as an attempt to keep Brazil underdeveloped and was characterised by Valverde (1971b) as being purely neocolonialistic.

It was therefore decisively rejected by, among others, the Comissão Nacional de Defesa e pelo Desenvolvimento da Amazônia (CNDDA), a group of patriotic Brazilians who opposed excessive foreign influence and strove to achieve a nationalistic integration and development of the Brazilian North (Valverde 1971b, 5–10). The Brazilian government clearly stated that the Amazon region would never be given up and that efforts must be made to integrate it as rapidly as possible with the rest of the country. It declared that it regarded the integration of the North as a task that must be carried out by Brazil with the means which the country considered to be the most appropriate.

The slogan of those carrying out the *Rondon Project* (see p. 53–53), "Integrar para não entregar" (integrate it in order not to lose it), expressed very concisely the wish of a great many Brazilians.

The threat to the region from foreign countries was incidentally a danger which aroused the vigilance particularly of the military. The military elite therefore also became the most passionate defenders of the integration and development of Amazônia and regarded this task as a matter of high priority. It was by no means impossible that, in earlier years, they had deliberately drawn the attention to various possible threats and tried to exaggerate their seriousness. In any event, some soldiers seized upon the border disputes between Venezuela and Guyana as an indication of the danger facing Brazil. Venezuela might be able to gain control of part of the Brazilian North (Rosenbaum and Tyler 1971, 425). Lastly, the military also condemned the plans of the Hudson Institute as a threat to national security and perhaps deliberately did so with greater vehemence than was necessary (Valverde 1971b, 10).

The desire to maintain and strengthen their own position undoubtedly played a part in the adoption of a stance by the military elite. Development of the Amazon region meant the possibility of the employment of troops in the pacification of Indigenous tribes, in the maintenance of order and in transport. Military engineers could also have an important share in road construction (Rosenbaum and Tyler 1971, 421).[15] Taking this into account, it is not improbable that the decision of President Medici to pursue more energetically the development of the Amazon region and to give a high priority particularly to the opening up of the region, was made under some pressure from certain military groups. Tyler and Rosenbaum pointed in this connection to the demands and criticism of General Albuquerque du Lima. He was once regarded as a

15 In 1973, five army battalions were stationed at Santarém, Cuiabá, Cruzeiro do Sul, Boa Vista and Porto Velho. For the activities of these army units, see p. 55–58.

possible threat to Medici's authority and the wind had to be taken out of his sails as quickly as possible (Rosenbaum and Tyler 1971, 426).

Population growth and the efforts to achieve integration of the North

One way of realising the economic integration and securing of the Amazon region against foreign occupation was through extensive colonisation. For this, manpower was needed, as indeed it was for various other development activities. The cheaper such manpower is, the better and, consequently, the great population growth was regarded by many Brazilians as not unfavourable. It would enable Brazil all the better to populate and exploit the still vast and scarcely inhabited interior relatively rapidly.

These Brazilians, therefore, did not wish to acknowledge the problem of rapid population growth and the need to restrain it. They pointed to the low average population density and to the enormous potential the country still possessed, thereby ignoring the fact that it was not only the existence of possibilities for expansion which were important, but also the pace at which an expansion could be achieved. Nor did these opponents of a population policy wish to recognise that rapid population growth was disadvantageous to rapid economic development and social progress.

Among the opponents was the Associação Médica do Estado da Guanabara. In the 1970s, this association opposed both the family planning activities of foreign missionaries working in the Amazon region and the Bemfam association.[16] Apart from pointing to the still low average population density in Brazil, the secretary of the medical society, Dr. Mário Victor de Assis Pacheco, pointed to the fact that it was precisely the "population explosion" which had enabled the country to achieve great things in the past, such as the building of Brasília and the construction of the Belém–Brasília highway. His thesis was that accumulated labour was the equivalent of capital and that, in view of the scarcity of the latter, Brazil must strive to obtain as much as possible from the former. Economic progress would benefit in consequence. He concluded that the people who were interested in family planning wanted to keep Brazil underdeveloped, so that it could be more easily exploited and the Amazon region be brought more easily under non-Brazilian influence (Pacheco 1972a, 82 f.).

Lastly, the same medical association even decided, during its first conference in 1972, again to condemn contraception strongly and to defend population growth on the grounds that it formed the basis for "ocupação e conquista do territorio brasileiro, fator indiscutível de desenvolvimento econômico, a exemplo do que ocurreu em todos os países desenvolvidos do mundo" ("occupation and conquest of the Brazilian territory, necessary, without discussion, for economic development, as has occurred in all developed countries of the world") (Pacheco 1972b, 107; author's translation).

One may ask whether such pronouncements, based on disputable arguments, were not largely inspired by self-interest, since the rate at which the population grew determined in part the prospects of a livelihood for doctors. In any event, the association did not forget its own interests, since the same resolution which condemned contraception also made a plea for better working conditions (Pacheco 1972b, 106).

Incidentally, it was not only certain groups of doctors who opposed a restriction of population growth. The Commisão Nacional de Defesa e pelo Desenvolvimento da

16 See particularly the publications of Mário Victor de Assis Pacheco.

Amazônia also rejected such a policy, while the Escola Superior de Guerra, the "brains trust" of the military elite, which largely determined the Brazilian development strategy, expressed its disquiet about an increasing use of contraceptives in 1972 (Pacheco 1972b, 108). The Brazilian government itself also several times plainly declared that the population growth did not need to be checked. The opening up of the Amazon region offered the possibility of avoiding the delicate question of population growth and also the chance to profit from that growth. It suited the Brazilian government very well, in fact, that a considerable increase was occurring at various places in the Amazon region. It was therefore noted with some satisfaction in certain official publications dealing with colonisation in the Amazon Basin that, in Altamira and district alone, 1000 new Brazilians were born in a single year and that a further 800 births were expected in the following months (Ministério da Agricultura n. d., *Desenvolvimento rural*, 11).

A much more realistic view of the demographic problems was taken by Roberto de Oliveira Campos, among others, who pointed out that one in every three or four children died during the first years of infancy in the North East in the early 1970s. He also pointed out that 4000 abortions were occurring in Brazil every day at the time (Morais *et al.* 1970, 127). His views and the views of those who thought like him found no official support, however.

Prestige and popularity considerations

Considerations of prestige also played a part in the efforts to integrate the Amazon region. Paulo Machado stated that the development of the North may be regarded as a "necessity of the Brazilian people" and he explained this as follows:

> When examining history, one notes that every nation has had a necessity for a great achievement in order to affirm itself as a nation. Many have found in war the heroic moment for their national union. Brazil, traditionally a peaceful country without any reason to engage in war, has found in the integration of the Amazon a great national achievement which has been able to attract the attention and preoccupation of every Brazilian. The conquest of the Amazon is, to a degree, a type of war fought within our own frontiers, where a bloodless war goes on in which the enemy is poverty, ignorance and disease (Machado 1973, 1–2).

Moreover, according to Machado, the integration of the Amazon Basin formed a unique opportunity for many Brazilians to escape from the strongly regimented and institutionalised life of the great cities and the more developed regions of the country. In the Amazon region one could show initiative as a pioneer, be creative, discover new sources of livelihood and enjoy more freedom. The development of the region formed a challenge and an adventure. Other people than Machado also believed that Brazil could prove, through the integration of the Amazon region, that it was not an insignificant nation but a country that was able to carry out difficult tasks successfully. Machado concluded: "All this explains the prompt and passionate adherence of Brazilians to the effort that the Government is making in the development of the Amazon" (Machado 1973, 1–2).

With regard to the latter statement, it may be remarked that one can speak only in part of spontaneity. In the early 1970s, the government systematically tried to convince the Brazilians that the opening up and development of the Amazon Basin formed one of the most important tasks for the Brazilian nation and that the whole country could benefit. They deliberately appealed to the feelings of national pride and exploited the characteristic of many Brazilians of feeling attracted by spectacular achievements. The opening up of the Amazon Basin was obviously such an achievement. Roberto de Oliveira Campos even characterised the striving for national integration through the opening up and colonisation of the Amazon region as something that had "apêlo mágico" ("a magic appeal") for broad layers of the Brazilian population and as a heroic solution for an "antiga tristeza" (i.e. the problems of the North East) (Morais *et al.* 1970, 112–131).

It was obviously of great importance to the government that the majority of Brazilians should show some enthusiasm, since this could only facilitate the realisation of the integration of the North. Moreover, the interest in the Amazon region could more or less convince the people that the development of the country was being tackled vigorously, and it could also divert the attention from other, less favourable aspects of government policy, such as lack of political freedom, torture, the continued existence of social abuses and the absence of radical land reform. The elite and the masses could be drawn closer together by a common ideal, thereby reducing the internal political and social tensions. The opening up and development of the Amazon region would therefore contribute not only to territorial and economic integration, but also to political integration, i. e. to that of the elite and the masses.

Tyler and Rosenbaum once expressed it as follows: "Once again a symbol of Brazilian grandeur has been created with which nearly the entire nation can identify" (Rosenbaum and Tyler 1971, 417).

The more successes the government had, the greater its popularity and the weaker the opposition. In other words, the stronger would be the position of the regime. According to Roberto de Oliveira Campos, the revolutionary movement of 1964 badly needed such a strengthening of its position in the late 1960s (Morais *et al.* 1970, 131).

Lastly, there was yet another motive that can be mentioned as underlying the Brazilian government's Amazon policy. This was the wish to obtain not only temporary popularity, but also lasting fame. Just as Kubitschek ensured that his name would live on through the building of Brasília, so may President Medici have hoped that he would become famous in posterity through his bold plans for the Amazon region. His spectacular road building programme, in particular, may have been partly grounded on this motive.

Concluding remarks

In setting out at the end of this chapter the various motives underlying *Operação Amazônia* and trying to draw up a balance, we may first of all remark that the fear that has been several times expressed of the loss of the Amazon region appears exaggerated. The more intensive occupation of the eastern Andes lowlands was in fact taking place slowly before the 1970s. There was certainly no question of a serious and acute threat from the west, nor from the north (Venezuela). Nor did this need to be the case in the following years. The danger that claims would be made on the region for colonisation by countries of the Third World should equally not be overestimated, since there were numerous practical objections to large-scale migration and colonisation. Even if these were indeed to occur, they certainly did not need to mean the end of Brazil's political control over the region. Brazil had succeeded in the past in integrating large numbers of immigrants into the resident population and would be able to do so again. With regard to the idea of colonisation by people from abroad, it should also be realized that large-scale occupation could lead to all kinds of unfavourable effects on the natural environment and that people in other countries were perhaps more afraid of a disturbance to the precarious ecological balance from large-scale clearings than the Brazilians.

We also consider that the danger of a possible economic subjection to the wealthy West was exaggerated, because there were several ways open to Brazil to avoid or limit this, at least if the country wished to do so. Moreover, such an argument lacked credibility as long as the frontiers were kept wide open to foreign investors.

One of the major objectives of the regime that was in power from 1964 was development, particularly in the sense of economic growth, including among its aims that of giving Brazil a more important place within Latin America and in the world as a whole. It seems to us, therefore, that the efforts to integrate the Amazon region must be viewed especially in this light. The government regarded the opening up and development of the North as an important means of accelerating economic growth. This policy obviously needed as far as possible to have the support and sympathy of a large part of the Brazilian population. In order to ensure this, the danger of a threat to, and a possible loss, of the region could naturally be used as one of the reasons.

For the military elite, national security and the preservation of sovereignty over the North was certainly an important motive, but it seems to us that its position was also primarily determined by the motive of economic growth. It clearly and repeatedly showed itself to be a supporter of a policy aimed at economic growth and, from the Escola Superior de Guerra, it exercised a strong influence on the strategy of the government, which was trying to realise that growth.

The fact that the military elite propagated particularly the development of the Amazon region to achieve this end may be attributed to the circumstance that the integration of this region, in addition to its economic growth potential, offered wide opportunities to increase the popularity and power of the military elite and the regime it supported. In the view of the then rulers, therefore, the integration of the North could make an important contribution to political stability. The latter could naturally also be achieved through a vigorous approach to the problem of the North East, but it would be much more difficult to achieve significant results there in the short term.

Lastly, there remains the question of to what extent social motives were important. Was the integration of the North also used as a means to reduce significantly the social problems of the North East? It is difficult to give a reasoned answer to this question at this point. In order to be able to judge to what extent the government was attempting to reduce social problems, the nature and the effect of certain development measures will first have to be analysed and attention will have to be paid to the colonisation process which was begun in the early 1970s. We shall be doing this in the next part of our study and will therefore be returning to this question in our concluding chapter. In anticipation of the latter, we may already remark that the "social" motives appear to be subsidiary to the economic and political ones.

Some development measures of the 1970s

Having reviewed in the last chapter the motives underlying the efforts to develop the Amazon region, in this chapter we shall be concerned mainly with certain measures that were taken in the 1970s to realise these efforts.

The establishment of SUDAM

As far as the activities of the federal government are concerned, we may mention first the establishment in November 1966 of a completely new development body: the Superintendência do Desenvolvimento da Amazônia (SUDAM).[17] The task of this body was to foster progress within its area of jurisdiction by such means as carrying out or initiating surveys and other investigations, drawing up plans, carrying out or initiating projects, encouraging private investment and coordinating the development activities of the separate states and territories. For this purpose, the SUDAM drew up a series of detailed plans covering a number of years, containing specific projects to encourage the various sectors of the economy, tourism, the infrastructure, the health services, education etc. The SUDAM was, in fact, a regional planning institution with the task of furthering as far as possible on all fronts the progress of the Amazon region (Kleinpenning 1972, 2 f.).

In so doing, its area of activity was not restricted to those regions traditionally regarded as belonging to the "North." It also extended as far as Mato Grosso north of the 16th parallel, Goiás north of the 13th parallel and to the part of the state of Maranhão west of the 44th meridian. This area is referred to as Amazônia Legal (see Fig. 1). It covered an area of 5,057,490 square kilometres, which is no less than 59 % of the total area of Brazil, while less than 8 % (6.94 million) of the country's population were resident there in 1968 (Silva 1966, 1).

17 The SUDAM replaced the Superintêndencia do Plano de Valorização Econômica da Amazônia, which had been established in 1953. The task of the latter service was to spend in a suitable manner the 3 % of the federal state income set aside annually under a constitutional provision of 1946 for the progress of the Amazon region, as well as other funds. The SPVEA never became more than a bureaucratic organ of government, which did not succeed in coordinating very much and which lacked the experts able to draw up and realise good investment plans. It also spread the investments too thinly. The organ achieved little during the thirteen years of its existence (Valverde 1971b, 3; Panagides and Vande Lage 1973, 9).

Figure 4. Priority areas and SUDAM-projects in Amazônia Legal (1972)

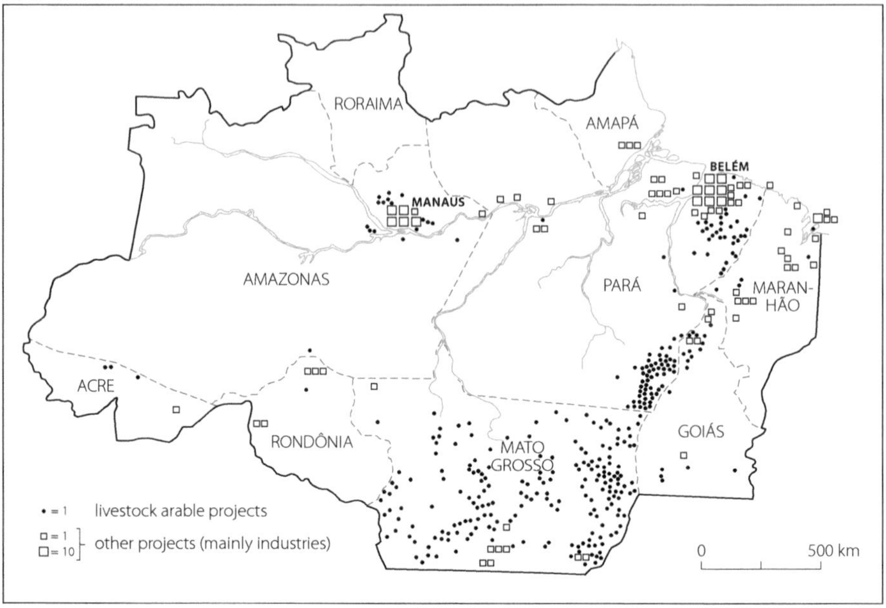

Source: Kleinpenning (1975) (author's own elaboration).

Orlando Valverde observed that such a large land area had never been entrusted to a development body before (Valverde 1971b, 2). The encouragement of the progress of such a vast region in fact formed an extremely onerous task for the SUDAM. It is not surprising, therefore, that this body wished to concentrate the government investments and the activities it was undertaking within the framework of its development plans largely in particular areas, the *areas prioritárias*. These were the more developed and densely populated regions. The priority areas covered 27 % of the area affected by the development plan, but contained 85 % of the population. 88 % of the livestock were to be found there. They accounted for most of the agricultural production and already contained the greater part of the infrastructure (see Fig. 4) (Lopes 1973, 43).

Financial incentives

Much attention was paid to the encouragement of private investment and it is in this field that the SUDAM had its most remarkable successes.

The investments in question were encouraged particularly by a series of fiscal measures devised earlier for the North East, but made fully applicable to Amazônia Legal in 1966 with the help of a number of amendments. By far the most important of the various *incentivos fiscais* was that natural persons and enterprises registered in Brazil could deposit 50 % of the money they owed in taxes with the Banco da Amazônia, which had functioned since 1967 as the official development bank for Amazônia Legal. This money could then be used for the financing of projects in the fields of arable and livestock farming, industry, infrastructure, health care, education or tourism, provided this was done within a stated time and the projects had been approved by the SUDAM. The investments could be made in newly established enterprises, but also used for the modernisation and expansion of existing enterprises.

Another provision, which partly compensated for the effect of unfavourable locational factors, gave firms established before 31st of December 1974 partial or total exemption from income tax for ten years. They could also claim exemption from import duties levied on machines and other requisites needed for the realisation of projects within the area under the jurisdiction of SUDAM. Lastly, they could also obtain exemption from duty on the export of certain products from the area (SUDAM/Banco da Amazônia 1972, 15; Panagides and Vande Lage 1973, 10). Besides the federal government, the states and municipalities also granted special facilities. The authorities also tried to make the establishment of new enterprises more attractive by the provision of infrastructure, mainly in the larger municipalities.

All these measures greatly encouraged the setting aside of taxation funds and gave rise to an increase in investments with non-tax money through the requirement that at least 25 % of the capital needed for the realisation of a project must come from other sources.

Up to June 1976, the SUDAM had approved a total of 528 projects for the establishment or modernisation of enterprises. The total investment involved was 14.571 billion cruzeiros, of which more than 51 % was "fiscal" money.[18] The Amazon region became at that time one of the areas where considerable investments were made. The most important task of the SUDAM was to encourage these investments and to control and canalise them.

A high proportion of the money came from the more developed South East. In 1970 nearly 81 % of the applications to take advantage of the *incentivos fiscais* came from the states of São Paulo, Guanabara, Rio Grande do Sul, Paraná and Minas Gerais. 58.4 % of the money involved in these applications came from the state of São Paulo and 13.9 % from the state of Guanabara. The total for the five states combined was 87.4 % (Miranda 1973, 7). Part of the money came from enterprises in foreign ownership, but it is difficult to discover the exact proportion.

The majority of the 528 projects approved until mid-1976 related to the agricultural sector (335); the second field of investments was industry, with 171 projects. Only 22 projects (which were intended to create a total of 8740 direct jobs) had been approved for *serviços básicos* and infrastructure. Up to the mid-1970s only a part of all these projects had been realised. Many still existed only on paper or were still in their initial phase. The industrial and agricultural projects will be discussed in the next chapter.

The establishment of a free trade zone

The federal government also tried to encourage the economic progress of North Brazil through the establishment, in February 1967, of a free trade zone for a period of 30 years. Initially the zone was restricted to the city of Manaus but, by 1968, it had already been extended to include the immediate vicinity, so that it eventually comprised almost the whole of the municipality and covered an area of about 10 000 square kilometres

18 Data supplied by the SUDAM (personal communication in 1976).

(SUDAM/Banco da Amazônia 1972, 39). Raw materials and the majority of industrial products could be imported into the zone from abroad without the payment of import duty.[19] Thus the facilities related both to articles intended for immediate consumption and to those used in industrial processing. Unrestricted export was also permitted. In addition, factory products were exempted from the tax on industrial goods.

The aim of these far-reaching fiscal facilities was to reduce various unfavourable locational factors, particularly in the industrial field, that would eventually arise in the heart of the Amazon region (*Boletim Informativo* 1971, 1).

The effects of the free trade measures will be evaluated in the next chapter.

The Rondon project

It was not only the government and business which began to show an increasing interest in the Amazon region in the late 1960s; there had also been a greatly increased interest since 1967 from university circles.

At the University of Guanabara the idea arose of involving the university more in the problems of the country's development. The plan gained the sympathy of many other institutions of tertiary education and of the government, which decided to encourage the participation of the students. This led to the emergence of the Rondon project, an assistance and development programme in which many institutions of higher education cooperated. From 1968 this project was under the direct responsibility of the Ministry of Home Affairs, which acted as the coordinating body. Up to March 1973 a total of over 34 000 students were reported to have cooperated in the project (Soares *et al.* 1973, I and II). This meant in practice that, during their vacations, students voluntarily spent 30–40 days elsewhere in Brazil in order to let their knowledge be used for improving the local living conditions. The Rondon project covered all the less developed parts of Brazil, but the North received the most attention up to 1973.

In order to ensure the realisation of the programmes and to guarantee greater continuity in the granting of assistance, a number of *campus avançados* were established. These were outposts where students and teachers could stay. There were already 14 of them in the Amazon region in June 1973 (*Boletim Informativo* 476, 28 June 1973).

The activities, an increasing number of which were carried out from these "campi," were mainly in the field of health, education, agriculture and livestock farming. They consisted both of direct assistance (e.g. medical help), and of research and other activities, such as resource surveys and assistance in cadastral work. The necessary programmes were drawn up by the institutions of higher education, in collaboration and consultation with the official bodies. They were carried out under the supervision of teachers. In some instances, the army gave assistance, such as providing transport or conveying food.

In addition to direct results on the spot, the Rondon project had the advantage of giving the students practical experience and of making them not only more professionally skilled, but also more aware of the many problems arising from the development of their country. The latter was certainly not the least important aspect. The confrontation with specific problems might lead to a change of mentality and to a greater social consciousness among those who would be in charge of affairs in the following

19 Weapons, ammunition, perfumes, tobacco, alcoholic drinks, and private motor cars were excepted.

decades. The attractive aspect of the Rondon project for the government was that it enabled it to harness an important category of the Brazilian people in the carrying out of its integration policy and fill them with enthusiasm for that policy. The project also meant that the government could give help cheaply to those areas where there had been less progress and there was a serious shortage of qualified manpower.

The government incidentally hoped, by means of the Rondon operations, to stimulate greater interest in working in the less developed interior territories of Brazil. The operations might lead to *interiorização da mão de obra*. Since 1972 this *interiorização* was one of the official objectives of the Rondon project. It formed a new activity, which was separate from the original programme, but had more or less originated from it, since it appeared clearly from the realisation of the assistance programmes that the lack of specialists was seriously jeopardising the continuity of the development process. At the same time, it was realised that this qualified manpower might be found among the young graduates who had become acquainted through one or more Rondon operations with the less developed parts of their country. Those in charge of the Rondon project had made it their aim for 1973 to persuade 150 specialists to work in the Brazilian interior (Soares *et al.* 1973, III, 3).

Increasing research activities

Universities and colleges were also involved in the development of the Amazon region through research programmes.

In 1972, Brazil began the realisation of the Programa dos Trópicos Úmidos, an extensive multi-disciplinary, mainly scientific, research programme, for which funds were made available within the context of the Programa de Integração Nacional (National Integration Programme, see p. 78) (Machado 1973, 13). These funds were used *inter alia* to finance soil investigations along the newly constructed roads.

The University of Mato Grosso, in particular, played an important part in the research programme, in collaboration with other bodies, such as the Instituto Nacional de Pesquisas da Amazônia at Manaus.

In order to assist the realisation of various parts of the programme, a start was made on the construction of the Cidade Laboratório Humboldt in Aripuanã, one of the most isolated municipalities of north-west Mato Grosso. In the first instance, about 1000 people were expected to come and live there in the heart of the tropical jungle, where they would carry out research not only in laboratories and experimental plots, but also in the jungle itself (Machado 1973, 14). The location was chosen so that various Indigenous tribes would also be accessible as a subject of research.[20] During a period of two years investments were made in the municipality of Aripuanã to the value of 40 million cruzeiros, mainly for the provision of infrastructure (*Boletim Informativo* 499, 18 September 1973).

According to Machado, all these developments stemmed from the consideration that "only education and research can guarantee the perpetuity of the new surge of progress that exists today in the Amazon" (Machado 1973, 20). Although much re-

20 The University of Mato Grosso was also to build a hospital in Utiariti, where Indigenous people could be treated, making allowance for their manners and customs (Machado 1973, 14–15).

search had been done in the Amazon Basin, nevertheless in many respects not enough was yet known about the region for development to be achieved in the correct manner.

Not only the universities, but also some research institutes began to do research on a much larger scale than before. We may refer here to the activities of the Instituto Nacional de Pesquisas da Amazônia (INPA) at Manaus, whose main interest was in the physical sciences, and to those of the Instituto Nacional de Pesquisas e Experimentação Agropecuaria do Norte (IPEAN) at Belém. The latter institute was concerned with soil and agricultural research. By 1975, it had already studied, *inter alia*, the agricultural potential of the soils along the Transamazônica and would also carry out soil surveys north of the Amazon, where work had begun on a second east-west link. The institute had a number of experimental plots in the Amazon region on which to carry out agricultural research.

Lastly, mention should be made of the research departments of the Banco da Amazônia and the SUDAM. The Bank carried out economic investigations with the aim of giving the government and investors the best possible advice. The field of research of the SUDAM was wider but here, too, the emphasis was placed strongly on research in the service of economic development. The *Núcleo de Altos Estudos Arnazônicos* of the university of Pará, also undertook research projects.

The extensive opening-up programme

In the late 1960s and early 1970s, attention was drawn to the Amazon region much more through the federal government's spectacular road building programme than through the measures discussed above. As early as 1958 the central government had begun to make the Amazon region more accessible by means of a road link between Belém and Brasília. This 2100 kilometre road was completed in 1960. In 1965 a further important connection was completed: that between Brasília and Porto Velho (Rondônia), via Cuiabá, the capital of Mato Grosso (see Fig. 5).

Figure 5. Road and general reference map of North Brazil (situation in late 1978)

Source: Kleinpenning (1975) (author's own elaboration).

Since then, the government has pressed on uninterruptedly with its policy for improving the infrastructure. Starting from the premise that there were many unnavigable rivers and that the waterways which were navigable were not assisting adequately the occupation of the region and were also making rapid communication impossible, it came to view the construction of more highways as an increasing necessity if the utilisation of the region was to be made easier. A start was therefore made on the construction of a road between Porto Velho and Rio Branco in the territory of Acre, as well as on the construction of a road from Porto Velho to Manaus. According to the original plans, these roads should have been completed at the end of 1970, but they were only finished a couple of years later. The road from Manaus to Porto Velho was asphalted at the beginning of 1974. This enabled one to drive from Porto Velho to Humaitá in three hours, while the boat trip previously took 25 hours.

Moreover, thanks to the activities of the army, a road link between Manaus and Boa Vista, in the territory of Roraima, was completed during the course of 1974. A continuation of this road to the frontier with Venezuela and Guyana was also completed.[21]

The most spectacular and, at the same time, unexpected road construction project dates from 1970 and was initiated by the Medici government, which regarded the improvement and expansion of the road network as one of the most effective means of fostering integration of the country. The project comprised the construction of two great highways through the heart of the Amazon region. They were financed mainly with funds made available through the Programa de Integração Nacional.

One road, about 1750 km long, ran from north to south and connected Cuiabá with Santarém, while the second road was planned to run from east to west south of the Amazon, linking Estreito, on the Rio Tocantins, with Humaitá, on the Rio Madeira. This second road has become known as the Transamazônica. It has a length of 2328 km and connects the principal population centres in the region south of the Amazon (Andreazza 1970, 18 ff.). Near Estreito the road connected with the Belém–Brasília highway and the road network of the North East. The latter was still in a very poor condition in various places in 1970, but it has been further improved since then (Morais *et al.* 1970, 1–25).

A start was made on the construction of the road from Cuiabá to Santarém, which did not connect directly with a single existing village, by units of the Brazilian army engineers, as early as the end of 1970. They worked outwards from Cuiabá and Santarém towards the army base of Cachimbo, in southern Pará. By October 1972, 690 km had been completed, mainly in the south. The whole road was planned to be finished in the course of 1974 (Ministério da Agricultura 1972a, 32).

The construction of the Transamazônica also began in September 1970, when four private companies started work on the 1254 km long section from Estreito to Itaituba. This portion of the road was completed in September 1972, when Brazil celebrated its 150th year of independence, and was officially opened to traffic. Regular services began to connect the larger centres.

The second, more westerly section of the Transamazônica, i.e. the 1074 km from Itaituba to Humaitá, was constructed by three private road building concerns.

21 The completion of this frontier link had already led to the import of Venezuelan industrial products into Boa Vista. The better accessibility had also resulted in an expansion of cattle farming, while farmers from the Northeast had begun to settle in the vicinity of the road (*Opinião*, 20 a 27 de agosto de 1973, pp. 4–5, "A Corrida para Roraima").

This portion was officially opened to traffic in March 1974 (Wozniewicz 1973, 16 f.). The third portion of the east-west highway runs from Humaitá via Porto Velho and Rio Branco to the Peruvian frontier. It was built by the army and was virtually completed at the end of 1973.[22]

Photo 1. Monument commemorating the fact that the Transmazônica reached Altamira[23]

Photo 2. Plaque unveiled when the Transmazônica reached Altamira

22 Some publications included this section with the Transamazônica, while others did not.

23 All Photos in this part by Jan M. G. Kleinpenning.

Photo 3. The Transamazônica just east of Altamira

Photo 4. The Transamzônica disturbed the normal drainage in several places

The army was also active elsewhere in this part of the Amazon Basin. It was working, for example, on an alternative connection between Humaitá and Rio Branco via Lábrea and building a road from Ariquemes to Guajará-Mirim, primarily to facilitate the exploitation and transport of cassiterite (Wozniewicz 1973, 31).

Most of the roads were initially not asphalted, but metalled to make them usable at all seasons.[24] Use was naturally much less easy and also much less safe in the rainy season than in the dry season, although dust was a much greater nuisance during that part of the year. The width of the roads was about 8.5 metres, at least where they had not been eaten into by erosion. They were, therefore, normal two-lane roads. The small rivers and streams were crossed by wooden bridges, but the large rivers, such as the Xingu, had still to be crossed by ferries in the early 1970s.[25] Initially, there were almost no service facilities, such as petrol pumps, along the roads. These were still almost wholly concentrated in the larger centres. In spite of this "austerity," large sums were spent on the construction of the roads. The total cost of the highway from Estreito to Humaitá and the Peruvian frontier was estimated at 810 million cruzeiros (Wozniewicz 1973, 30–32).

A more recent road building project gave rise to less sensation, because many people regarded it as the logical continuation of the earlier activities, but this did not mean that it was less ambitious. It related to the construction of the Perimetral Norte. As appears from Figure 5, this road opened up the little known, little used and extremely thinly populated region north of the Amazon.[26]

The contract for the construction of the section from Macapá to São Gabriel de Cachoeira and the Colombian frontier was granted to six companies, five of which were also involved in the construction of the Transamazônica. The work began in August 1973. The costs of this 2586 km highway amounted to 884 million cruzeiros. The section running from Cucuí, on the Venezuelan frontier, via São Gabriel de Cachoeira to Cruzeiro do Sul is 1629 km long and was built by the army.

The total length from Macapá to Cruzeiro do Sul is 4215 km and the costs were estimated at 1100 million cruzeiros (*Boletim Informativo* 381, 10 November 1972). The completion of the whole road was planned for the end of 1977, which meant that the Perimetral Norte was also expected to be built at a fast rate. Following this, a further highway was planned to be built between Santarém and the Surinam frontier (continuation of the road from Cuiabá-Santarém).

In the longer-term future, these roads would naturally not be the end of the story. The highways described above were only the beginning of the intended opening-up and integration. They would form the main road framework and would obviously lead to the construction of a number of secondary roads.[27]

---

24 A start had been made on asphalting the Belém–Brasília highway, a project that had to been completed by the end of 1973 (*Boletim Informativo* 278, 4 May 1972).

25 The traffic capacity of the roads was determined from estimates of future traffic flows. It was assumed that, in 1980, from 50 to 400 vehicles would use the Transamazônica daily with the usual number at between 50 and 150 (Wozniewicz 1973, 4).

26 Excluding Manaus, the population north of the Amazon was estimated at about 400 000. This was less than one inhabitant per 3 square kilometres. The region covers about 15% of the total area of Brazil ("A Nova Epopeia da Perimetral Norte," *Rodovia* 301, Jan.–Feb. 1973, pp. 26–29).

27 The employment which was temporarily created by these road building projects was not very great, since the operations were highly mechanised. Detailed information is lacking. Although much tree-felling could still be done better by hand than with machines, only a few thousand workers would be required. In March 1971, 5200 people were employed along 980 km of the Transamazônica (*Rodovia*, 290, May–June, 1971, p. 63).

There would also be connections with roads which had been or were being built in the neighbouring countries. We have already pointed out that the Transamazônica was planned to connect with the highway from Pucalpa to Lima. In 1970, all but about 135 km had been completed (Morais *et al.* 1970, 45). There would also be a road from Caracas via Ciudad Bolivar to the Brazilian-Venezuelan frontier, to connect with the almost completed road from Manaus to Boa Vista. As the result of an agreement with Guyana, a link with Georgetown was also planned, while a link was assured with La Paz through an agreement with Bolivia. A road between Macapá and the frontier with French Guiana had already been in existence for some time in mid-1973.

The routes of the Transamazônica and the Perimetral Norte were planned not only to release various larger population centres from their isolation, but also to connect the points from which the tributaries of the Amazon are navigable. The aim was to integrate road and water transport and to encourage a more intensive use of the many navigable waterways. Along the Transamazônica river ports would be constructed or improved at Carolina, Imperatriz, Marabá, Jatobal, Altamira, Santarém, Itaituba, Humaitá, Porto Velho and Boca do Acre (Andreazza 1970, 7). Financially and technically approved plans already existed in mid-1973 for the improvement of the ports near Porto Velho, Altamira, Santarém and Itaituba (Boghossian n. d., 14; *Boletim Informativo* 453, 2 April 1973). The construction of the Perimetral Norte would be complemented by the provision of port facilities at Macapá, Caracaraí, Benjamin Constant and Cruzeiro do Sul.

This encouragement of inland shipping formed another aspect of the integration policy being pursued by the Brazilian government in the early 1970s. In order to improve communications, the government also extended and improved the post and telegraph network and constructed more airports. It was planned to build 126 new airstrips during a period of ten years and 50 of these had already been completed at the end of 1973 (SUDAM/Banco da Amazônia 1972, 10–12; Amazônia – modelo de integração 1973).

Provisional evaluation of the effects of some development measures

The developments in the Manaus free trade zone

The institution of the free trade zone led immediately to a great increase in the import of all kinds of consumer goods, both from abroad and inside Brazil, because such goods could now be offered to the consumer considerably more cheaply than elsewhere and than hitherto. Trading activity increased greatly in a short time as appears from the fact that the number of registered trading undertakings rose from 458 in 1968 to 2600 at the end of 1974.[28] Numerous new shops were opened and the existing ones considerably expanded their activities or turned to the sale of other articles that were more in demand and more profitable. This often resulted in a blurring of the distinction between different classes of shop. Because of this expansion and reorientation of the retail sector, Manaus was generously provided with a variety of commodities from home and abroad, which altered the situation radically. Previously, the provisioning of the city had been inadequate in many respects, including that of essential food supplies.

In a short time, the commercially somewhat inert and sleepy Manaus was transformed into a dynamic urban centre. By mid-1973, the central area was dominated by modern shops where one could buy a great variety of goods, such as American canned foods, Swiss watches, Persian carpets and Japanese transistor radios.

Tourism increased. The possibility of acquiring cheap radio and television sets, record players and other electrical goods, in particular, exerted a strong attraction. Not only Brazilians, but also foreign tourists, used the opportunity to combine a visit to the unknown city of Manaus and the neighbouring tropical jungle with the purchase of a number of relatively cheap consumer goods. People who visited Manaus for business reasons also almost always used the opportunity to take away particular articles for themselves or for friends and acquaintances. Consequently, the customs officials were fully occupied in keeping the large flow of all kinds of cheaply purchased goods to other parts of the country as far as possible within the permitted limits. The modern airport was often so congested that it was best to arrive there well before departure time.

The establishment of the free trade zone, apart from the creation of employment, was not equally favourable for all layers of the population. The price reductions applied mainly to durable consumption goods, which only people from the higher income

28 Information supplied by SUFRAMA.

classes could afford. The clientele, therefore, largely consisted of the more prosperous inhabitants of Manaus and of the many, more well-to-do, Brazilians from other parts of the country, who almost always made use of a visit to Manaus to acquire luxury goods. Food prices and rents, on the other hand, fell hardly or not at all, so that the advantages for the lower income classes remained limited. It is therefore not surprising that there remained a large informal sector in Manaus.

A further unfavourable aspect was that the wide availability of all kinds of commodities tempted the local Brazilians to raise their level of consumption and to spend their money on goods that were far from essential. The purchasing power of the majority of the population was modest and many people did not have an immediate need for a great number of articles, such as television sets and electric shavers, but they were more or less tempted to buy through the abundance of such articles and the facilities for hire purchase.

Another negative side of the commercial revolution was that the retail sector expanded so much that there was heightened competition, with the shopkeepers often anxious to sell mainly those articles that were most profitable. Various poor and mediocre goods also found their way on to the market in the late 1960s, including clothing that was not suitable for the hot, humid climate (Martelli 1969, 14). The import of foreign canned goods and other foods also made difficult the disposal of small surpluses of certain agricultural products from the immediate neighbourhood, because they were of less interest to the shops of Manaus (Martelli 1969, 18).

Another less favourable development was the rapid increase in the population. The increased economic activity resulting from the free trade status of Manaus tempted many Brazilians to migrate from the surrounding countryside. During the period 1960–1970 the population of the Manaus municipality increased from 175 300 to 314 200.[29] Employment expanded considerably, especially since trade also stimulated other activities, such as construction, but did not keep pace with the population increase, so that many city dwellers led a poverty-stricken existence (Filha 1971a, 79 f.). For these poorer people, in particular, the generous supply of goods in the shops created a painful tension between needs and the possibility of satisfying them.

As a result of the revival of trade, industry and tourism, Manaus experienced a building boom. Skyscrapers began somewhat hesitantly to contribute to the appearance of the city. During the period 1967–1971 a rise of nearly 400 % was recorded in the activities of the construction industry.[30]

The aim of the free trade measures was not so much to encourage trade, consumption, and tourism, as to accelerate the pace of industrial development. Industrialisation had indeed begun partly as a result of the financial incentives offered by the SUDAM, from which the firms in Manaus were also able to benefit. A number of enterprises had already established themselves in and around Manaus or were intending to do so. In a few years the range of industries became more varied and extensive. Whereas, until a short time before, Manaus had been little more than a collection and distribution centre, it was now also becoming an industrial centre of regional significance. One of the most remarkable industrial projects of the 1960s was the establishment of an iron

29 Figures derived from *Sinopse estatística*.

30 The figures used in this section were largely derived from *Anuário Estatístico* (1974).

and steel complex.[31] The building of a petrochemical complex was one of the plans of the mid-1970s still to be realised.

The "climate" for the establishment of industries was favourable in various respects. Apart from the financial facilities and the relatively cheap manpower, there were the good port facilities, the central location in the Amazon region, the relatively favourable communications (Manaus was becoming increasingly a nodal point of roads), the presence of some infrastructure, including a small refinery, the existence of a university and the occurrence of various industries which could function as suppliers or customers.[32] The SUFRAMA (Superintendência da Zona Franca de Manaus) was trying to make the locational conditions still more favourable through the expansion and improvement of the infrastructure. Many Brazilians, therefore, looked forward to the industrial future of the largest urban centre of the state of Amazonas with some confidence.

During the period 1968–1974 the SUFRAMA approved a total of 138 industrial projects, 97 of which were in process of execution or already completed at the end of 1974, while 41 had not yet commenced. The total investment for all the projects was 2.229 billion cruzeiros. The number of jobs to be provided directly was 26 400 (*Projetos industriais aprovados 1968–1974*, 1975). The industrial development was taking place partly in a *distrito industrial* (which covered an area of 664 ha and was provided with the necessary infrastructure) and partly outside this industrial district.

Apart from a number of industries supplying local needs or processing regional raw materials (such as timber, jute, hides, precious stones and gold), the projects related largely to enterprises which had

a) great interest in tax-free imports of raw materials from abroad, or in the exemption from value added tax (which was considerably higher in Brazil for luxury goods), and
b) manufactured goods which could be transported over long distances because of a favourable weight-value ratio.[33]

Important branches of industry, therefore, which were present in the free trade zone or would be established there, included textiles and clothing (mainly artificial fibres), electronics (radio and television sets and calculators) and other luxury goods, such as jewellery, watches, alarm clocks and optical products.

The firms specialising in these articles derived their raw materials or semi-manufactures largely or entirely from other parts of Brazil or from abroad, so that there were relatively few or no "backward linkages" with regional and local concerns. This meant that the "multiplier effect" was small as far as employment was concerned. According to Mahar (1976), the need for packaging materials had created "forward linkages," but in general these also were limited. This was all the more so because the local

31 The plan for building the complex dates from before the institution of the free trade zone. It came into operation in March 1972 and had an annual capacity of 60 000 tons. Iron ore was drawn from the region of Jatapu on the Rio Negro. Various raw materials, such as lime and manganese also came from the Amazon Basin. The fuel was charcoal.

32 The refinery had been in operation since 1957 and used oil from Peru and Venezuela.

33 The following is partly derived from Mahar (1976).

commerce was concerned mainly with the sale of imported end-products and much less with the sale of locally produced manufactured goods. These were destined mainly for the markets in the Centro-Sul and abroad.

If one adds to this the fact that by no means all of the approved projects had been fully realised and that the majority of the industrial enterprises were owned or would be owned by firms or individuals from other parts of Brazil or from abroad, thus resulting in an outflow of profits, the conclusion appears justified that the effects of the industrial policy until the mid-1970s could not be judged to be wholly positive.[34]

Since the free trade led to greater competition for home industry and the import of electrical equipment, in particular, proved to be disadvantageous for Brazilian industry, there was, in the mid 1970s, a great risk of a limitation of the free trade measures. This possibility was one of the reasons why various foreign firms, including Japanese ones, had decided to set up assembly plants for radios, colour television sets and other electrical products (*Amazonas, porta aberta para o futuro* 1972).

Partly because of the incipient industrialisation, imports and exports considerably increased in the late 1960s and early 1970s. In 1972, goods to the value of 1.4 billion cruzeiros were imported into the Zona Franca de Manaus, while the value of exports was 597 million cruzeiros. In 1968 the value of imports was still only 225 million, while exports amounted to 112 million cruzeiros in 1967. This meant that imports increased sixfold in a few years, while exports increased nearly fivefold.

Calculated by value, 60.5 % of the imported commodities originated from Brazil and 39.5 % from other countries. In 1974, about 60 % of the Brazilian goods came from São Paulo and Guanabara and only 13 % from the North. The relationship with the local economy was therefore weak. Apart from raw materials and semi-manufactures for the finishing and assembly industries, the imports consisted largely of durable consumer goods to be sold by the many traders of Manaus. They found a market because of the growth in incomes, the population growth, the rise of bargain tourism and the lack of adequate local industry. A considerable share was accounted for by goods regarded as luxury articles by the Brazilian government and so subject to high taxation outside the free trade zone.[35]

62 % of the foreign goods came from the United States, Japan and Panama. Only 13 % of the outward movement of goods was to other countries; 36 % went to Western Amazônia and 51 % to the remainder of Brazil.[36]

About 60 % of the outward movement of goods destined for the remainder of Brazil was intended for São Paulo and Guanabara. It consisted for a considerable part of goods from the primary sector, such as rubber and jute. The part played by manufactures in 1973 was still a modest one, although it was gaining in importance.

Foreign exports had increased partly as a result of the free trade facilities. They still included many primary products. Manufactures accounted for only a modest share in the early 1970s.

The value of the incoming goods considerably exceeded the value of those going out (1119 and 0.421 billion cruzeiros, respectively, in 1973). Mahar concludes from this that much of the extra income that was received in the free trade zone as a result of the

34 As elsewhere in Brazil, the enterprises there may not be more than 50 % foreign-owned.

35 See for more details Mahar (1976).

36 Figures derived from *Anuario estatístico* (1975).

growth in trade and industry drained away to São Paulo and Guanabara. Only when industry had become more developed in Manaus would there be a more favourable balance.

The figures given here naturally relate only to the officially registered trade movements. In addition, there was a good deal of smuggling in spite of government efforts to limit it. Tobacco, perfumes and alcoholic drinks were not exempted from import duties, but entered in fluctuating quantities as contraband. The legal requirements were also evaded in respect of the export of the dearer consumer goods. The great extent of the free trade zone (10 000 sq km) incidentally did not make easier the control on imports and exports.

The expansion of trade, industry, tourism, construction and related activities, such as banking, created fresh employment, but the population also greatly increased, mainly as a result of the increased migration from the rural areas to the city. Consequently, there was still a lack of adequately paid work. No figures are available of total employment, but there are some data relating to the industrial sector. In June 1968, 222 industrial enterprises employed only 6566 people (Williams 1971, 21), which was, of course, only a very modest proportion of a total work force estimated at from 90–100 000. The majority of the working population had therefore to find a living in the tertiary sector. In 1973 the number of industrial jobs probably totalled 10 000.

The 96 industrial projects approved by SUFRAMA up to 6 July 1973 were expected to create an estimated total of 16 759 jobs, but this would not be achieved until after several years, even if all the plans were fully realised (*Projetos industriais aprovados 1968–1974* 1975). Many projects still existed only on paper or were in the first stages of implementation. Since the commercial sector was already well-filled, the future growth in employment would be largely determined by the rate of expansion of industrial activity.

The largest employer would be the SIDERAMA iron and steel works, which employed 480 men in its initial phase, but was expected to provide 1132 jobs when operating fully. The second industry in terms of employment (situation in July 1973) was a jute processing factory, which would employ 1086 workers. Most enterprises employed, or would employ between a few dozen and a few hundred workers, which meant that the greater part of industry consisted of small to medium-sized firms, whose contribution to the ultimate expansion of employment was not very great (*Projetos industriais aprovados 1968–1974* 1975).

Apart from industrial expansion, an effort was also made to increase agricultural production in the vicinity of Manaus. The intention was for medium-sized and large holdings to practise livestock farming and commercial arable farming. It was expected that the arable holdings would produce not only commodities for the urban market, but also for the national market and for export (such as guarana, pepper, cocoa, rubber and fruit). The actual developments until 1974 were modest. Although a *distrito agropecuário*, 560 000 hectares in extent, had been defined near Manaus, very few holdings had been established there.

In the mid-1970s, the SUFRAMA had plans for allocating approximately 10 000 hectares for intensively farmed 100 ha. holdings, 150 000 hectares for commercial arable enterprises of between 500 and 3000 ha, 250 000 ha to livestock fazendas of between 3000 and 15 000 ha, and the remainder mainly to large forestry enterprises. These are only provisional figures, but they show clearly that the aim was to achieve modern, large-scale agriculture and forestry. The exploitation of the forests was to be directed, among other things, at the manufacture of cellulose and paper.

To summarise the foregoing, we may say that the developments in Manaus up to 1976 as a result of the free trade facilities had both positive and negative aspects. The following may be regarded as favourable consequences:

- the cost of living fell;
- incomes became higher;
- the urban market was better supplied with certain commodities;
- employment was expanded as a result of the growth of trade, tourism, the construction industry, manufacturing and banking;
- overt unemployment decreased.[37]

Opposed to these positive effects, however, are a number of negative aspects, *viz.*

- the developments were rather artificial, i. e. they were mainly the result of an extensive import trade, involving high transport costs, built up to profit from a favourable fiscal climate;
- the economic growth in Manaus showed few signs of diffusion through the region as far as employment and distribution of incomes were concerned. It was a development in an enclave. There had even been an inflow of capital from the region into Manaus during recent years and a considerable loss of labour from the surrounding countryside as a result of rural-urban migration;
- the assembly plants which put together parts from abroad could form a threat to the Brazilian balance of payments, especially since it was not certain whether these industries would be able to compete on the world market;
- industrialisation was only slowly gaining momentum, so that its contribution to the development process was still small;
- the imports had resulted in greater competition for the industries of Manaus and the rest of Brazil;[38] A number of older firms in Manaus consequently had to close their doors (Rosenbaum and Tyler 1971, 423);
- the development of trade had resulted in the large-scale legal and partly illegal import of many luxury articles, which made an attack on the foreign currency reserves and catered mainly for the needs of the more well-to-do Brazilians;
- an increase in the wants of many residents and visitors to Manaus as a result of the confrontation with a large number of commodities, when these wants could by no means be satisfied. The lower income groups, in particular, were unable to benefit;
- the effects were in general much more limited for the lower income groups than the higher, bearing in mind the fall in the cost of living;
- a considerable share of the advantages of trade and industry was to the benefit of entrepreneurs from the South East;
- the great increase in migration from country to town, which led to the depopulation of some areas of the countryside and perpetuated the employment problem in Manaus.

37 It was mainly as a consequence of this that the population of Manaus increased from 175 300 to 396 667 during the period 1960–1974.

38 It was recently decided to revise various aspects of the free trade facilities (*Boletim Informativo*, 7 June 1976).

Mahar therefore pleaded for a development strategy which would encourage enterprises to make more use of local and regional raw materials. The effects on the regional economy would then be much stronger.

The results of the industrialisation policy

Table 3, which shows the distribution of the industrial projects approved by the SUDAM up to 1st January 1973, gives an impression of the regional differences in industrialisation. It appears from Figure 3 that the great majority of the industrial projects in the states of Pará and Amazonas had been or were being realised in Belém and Manaus, respectively, or in the near vicinity of these centres.

Table 3. The number of industrial projects (new establishments or extensions) approved by the SUDAM in Amazônia Legal up to 1st Jan 1973

State/Territory	No. of industrial projects approved	Total investment in cruzeiros x 1000	Expected no. of new jobs
Acre	1		97
Amapá	5		1405
Amazonas	36		9591
Goiás	7		830
Maranhão	23		3076
Mato Grosso	7		1422
Pará	83		18 344
Rondônia	5		660
Total	167	2 449 812	35 425

Source: Lopes (1973, 50).

By comparison with Manaus, Belém, the largest urban centre of the Amazon region, had a more favourable locational climate for industrial enterprises, despite the fact that it lacked the attraction of free trade regulations. It lies closer to the more developed and more densely populated parts of Brazil, which is an advantage for the supply of raw materials and the marketing of the finished products. The city itself had 776 000 inhabitants in 1974, while a considerable proportion of the population of the Amazon region (ca. 25 %) lived in the Belém-Bragança district. Consequently, there was a much greater market potential for industry on the spot and in the surrounding area than in Manaus. Lastly, we may refer to the better and more extensive infrastructure and to the existence of road connections with the Centro-Sul region. As a result, Belém attracted more industries in the late 1960s and early 1970s than Manaus did.

Manaus was smaller than Belém and did not possess a densely populated hinterland, but, with its 397000 inhabitants, it was the second population agglomeration within Amazônia Legal. Further, in comparison with the smaller centres of the Amazon region, Manaus possessed relatively good and extensive services. The wide range of free trade facilities had also considerably improved the locational climate since 1967.

The concentration of industrialisation noted here in and around the two largest cities is understandable, but a consequence was that the development of the principal urban centres was still further increased, so that the disparity with the surrounding countryside became in many respects greater rather than less. These increasing differences also intensified migration to the cities, at a time when the drift from the countryside was already largely directed towards the two centres.

The government tried to give greater stimulus to a few smaller centres in order to slow down the migration to Manaus and Belém, but the differences in the level of urban development were still so great that hardly any success had been achieved by 1975. Consequently, in spite of the industrialisation in both cities, there was still an unfavourable balance between employment and the demand for work and the poor quarters of the two places continued to grow.

During the period 1960–1970, the population of the municipality of Manaus grew from 175300 to 314200, an increase of 79.4%. The state of Amazonas, of which Manaus is the capital, increased in population from 721200 to 960900.[39] It may be deduced from this that the area not forming part of the capital grew at a much slower rate. There was a heavy migration from the rural areas and the small towns to Manaus. This was partly the result of the difficult situation in which the extractive economy found itself and the unattractive living and working environment in many places, but it was also the result of the increasing attraction of Manaus, which had been revitalised, *inter alia*, by industrialisation.

Between 1960 and 1970, Belém grew from 402000 to 642500, which is an increase of about 60%. The whole of the state of Pará increased in population from 1551000 to 2197000, which means that the area not forming part of the capital had a population increase of 405700 (*Sinopse estatística do Brasil* 1971). In relative terms, this was also a less rapid growth than that which occurred in Belém.

A direct consequence of the heavy migration flow was that still greater pressure was placed on the already inadequate urban facilities. Like the SUDENE, the SUDAM also encouraged the improvement of water supply and sewerage systems etc., but it did not succeed in expanding and improving the infrastructure sufficiently to alleviate the residential environment of the population. Whatever was achieved was rapidly overtaken again by the population growth and large sections of the population continued to be deprived of basic amenities.

A look at the totals in Table 3 shows that the policy of encouraging industry by means of *incentivos fiscais* and various other measures had achieved only modest results by 1975. Industrialisation in Amazônia Legal was, in fact, still in its infancy, especially since many projects had not yet been realised or had been realised only in part. In the North East the SUDENE was forced to admit that, in spite of an active industriali-

39 Figures derived from *Sinopse estatística do Brasil* (1971).

sation policy, it had not been able to achieve an adequate expansion of employment. The SUDAM had likewise not been successful in Amazônia Legal. A radical change in this situation was definitely not be expected in the short term, since the conditions for industrialisation were more unfavourable in the North than in the North East.

The slow expansion of industrial employment was incidentally not entirely the consequence of unfavourable locational factors. Another fact is that the policy of the Brazilian government was not calculated to create a big demand for industrial labour. The financial incentives were creating a favourable investment climate, while the other conditions remained relatively unfavourable to industrialisation. These included the lack of skills of much of the potential labour force. Consequently, capital-intensive industries were the most attractive. Such firms derived the maximum benefit from the tax facilities and were not greatly dependent on the scarce available skilled labour supply. This meant that Brazilian and foreign industrialists and other sectors of the population owning capital profited from the financial incentives, while there was only a modest improvement in the opportunities for the mass of the population of the North. An approved industrialisation project produced on average 212 jobs. It was expected that the 171 projects which had been approved up to 1976 (during a ten year period) would give rise to a direct increase in employment of 43 826 jobs, at least when all the projects had been fully realised, which was by no means the case.[40] The average investment required to achieve this result was no less than 69 154 cruzeiros per job.

In order to form a correct picture of the employment effects, it should incidentally be noted that the number of direct jobs mentioned here will have to be reduced by the number of jobs that disappeared as a result of the closing of less viable and often smaller enterprises, which were not able to compete. No research has ever been done on the magnitude of this effect. Nor were any reliable data available about the indirect employment which was to be expected or had already been created. There was probably relatively little of this, since many firms had only a few linkages with other industrial undertakings. This applied in any event to many new firms in Manaus and had also been observed among a lot of the firms established in the North East to benefit from fiscal advantages. The situation in Belém, Manus and other places was therefore probably similar.

It may be concluded that the population of Amazônia Legal had so far experienced only modest advantages from the policy of encouraging industry. There had been no great improvement in urban employment.

A considerable part of the capital with which approved SUDAM projects had been or were being realised came from the Centro-Sul. In 1970 as much as nearly 81 % of the applications for the benefits of the *incentivos fiscais* came from São Paulo, Guanabara, Rio Grande do Sul, Paraná and Minas Gerais. The amount of tax money involved represented more than 87 % of the total applied for.[41] The picture has not changed since then. This means that a considerable part of the profits to be earned by the industrial projects will benefit industrialists and other capital-owning population groups in the South East. Since part of the industry there was in foreign hands, part of the profits

40 An unknown proportion of the jobs is already included in the employment to be created by the 138 projects approved by the SUFRAMA, since the enterprises in Manaus are able to benefit from the facilities of both the SUDAM and the SUFRAMA.

41 The projects concerned include both industrial and others (Miranda 1973, 7).

additionally flowed to foreign countries. As far as industry was concerned, the North threatened to become increasingly a dependency of the South East.

This was all the more so since various industries which were established in the North through local initiative were threatening to fall into the hands of industrialists from the more developed South East or from the United States. The weekly paper *Opinião* pointed out at the time that a number of enterprises had already been sold or would shortly be taken over. Among the examples given were FASA (match industry), Parquet do Pará, SIDERAMA (iron and steel industry) and ESTANAVE (shipbuilding). The industries concerned were generally those on the verge of bankruptcy or, in any event, those which had financial problems as a result of unfavourable production circumstances, such as increasing competition from South-Eastern industry, the low purchasing power of the population and insufficiently skilled personnel. The paper also pointed out that the Banco da Amazônia was not unfavourable to such sales, since it did not find the continual advancing of credit to economically unhealthy enterprises attractive. It is not surprising, therefore, that the SUDAM also tried to encourage the merging of regional enterprises with larger and more modern concerns. The majority of the undertakings which had lost their independence by 1975 passed into the hands of industrialists from São Paulo.[42]

The expansion of large-scale livestock farming

Examination of developments in the agricultural sector reveals that there was a considerable expansion of cattle farming in the late 1960s and early 1970s. Glaser pointed to the obtrusion of large-scale cattle farming near the Belém–Brasília highway and the road from Cuiabá to Porto Velho, among other places (Glaser 1971, 22–24). Figure 4 shows that the livestock farming projects of the SUDAM were concentrated predominantly on the southern and eastern fringe of Amazônia Legal (central Mato Grosso, northern Goiás and eastern Pará). These are areas which, although situated within Amazônia Legal, actually lie on its periphery. This means that the vegetation in many places is not as dense as in the more central part of the Amazon basin. It mostly consists of *cerrado*, *cerradão* and *mata fina*, i.e. of tree savannas and a tropical forest forming a transition to the *selva*. This southern peripheral zone is relatively favourably situated in relation to the more populated areas of Brazil, so that the transport of meat and animals was not too difficult and expensive. Besides relatively favourable communications with the consumer markets in the South East, North East and North (Belém), these regions possessed the advantage of being relatively easily accessible for the owners of the *fazendas*, who largely lived in South-East Brazil. Although they were absentee owners, they could nevertheless remain well-informed about the fortunes of their estates.

The new – or modernised – enterprises concentrated mainly on beef production. In most enterprises arable farming was either subsidiary or completely absent. The *fazendas* were planned on modern lines, as appears from such things as the purchase of highly productive breeds of cattle, the laying down of fenced "leys" and measures to combat disease. In this respect their management differed from that which had traditionally characterised livestock farming in the region (Pinto 1971, 14).

42 *Opinião*, 20 a 27 de agosto de 1973 pp. 8–9 ("O sul vai ao norte").

During the 1960s circumstances had been generally favourable for the expansion of livestock farming in Brazil. There was a still increasing demand for meat, both on the home and the foreign market (Ramalho 1971, 41). This growing demand could be met through the intensification of livestock production on the existing grassland area, but in many instances it proved more advantageous not to intensify, but to expand the area of grazing land in those regions where land prices were still low. Since the land had been made still more accessible around 1970, an expansion of livestock farming became possible in a considerable part of the interior. Certain parts of the Amazon region now also belonged to the zones which were attractive for conversion to pasture lands.

Table 4. The number of farming projects approved by the SUDAM in Amazônia Legal up to January 1st, 1973

State/Territory	No. of projects	Total area in hectares	Investment in cruzeiros x 1000	Expected no. of jobs
Mato Grosso	184	5 049 000		9622
Goiás	25	1 599 000		1043
Pará	91	1 408 000		3515
Amazonas	12	115 000		436
Rondônia	1	30 000		60
Maranhão	5	73 000		139
Roraima	-	-		-
Amapá	-	-		-
Acre	-	-		-
Total	318	8 274 000	2 445 843	14 815

Source: Pinto (1971, 14).

For various reasons preference was given in many places, particularly in the Amazon region, to livestock farming over arable farming:

- the soils proved to remain productive for much longer when used for grazing rather than for arable farming;
- arable farming required more labour, which was still scarce in large parts of the region;
- cattle are mobile and could therefore be transported more easily to the centres of consumption than was the case with arable crops;
- certain other conditions also, such as the level of prices, made livestock production more rewarding than arable farming (Glaser 1971, 24).

It was indeed not only farmers who found cattle farming considerably more attractive than arable farming. It was also attractive to those who thought in terms of national security because, in its extensive form, it required large areas of grazing land. This made extensive livestock farming a source of livelihood that enabled considerable areas of land to be taken into use with relatively little effort. Just as the Portuguese were once able to occupy a large part of eastern Brazil by using it for extensive cattle farming, so now a part of the vast Amazon region could be integrated into the economy with relatively little manpower and thereby protected from possible foreign occupation.

As had often been the case in the past, the recent expansion of livestock farming was again concerned with an activity that was practised almost entirely on large or very large holdings. As long as land prices remained very low, extensive grazing was the most attractive practice. Livestock farming could also be managed more rationally on a large holding and business credits obtained more easily. In addition, certain measures that were necessary for modern farming practice in a tropical environment, such as the purchase of high-grade breeds of cattle and the combatting of cattle diseases, were an expensive matter, within the means of only financially strong entrepreneurs. Such people were also able to bear more easily the loss of cattle, which was still great in the humid tropical environment because of various diseases. The dominance of the large enterprises in Amazônia, however, was by no means only the result of economies of scale. The financial facilities of the SUDAM also greatly contributed in the early 1970s to making a more capital-intensive form of livestock farming attractive. The new agricultural holdings consequently had areas ranging from thousands to tens of thousands of hectares. They were owned by wealthy individuals or undertakings (often limited companies), which possessed the necessary technical knowledge to enable them to farm by modern, rational methods. The developments were therefore the same as those observed by Brücher in Colombia, where the expansion of the modern type of livestock farming was realised through the establishment of large, well-capitalised holdings.

It is incidentally not surprising that the favourable investment climate often resulted in over-hasty and ill-considered action. Insufficient study was made of possible difficulties, with the result that many of the projects had made insufficient progress. The SUDAM had not taken enough measures to prevent this.

The main beneficiaries of these large-scale ranching enterprises were the capitalists and large businesses of the Centro-Sul. It was mainly these people who had found in cattle ranching an attractive field of investment for their tax money, thanks to the fiscal facilities of the Brazilian government. Even many industries and banks which originally had nothing to do with cattle farming had begun to invest in ranching enterprises. Examples were Camargo Corrêa (a building firm), Liquigas, Nestlé, Goodyear, Eletrobras and Volkswagen do Brasil. Among the investors were many large concerns in which much foreign capital had also been invested. This meant that some of the profits from these projects would again flow abroad.

A few figures will illustrate the importance which the *incentivos fiscais* had for the development of livestock farming. According to Table 4, a total of 318 farming projects had been approved by the SUDAM up to 1st January 1973. In 1976 it had approved 335 projects. Detailed figures would show that nearly all of these were livestock farming projects. These involved a total investment of 7200 billion cruzeiros, of which 5500 billion (i. e. 73.64 %) consisted of money owed in taxes.[43] The remainder was the applicants' own capital or could be obtained from other sources. These combined investments accounted for no less than 39 % of the total investments involved in all the projects approved by the SUDAM up to January 24, 1973 (industrial projects, 38 %) (Lopes 1973, 50). This shows clearly that livestock farming was one of the most attractive sectors in which to make capital productive in Amazônia Legal.

Livestock farming was, in fact, one of the most dynamic sectors of the Northern economy in the early 1970s. Various official Brazilian publications, therefore, stated that the SUDAM's *política de incentivos fiscais* was a great success, especially in the livestock farming sector. Thanks to the *incentivos fiscais*, in particular, and the way in which the SUDAM used these facilities, there was a spectacular expansion of livestock farming.

The total area of the 335 projects which had been approved by the SUDAM was no less than 7 860 846 hectares, giving an average of 23 465 hectares per project. The average investment was 15 569 million cruzeiros. Condurú mentioned that some of the projects exceeded 30 000 hectares in area (Condurú 1973, 10). Some comprised an area of several hundreds of thousands of hectares. A well-known example in this connection was Ometto from São Paulo, a company which owned 678 000 hectares. Its cattle ranch (Fazenda Suiã Missu) had 30 000 cattle in the early 1970s, but an increase to 125 000 was anticipated (Wagley 1974, 9). Among the most powerful enterprises was the Companhia de Terras da Mata Geral, which was responsible for five large livestock farming projects. Another important group was that of São Paulo e Celso Garcia Cid, which had already purchased 800 000 hectares in the North at the end of the 1960s (*SUDAM, 6° aniversario da SUDAM* 1972, 2).

Realisation of the 335 projects would make possible a cattle population of more than 6.2 million head. This expansion would better enable Brazil to meet the increasing home demand for meat and to develop as an exporter. Against this positive aspect it should be remembered that larger exports also meant a greater dependence on external markets.

Many *fazendeiros*, in laying down pastures, made use of arable farmers, with whom they concluded share-cropping contracts. They permitted the share-croppers to practise shifting cultivation for two or three years. After the land had been burnt over a few times it was suitable for the sowing of grass and was taken into use for grazing. In this way the *fazendeiros* came quite cheaply into the possession of grazing land, especially since they also obtained a large proportion of the harvest (mainly rice) within the terms of the share-cropping contract. The share-croppers, however, found work for only a limited period of time and, after a few harvests, had to seek a living again on another piece of land. The result of this situation was that arable farming provided work only temporarily and to a limited degree (Glaser 1971, 29).

Clearing sometimes took place in a different manner. On the King Ranch, about 300 miles south of Belém, about 180 000 acres were cleared of forest with the aid of heavy tractors, between which were stretched iron chains. Because the latter had heavy iron balls attached to them, they remained close to the ground as they were drawn forward by the tractors and uprooted a large number of trees in a short time

43 335 approved agricultural projects, concerned with the expanding of beef cattle, involved an investment of 5215 thousand million cruzeiros.

(Foland 1971, 72). In such cases the clearing of the land provided relatively little work for temporary labour.

Apart from machines, in order to speed up the work, use was also made of defoliants distributed by DOW Chemical and said to be derived from the stocks laid up by the Americans for the war in Vietnam, although differing somewhat in composition.

The maintenance of the pastures and the tending of the cattle was usually limited to what was strictly necessary, so that cattle farms of thousands of hectares gave employment to only a few men. Glaser states that it was not unusual to find 1 cowherd looking after 250 animals, and the C.E.A.S. report gives the example of a holding of 200 000 hectares with only 300 workers (Glaser 1971, 33; *Amazônia – integração e marginalização* 1973, vol. 1, 19).

Table 4 shows that the expansion of employment from the realisation of 318 projects was estimated at only 14 815 jobs, or one job per 560 hectares. It also has been calculated that the 335 projects approved up to 1975 since 1966 would provide direct employment for a total of only 16 851 people (if they are fully realised).[44] This gives an average of 50.3 jobs per project or 2.3 jobs per 1000 hectares. Labour requirements after the initial clearance phase were extremely low. This means that there was scarcely any reduction of population pressure as a result of the projects. They encouraged, moreover, the further expansion and consolidation of large estates.

It has been stated in defence of the labour-extensive land use that the labour supply was small in the thinly inhabited territories. This was certainly true in the 1960s and 1970s, but the reason is that the economic activity in the past consisted largely of extensive livestock farming, which provided hardly any employment. It prevented large-scale migration to the interior. The further expansion of labour-extensive types of farming that occurred in the 1960s and 1970s was, in fact, only consolidating the existing situation in the countryside. It could result in an intensification of land use being made more difficult in the more distant future, thereby preventing a rise in the absorption capacity of the agricultural sector. This expansion of labour-extensive land use constituted, in fact, one of the major negative aspects of the development at that time.

By the end of 1973, the large livestock holdings occupied only a modest proportion of the Amazon region, but more disturbing than the small proportion was perhaps the fact that the creation of extremely labour-extensive large-scale holdings (often on land suited to arable farming) seemed to be increasingly possible, and this in a country where the system of large estates had been a significant factor in the emergence of underdevelopment and where the prevention of the further expansion of such estates might be an important means of avoiding an accentuation of the underdevelopment.

Although there had been a less rapid expansion of livestock farming in Amazônia Legal during the two or three years before 1973, one may not conclude from this that the process of occupation would shortly afterwards no longer be largely dominated by livestock farming. It was probable that, in the following years, much forest land would still be converted into pasture and that this would often take place within the system of large-scale holdings. The following are the arguments, not necessarily in order of importance, for this expectation:

44 Data supplied by the SUDAM.

- The SUDAM was still creating through the incentivos fiscais an attractive investment climate, although certain recent provisions had made it somewhat less favourable than during the late 1960s.[45]
- There would continue to be a good market for cattle products, both at home and abroad, during the following years, so that investments in livestock farming would certainly yield a return (Ramalho 1971, 41). In many instances, livestock farming would be more profitable than arable farming and involve fewer problems of realisation than industrialisation.
- The accessibility of the Amazon region would be considerably improved in the near future through the realisation of the great highway construction projects. The roads that had been completed until then had always resulted in a marked expansion of livestock farming.
- The experiences with the breeding of zebus and with crossings between zebus and "European" cattle races had until then been favourable and had created breeds that were well adapted to the humid tropical climate.
- It was also being increasingly realised in Brazil that many tropical forest soils were little suited, because of their poverty, to simple forms of arable farming (shifting cultivation), but that they lent themselves quite well to the practice of livestock farming. Glaser noted that the recently laid down pastures still showed no signs of exhaustion after several years despite a lack of the application of fertilisers, while arable fields did show such exhaustion. Experts of the IPEAN reached similar conclusions in respect of land that had been taken into use about ten years earlier. Their findings agreed with those of Brücher in Colombia. Glaser added the comment that the forest soils of the Amazon region were better suited to livestock farming than the savannah lands of western Brazil. This is why some cattle farmers had already sold their holdings in the latter region in order to start new, larger and more modern fazendas in the more northerly areas (Glaser 1971, 25–30).
- Part of the tropical forest lands had already come into private hands, so that large estates already existed in various places. Moreover, it was still possible to acquire large areas of land cheaply by legal and illegal means (*Bispo ataca marginalização...* 1971, 141 ff.).
- The Brazilian government supported a further expansion of the large livestock holding run on modern lines by skilled proprietors. As a result of such expansion large areas of land were occupied in a short time and Brazil was also able to develop into one of the world's largest meat producers and exporters. In order to achieve this, the government was thinking both of an expansion of livestock farming in those parts of the Amazon region which were already occupied, as well as an expansion into regions where no modern livestock farming projects had previously been realised (including Acre and Roirama) (Tocantins 1973, 5).

Experts of the Banco da Amazônia had already begun mapping and survey work for the purpose of realising specific projects. Brazil also hoped to be able to carry out a programme of incentives with money from the International Bank for Reconstruction and Development. This would require a sum of about US$ 500 million (*Boletim Informativo* 489, 14 August, 1973). It was by no means unlikely that, in the near future, foreign

---

45 For further details see "Conclusions: Looking back and looking ahead."

capital would be called upon to a greater extent, since the desired expansion could be more speedily realised with the support of foreign investors and it might also be easier to gain export markets.

The expansion of large-scale livestock farming just described certainly did not occur wholly without conflict and social injustice. The rural population frequently experienced the disadvantages of the expansion of large estates encouraged by the policy of the government. Land was often bought up at low prices by aggressive real estate brokers, who resold large areas to interested capitalists. *Posseiros* (squatters), who settled in many places on uncleared land to make a living from a little subsistence agriculture, were often found to be a hindrance to the creation of large holdings or the exploitation of large estates. As a result they were expected to leave or to sign a declaration that they would leave the land within a short time. In favourable instances they received compensation, although little account is taken of the fact that the clearances of the *posseiros* considerably facilitated the creation of grazing land. In many instances, however, they simply had to disappear, willingly or otherwise. Many owners of large estates had no compunction in destroying the harvest, setting fire to the *posseiro's* homestead or using other forms of violence to make clear what was expected of the occupants. Generally *pistoleiros* were employed for the purpose. The police were often unaware of these cases, or heard of them too late or even turned a blind eye, choosing in so doing the side of the big landowner. The latter incidentally often also applied to other government functionaries, such as magistrates and governors.[46] Such conflicts between *fazendeiros* and squatters were expected to continue, especially where land was taken into use that was already accessible and could therefore easily be occupied by simple shifting cultivators.

The position of the shifting cultivators was scarcely more favourable than that of the squatters when they had the status of tenant farmers. Although the tenants did not run the risk of being driven from the land totally unexpectedly, they had to be satisfied with unfavourable tenancy terms. According to Alberto Tamer, many tenants had to give up one half of the rice harvest to the landowner, who had the advantage that, after a few years, he could use the land for grazing (Tamer 1971, 91 ff.).

It also appeared that the expansion of large-scale livestock farming led to a number of reprehensible practices in order to obtain labour for the necessary reclamation works. There was, in general, little enthusiasm to go and work in the interior of Brazil as a labourer, mainly as a result of the unfavourable working conditions. Consequently, manpower was scarce in many areas. Nevertheless, quite a large number of workers was sometimes required for a period of time, such as during the laying down of a cattle *fazenda*. This meant that the *fazendeiros* had no choice but to pay higher wages or resort to recruitment by trickery. They often chose the latter alternative. As a result, all kinds of inadmissible crimping practices occurred.[47]

The crimps (*gatos*) often operated in common lodging houses, simple cafes and brothels in the small towns along the road from Belém to Brasília and in the larger and smaller centres of the North and North East. They usually recruited the necessary manpower by promising poor wretches who had little to lose high wages and other favourable working conditions. Sometimes they also repaid temporarily the debts of the prospective labourer. The *empreiteros* caried the responsibility for this procedure,

46 See also Glaser (1971, 27 ff.).

47 A description of these practices to be found in the article by Coutinho and Barbosa (1973).

which meant that the landowners did not run the risk of serious trouble with the law if the means by which the workers were recruited were unexpectedly discovered.

Some labour contractors not only recruited the workers, but also saw to the transport to the area where they were required and took charge of the clearance work to be carried out. In such instances, the *empreitero* bore all the responsibility and this was often acceptable to the landowners. The latter had only to pay the contractor the agreed sum and they did not run the risk of coming into conflict with the law when it unexpectedly appeared that the workers had been recruited in a reprehensible manner. Other labour contractors, on the other hand, simply delivered workers to the *fazendeiro*, who then himself had to ensure that the necessary work was satisfactorily carried out.

Generally, the promised high wages were not paid and, in spite of promises to the contrary, deductions were usually made from earnings for meals and the cost of transport. In consequence many labourers received very little for their work. This was even more the case if they had also been compelled to buy their necessities at high prices in the *fazenda* shop. The undesired departure of workers was prevented by not paying the wages until the end of the term of employment or by the use of armed guards. Anyone who tried to flee ran the risk of being shot and finding a grave in the forest. The meals were often bad and monotonous. All kinds of basic facilities were lacking, such as medical treatment centres to deal with illnesses and injuries arising from the heavy work. Anyone complaining about his health was sometimes more likely to be injected with alcohol than to receive adequate treatment. Stated briefly, it often happened that all social laws were trodden underfoot. The police and legal authorities took insufficient action against these abuses of power by big landowners, *empreiteros* and land speculators, while the SUDAM failed to check what happened in the projects it had approved. Consequently, there were frequent reports in the Brazilian press which showed that their reprehensible practices were by no means a thing of the past. That these were not at all isolated occurrences appeared, for example, from the fact that North Brazilian bishops felt it necessary to discuss in detail the behaviour of the *fazendeiros* and *empreiteros* and to make a protest to the government.[48] They also considered what could be done about it by the church at the local level. The increasingly frequent defence of the poorer classes by the church had already caused difficulties for various bishops and led to the issuing of threats against several church dignitaries.

Valverde has observed with reference to these conditions that, in 1972, *nordestinos* and other poor Brazilians were still misused. In his view, conditions of slavery existed, as they had done during the rubber-gathering period. Apart from being noted by the geographers Valverde and Glaser, these abuses were incidentally also noted by Dom Pedro Casaldáliga, the bishop of São Felix (in N.E. Mato Grosso). As a result of the Brazilian government's *incentivos fiscais* many large livestock farming enterprises were being established in his diocese, but the local population experienced various serious disadvantages from them. The land was bought up at low prices by land agents, who resold it in large parcels to interested, wealthy individuals. As a result, the squatters were forced to leave the land, while those who were later able to come and work on the land as labourers were shamelessly exploited.

Many of those in search of work were aware that *gatos* operated on the labour market and sometimes already knew from first hand that the fine promises meant little,

48 Their discussions led to the appearance of the publication "Pastoral da Terra" (1976).

but use was still repeatedly made of the services of crimps. Other possibilities of finding work often scarcely existed.

It need hardly be said that in areas where an atmosphere of violence, aggression and exploitation surrounded the small farmers and workers, the Indigenous were also a much-threatened population group. They, too, were often driven off the land or were simply rounded up.

Valverde made the suggestion that the government should take charge of the recruitment of labour in the larger population centres. He also proposed that the *fazendeiros*, who were able to establish or modernise estates with taxation money as a result of the government facilities, should be compelled to recruit their workers exclusively through the official labour bureaux. A third suggestion of his was that the government should control the working conditions. Unfortunately, many practical difficulties stood in the way of the realisation of these suggestions, which probably partly explains why the abuses were not been firmly dealt with.[49]

The expansion of tropical tree and shrub crops

The expansion of tropical tree and shrub crops which was considered possible was still at its very beginning in the mid-1970s. There had not been, in recent years, any noteworthy increase in the cultivation of oil palms, rubber, cocoa, pepper or other perennial crops, although steps were being taken to bring about such an increase.

As far as natural rubber was concerned, Brazil was trying to double production by 1980, so that imports would be unnecessary. In order to achieve this, a start was made in Belterra (area of the former Ford plantation) with making provision for the raising of 1 million young rubber trees. Apart from in the area near the road from Cuiabá to Santarém, it was the intention to encourage rubber cultivation in Acre. A start was also made near Altamira with the growing of 200 000 young pepper plants and cocoa trees were being raised near Altamira and Manaus, among other places. Preparations were also being made for a rapid expansion of the areas for coffee and sugar cane. The cultivation of oil palms was limited to experimental plots of a few thousand hectares at the time.[50] An effort was made to intensify the cultivation of babaçu palms within the context of an experimental project in the municipality of Governador Archer (10 000 hectares).

Special credit facilities had already been made available to encourage the commercial cultivation of these and other crops in future years.

49 The foregoing is derived mainly from the publications of Glaser (1971) and Valverde (1972), as well as from the anonymous article *Bispo ataca marginalização…* (1971).

50 Figures in this section derived from Ministério da Agricultura (1972a, 26 f.), and from *A Sudam e a cultura do dendê na Amazônia* (n. d., 7).

The development of forestry

In order to be able to exploit the forest more intensively in the future, the SUDAM began to make further studies of the forest resources. In so doing, it was studying particularly the potentialities for the use and regeneration of the tropical forest. It was also experimenting with reafforestation. In addition, it began to train foresters and workers for the woodworking industry. Lastly, studies were also made of modern, mechanised extraction and processing techniques (*Industrialização de madeiras* 1970).

In the forestry sector, too, the development process was only at its beginning. Timber exploitation was still relatively modest. The North still provided only a small proportion of the total quantity of timber felled in Brazil, although an expansion of timber exploitation had been recorded in recent years.

It was not only in the livestock farming sector, but also in that of forestry that enterprises of tens of thousands of hectares had already been created. Here, too, a number of circumstances related to the nature of the environment had made the establishment of large enterprises advantageous. The industrial complexes mentioned earlier would certainly require more than 100 000 hectares in order to function properly. The encouragement of such undertakings had already been recommended by experts of the FAO, who had surveyed part of the Amazon Forest. In their view, enterprises with very large areas of forest at their disposal, permanently or for a very long period, such as a century, would be more interested in total utilisation and reafforestation than would small enterprises with short-term exploitation rights (*Levantamentos florestais realizados pela missão FAO na Amazônia – 1956/1961*, 1974, 1, 10; Knowles 1971, 18 f.). The establishment of large enterprises was also encouraged by the financial facilities of the Brazilian government, which created an attractive climate for the large, capital-intensive enterprises.

Among the most important undertakings was that of Georgia Pacific (Companhia Amazônia de Laminados), which purchased 640 000 acres of forest in the municipality of Portel, mainly with the intention of starting the large-scale manufacture of veneers and plywood (Foland 1971, 72; Filha 1971b, 76).

Bruynzeel Madeiras S.A. (BRUMASA) owned about 200 000 hectares of forest on the island of Marajó and in Amapá and produced annually about 25 000 cubic metres of plywood, chipboard and other wood products (Panagides and Vande Lage 1973, 24).

These enterprises had purchased forest in parts of the Amazon region where surveys had already been carried out (by experts of the FAO and others). It was then demonstrated, *inter alia*, that the stands of forest on the island of Marajó were of great importance. According to Irene Garrido Filha, these enterprises knew very well, therefore, what they were buying (*Levantamentos florestais realizados pela missão FAO na Amazônia – 1956/1961* 1974, vol. 1, 10; Filha 1971b, 76).

A third great enterprise was *Jari, indústria e comércio*, forming part of the National Bulk Carriers group. It had bought 1.21 million ha. of land in the municipality of Almeirim (Pará), with various aims in view, including timber production. The firm was experimenting with the planting of *Gmelina arborea*, a tree that flourishes in the Amazon Basin, grows rapidly and is a suitable raw material for paper manufacture. Some 80 000 hectares were already reported to have been planted by 1969 (Martelli 1969, 136; Falesi *et al.* 1972a, 62).

In addition, there were various smaller enterprises, both Brazilian and foreign, which were exploiting the forests for the extraction of timber and the manufacture of wood products, thereby profiting from the Brazilian government's *incentivos fiscais*.

From August 1973, the export of round timber on a large scale was no longer possible. The timber had first to be processed before it could be exported. This measure could encourage the processing industry still further.

The developments in the mining sector

Since the end of the Second World War, the emphasis in the mining sector had been entirely on the exploitation of manganese and tin ore. Rich manganese deposits occurred near Serra do Navio, in Amapá. Their exploitation began in the 1950s after the construction of a railway between the deposits in the interior and the port of Macapá, and after the port facilities had been expanded. The first shipload of manganese ore left the port of Macapá in 1957. In 1969, the Brazilian–United States undertaking which owned the concession exported 1.4 million tons. At that time, manganese ore had been the North's most important export for some time and it accounted for 37.6 % of the total value of exports from the region in 1970 (Kleinpenning 1973, 148; Panagides and Vande Lage 1973, 8).

A more recent development was the rise of tin mining of Rondônia. This was mainly the result of the opening of a road link between Porto Velho and São Paulo in 1965, which first made it possible to transport the ore by lorry to the processing plants in South-East Brazil (Volta Redonda). In 1960 Rondônia produced only 49 tons of tinstone. Rubber, Brazil nuts, hides and skins and a few kinds of vegetable oil were still the most important exports from the territory. In 1973, the first place was occupied by tin ore. Production in 1970 was estimated at 4000 tons. Mining would be expanded still further in later years and, in order to facilitate this, the army had already constructed a road to link Ariquemes with Guajará-Mirim. Consequently, it was no longer necessary to transport a large part of the ore in small aircraft to the collection centre at Ariquemes, but it could be loaded directly into lorries (Kleinpenning 1973, 148–149).

Various other roads had also been built in the years before 1973 to make the ore reserves more accessible.[51] Moreover, as a result of extensive exploration, much more had become known of the mineral wealth of the Amazon basin. Up to 1973 the SUDAM had approved 20 private mining projects involving an investment of 700 million cruzeiros (SUDAM/Banco da Amazônia 1972, 19). Nevertheless, one could not yet speak of a spectacular expansion of mining. Government and private projects were still at the stage of further exploration and preparation. However, a considerable intensification of mining could be expected in the years to come.

It was expected that the exploitation of iron ore, in particular, would become of great importance. In order to facilitate the winning of the enormous reserves in the Serra dos Carajás, the Companhia Meridional de Mineração was established in 1970. 51 % of the shares of this company were held by the Brazilian Companhia Vale do Rio Doce and 49 % by the American concern United States Steel. The daughter company

51 The Transamazônica had already made it possible to transport workers and materials as far as Marabá, i. e. 150 km N.E. of the Serra dos Carajás.

carried out detailed exploration and also prepared the exploitation in other ways. Studies had already shown that the transport of the ore could be achieved most expeditiously by means of a railway line to the port of Itaqui, which is situated near São Luis, 970 km from the mining area. Construction of the railway began in 1974.[52] At the time, 500 hectares of land near Itaqui had already been reserved for the construction of an ore port (*Boletim Informativo* 494, 30 August 1973). It was hoped to begin mining the iron ore in 1978 and to achieve a production of 40 million tons.

At first the greater part of the ore would be exported. The *Companhia Vale do Rio Doce* would be responsible for the export of the ore, but certain rights were reserved to United States Steel. It would have the option of purchasing up to one half of the production at a price adjusted to the market situation. In addition to export, there might also be some processing within Brazil. In any event, the idea had already been put forward of establishing one or more steelworks on the northern coast, such as near São Luis.

The effect of the development measures discussed above. Summary

In the preceding sections attention has been paid to a few developments closely related to the measures taken by the government to integrate the Amazon region more closely into the national economy.

As far as the free trade measures are concerned, it was observed that these had led to an increase in commercial activity in and around Manaus, to further industrialisation, to the growth of tourism and to expansion of the construction industry. The consequent expansion of employment, however, was relatively slight. The free trade facilities led to a strong migration from the country to the city and this, together with the natural population increase, meant that the demand for work in Manaus outstripped the growth in the number of jobs, so that many inhabitants still led a poverty-stricken existence. Other negative aspects of the recent developments were the loss of foreign exchange, the increased competition for the traditional retail sector and the increased competition for regional and national industries. It is not possible, therefore, to pass a purely favourable judgement on the developments that occurred in Manaus up to the early 1970s.

As far as the longer-term future was concerned, much depended upon the degree to which labour-intensive industries could be persuaded to establish themselves in the heart of the Amazon region, where the locational climate was still relatively unfavourable in spite of all the government facilities.

A second strongly growing municipality in the early 1970s was Belém, which was the main area where industrialisation was stimulated by the *política de incentivos fiscais*. As in Manaus, however, the growth in the number of industrial jobs could not keep pace with the increase in population, so that the employment situation still gave cause for concern. A considerable proportion of the active population had to find a living in the tertiary sector, which showed clear signs of overcrowding.

In the agricultural sector the *incentivos fiscais* led mainly to an increase in the number of large livestock holdings. A positive aspect of this development was that livestock farming was beginning to take on a more rational and modern character, with better

52 It was estimated that about 10 000 workers would be needed for this.

production techniques being introduced from the South East. The large cattle ranches established at the time, therefore, made a relatively big contribution to the increase in agricultural production. The other side of the picture, however, was that the large holdings created very little employment and, because of their extensive grazing methods, they appropriated large areas of land. By doing so they limited the opportunities of small farmers (squatters or tenants) to find a living in the agricultural sector. Labourers had to accept unfavourable working conditions.

In the forestry and mining sectors, too, the *incentivos fiscais* encouraged capital-intensive, large-scale enterprise and the expansion of employment in these branches of the economy was also still very modest. Part of reason for this, incidentally, was that the projects had not yet been realised or only partially so.

The effects of the financial incentive measures on employment, therefore, were limited. The 502 projects approved by the SUDAM up to 1st January 1973 would create an estimated total of only 53 110 jobs, but this number would only be achieved when all the projects were fully realised (Lopes 1973, 50).[53] The financial incentives did not help to improve the existence of large numbers of migrants from other parts of Brazil, such as the North East. Their contribution to the solution of the socio-economic problems of the North East was virtually non-existent.

The conclusion seems justified that the Brazilian government, in its policy for the Amazon region, has been guided little or if at all by social motives, i.e. by the wish at least to increase and improve the opportunities of livelihood for the least well-off sections of the population. In our view, it aimed primarily at economic growth, the advantages of which have so far largely benefited the business community and the moneyed classes from the Centro-Sul and abroad who found an attractive investment climate in the North. As a result, the Amazon Basin was drawn more firmly into the sphere of influence of the more-developed South East and became more dependent upon it. For the mass of the population little changed.

The business groups from the South East were naturally most interested in the development of those zones situated nearest to the South East and the other more populated parts of Brazil. Such zones are favourably located in relation to the markets and can be reached most easily and frequently by the entrepreneurs. It is understandable, therefore, that the expansion of livestock farming occurred mainly on the southern fringes of Amazônia Legal and along the major highways, such as that from Belém to Brasília. It is also understandable that industrialisation was strongly concentrated in and around Belém. As a result, the spatial contrasts increased in the North.

The measures discussed above were probably also taken in the expectation that, thanks to the effects of economic growth, the government's prestige would be increased at least among the elite, if not among all levels of the population. The government may also have considered that they would help to accelerate the occupation of the Amazon region. The cattle ranching projects, in particular, within the framework of which large areas are cleared, were by no means unimportant when viewed as part of a strategy for greater national security.

53 Apart from the 167 projects in the agricultural sector, this figure includes 17 projects for *serviço básico* (jobs provided: 2879).

The danger of an increasing dependence on foreign countries

One of the possible dangers of Brazil's development measures could be that the country will become unhealthily dependent upon foreign countries.

From the early 1970s foreign capitalists interested in forestry and livestock farming enjoyed attractive terms for investing in Brazil. They also obtained large areas of land with the intention of exploiting the forest or taking up livestock farming (Georgia Pacific, Bruynzeel).

Foreign companies were also greatly interested in the mineral wealth, particularly the North American firms, whose market is largely in the United States, which is relatively near northern Brazil. United States Steel had already assured itself of an important share in the exploitation of the vast iron ore reserves in the Serra dos Carajás. Bethlehem Steel had large interests in the Indústria e Comércio de Minérios S.A. (ICOMI), which had control of the manganese exploitation in Amapá. Billiton had already obtained various concessions in Rondônia for large-scale tin mining as soon as the international market situation made this desirable and the Brazilian government had found a solution for the problem that the better deposits were occupied by simple tin-washers. A start had already been made with mining on a modest scale (Kleinpenning 1973, 149; Foland 1971, 74). In the Valle de Trombetas, where important bauxite deposits occur, three foreign concerns had already begun exploitation, namely, ALCOA (the most powerful firm in the field of bauxite mining), ALCAN (another large firm) and National Bulk Carriers. The latter firm had purchased about 1.2 million hectares of land on the left bank of the Jarí. The other companies had also acquired large areas of land and, according to Irene Garrido Filha, they knew very well what they were buying. The presence of minerals was an established fact (Filha 1971b, 76).

It is not precisely known which part of the Amazon region had come into the hands of foreign owners as a result of this interest in forestry, livestock farming and mining, but a parliamentary investigation of 1968 showed that 11 million hectares were involved in Pará, Amazonas and Roraima alone (Martelli 1969, 136). In reality, the areas were probably much greater. The fear of some Brazilians that the greater part of the North would gradually fall into the hands of foreign interest groups was not completely unfounded, therefore.

Various provisions existed to limit and place conditions on the purchase of land by foreigners or foreign undertakings. For example, a foreigner who purchased land had to come and live in Brazil within three years and to exploit the land. A further provision was that foreigners or foreign firms were not permitted to own more than a quarter of the municipality in which the land was situated. Moreover, persons and undertakings of one nationality were not allowed to jointly own more than 40 % of the land in a single municipality. In the past, however, such restrictive measures had been repeatedly evaded and it was by no means unlikely that they would be evaded again in future years ("Lei sobre venda de terras á estrangeiros" 1971, 110–114).

One may ask, therefore, whether the Brazilian government's development and integration policy, which had as one of its official aims the avoidance of too much foreign influence, would not in practice lead precisely to a greater dependence on foreign countries. In view of the large amounts of capital and know-how required for primary production along modern lines, and in view of the dependence on foreign markets for minerals, timber and livestock products, it would not be easy, in any event, for Brazil to pursue a policy that would enable it to remain complete lord and master of the riches of the Amazon region.

A circumstance that could encourage still further the flow of foreign capital was the fact that extensive foreign investments also had an important political advantage. They made possible a further economic growth, but they did not lead to a proportionate increase in the power of the national business community. In the view of Tyler and Rosenbaum this could encourage the stability of political power relationships and such stability would not be unwelcome to the Brazilian rulers (Rosenbaum and Tyler 1971, 421).

The criticism of the road building plans

It has appeared from the above that there were reasons to doubt whether the various measures to stimulate the economy would lead to a reduction of the state of underdevelopment and of the economic dependency of Brazil. Serious doubts were also expressed both in Brazil and elsewhere as soon as it became known that the government had spectacular and expensive plans for opening up the Amazon Basin by means of a number of great highways. The proposed construction of the Transamazônica, in particular, gave rise to a great many negative reactions. In Brazil, Alberto Tamer and Roberto de Oliveira Campos, especially, expressed serious doubts.[54]

We can summarise their criticism and that of various other Brazilians and foreigners point by point as follows:

- The decision to build the Transamazônica was taken before the plan had been fully studied. The project was not the result of a detailed cost-benefit analysis of various alternatives. Nor was it considered whether the plan should have a high priority in relation to other road building projects in Brazil.
- Consequently, there could be a great danger of the road building projects leading to an enormous waste of money. Even if this did not happen, very large investments would still be required, which would make very great demands on the country's resources, perhaps even too great demands.
- The building of roads was not necessary for a more intensive exploration of the mineral resources. Such exploration could be carried out much more quickly and completely with the aid of modern air photomapping methods. Nor were the roads necessary for transporting the ores. This could be done much more cheaply by rail or waterways.
- The construction of a road like the Transamazônica was certainly not necessary for strategic reasons. Other countries also had vast areas that were scarcely inhabited and not served by roads, but they were able to control them. Examples are the north of Canada and the Soviet Union. If the building of roads was nevertheless considered necessary for strategic reasons, it would probably have been more sensible to build north-south than east-west routes, since political and economic power were concentrated in the Centro-Sul region.

54 See their publications about the Transamazônica (Tamer 1971; Morais *et al.* 1970).

- The Transamazônica would connect a scarcely inhabited and economically undeveloped region with a poor, over-populated and economically weakly developed region (the North East), which would be of little advantage for the progress either of the North or the North East. Roberto de Oliveira Campos characterised the Transamazônica as the link between a deserto árido and a deserto úmido (Morais *et al.* 1970, 108). In his view, the Amazon region would have been much better served by connections with the South East of the country, from where ultimately the most important growth impulses had to come. The comparison that was made more than once, in official publications and elsewhere, between the Transamazônica and the Belém–Brasília highway and the conclusions which were drawn in respect of the future development of the Amazon region were highly disputable, since the Belém–Brasília highway connected totally different regions.
- If it was intended to create more employment for the North East in the public works sector by means of the Transamazônica, only small numbers of workers would be able to benefit, since the road-building operation was highly mechanised. It would have been much better to undertake reafforestation, irrigation works, further road building projects and similar activities in the North East.

Although the criticisms noted above may be regarded as valid in several respects, we nevertheless do not wish to use them as a basis for deciding whether or not the road building projects were justified. It seems to us that the latter is determined primarily by the extent to which the Brazilian government has succeeded in later years in achieving an extensive and successful colonisation that could make a real contribution towards solving the existing socio-economic problems, particularly those of the North East. We consider, therefore, that we cannot give a judgement of the road building projects until after a more detailed study of the colonisation plans and of the activities that were realised. In the following chapters much attention is devoted to these subjects.

The colonisation plans and the objections to them

The origin of the colonisation plans

The colonisation plans for the Amazon region took shape in 1970, at a time when the North East was again afflicted by an abnormal drought. It appeared clearly that the Superintêndencia do Desenvolvimento do Nordeste, which had been established in 1959 to further the integrated development of the North East, had not been able during the 1960s to develop the region socially and economically sufficiently to limit the harmful effects of severe droughts.

President Médici visited the North East personally at that time to acquaint himself with the disastrous consequences of the abnormal drought. As a result of that visit, he declared that the Amazon region should be opened up by roads to enable a large number of *nordestinos* to find a better life there. The building of roads would also provide employment for *nordestinos* and it was expected of the road construction contractors that they would hire their labour mainly from the North East. Just as the building of Brasília and the construction of roads to the new capital had provided work for tens of thousands of *nordestinos*, so would the new highways across the Amazon region provide employment for many.

The plan for opening up the Amazon region was not new. In 1969, Eliseu Resende, the director of the Departamento Nacional de Estradas de Rodagem, had already published a study in the *Revista Econômica do Jornal do Brasil* on "O Papel da Rodovia no Desenvolvimento da Amazônia." In this article he referred, *inter alia*, to the increasing population pressure in the North East, to the inadequate accessibility of Amazônia by navigable waterway and to the necessity for government measures to bring about a more intensive occupation of the vast and still almost uninhabited North. He also made a few concrete proposals in the article, including an east-west link (Transamazônica), but made it clear at the same time that his *departamento* possessed insufficient funds to realise the rapid opening-up of the Amazon region and that there were road building projects which merited a higher priority. In his view, therefore, the great highways linking up the North could be constructed only gradually, i.e. in short sections (Resende 1971, 288 ff., especially p. 293).

The unexpected drought of 1970 brought about a change in the situation, causing President Médici to decide to give the highest priority to the construction of the Transamazônica and the road from Cuiabá to Santarém. This decision to give effect to the recently launched plans for opening-up Amazônia in the very short term came as a complete surprise to many. Many people were also surprised by the colonisation projects, especially as the government did not yet have detailed plans at its disposal. In the past, special measures had more than once been taken after periods of extreme drought to lessen the problems of the North East, but they had never yet gone so far as to include large-scale colonisation in the still thinly-populated areas of North Brazil.

In June 1970, the government introduced the Programa de Integração Nacional (Decree 1106 of 16th June 1970). One of the points of this programme was that a sum of 2000 million cruzeiros should be invested during the period 1971–1974 in the areas under the aegis of the SUDENE and the SUDAM, to be used not only for further industrialisation and agricultural development in the North East, but also for the construction of the two highways referred to above and for colonisation along their margins (*TransAmazônian Highways* 1970, 11 and 14).[55]

Nor were these spectacular colonisation plans in fact original, since at other moments in Brazilian history there had been thoughts of reducing the problems of the North East by encouraging the migration of *nordestinos* to the Amazon region. After the disastrous drought of 1877 Pedro II offered the *flagelados* free transport to the ports of Belém or Manaus (Morais *et al.* 1970, 115). The idea had been toyed with at various times subsequently. What was new in 1970 was the decision actually to make use of the colonisation potential.

The objections to the colonisation plans

Like the road construction projects, the colonisation plans gave rise to immediate criticism. Alberto Tamer and Roberto de Oliveira Campos at once called in question the necessity for colonising the Amazon region and also feared that such colonisation would be far from successful.[56] Other people also made written and verbal criticism of the plans and so put a damper on the almost lyrical enthusiasm with which the road building and colonisation plans were announced and defended. The criticisms are summarised in the sections below.

The availability of land elsewhere

One of the first objections was that there were still ample possibilities for colonisation near the existing highways in the Amazon region, such as the road from Belém to Brasília and that from Cuiabá to Porto Velho. Similar possibilities were seen in Goiás and Mato Grosso, where large areas were put into use for extensive livestock farming at the time.

It was also pointed out that there were still large areas of land available for colonisation in the state of Maranhão. This region possesses a natural environment that differs less from that of the North East than does the Amazon region proper, while

55 In the following year the government announced the Proterra programme, which formed part of the Programa de Integração Nacional and included further measures for the development of agriculture in the North and North East.

56 See their publications relating to the Transamazônica (Tamer 1971; Morais *et al.* 1970). Some of the criticism is to be found, in briefer form than what follows here, in the publications included in the list of references. It is derived from short newspaper articles and conversations with Brazilians.

colonisation had also already been taking place there for several decades. There was a considerable migration to the region from the neighbouring states of Piauí and Ceará, in particular. Another important advantage of Maranhão was the fact that it is situated much closer to the North East, which meant that the problem of isolation and of the great distances to the more densely occupied areas of Brazil were felt much less keenly there than in the North proper. This closer location was advantageous, for example, in the marketing of agricultural surpluses (Morais *et al.* 1970, 123; see also Tamer 1971, 91 ff.).

A colonisation study instituted by the SUDENE in 1972 showed that, in the zones of Itapecuru, Gurupi and Alto Parnaíba alone, a total of at least 48 000 families would be able to find a living (Apote *et al.* 1972, 55).

In view of all this, it is not surprising that, after the colonisation plans were announced, it was quickly concluded that the government would do better to use the money, not for road building, but for an intensification and improved organisation of colonisation in Maranhão, especially since a number of colonisation projects were already in progress there, so that it could draw upon some experience in the field.

The low level of education of the *nordestinos*[57]

There was also doubt from the beginning as to whether the *nordestinos*, from whom the government expected a great deal of interest in the colonisation projects in the North, were the most suited population group to realise a successful colonisation scheme. The *nordestinos* had, in general, little education and many were even illiterate. By no means all of them yet saw the necessity of education for their children, with the consequence that they often kept their children at home as soon as there was work to be done on the land.

Moreover, many *nordestinos* had an extremely limited knowledge of agriculture. Many employed traditional agricultural methods, not only when they practised farming in the North East or in Maranhão, but even when farming in the Amazon region. The *nordestinos* who were established in Amazônia in about 1970 almost without exception turned to simple, shifting cultivation. Some of them did not see the value and the necessity of more intensive production techniques, since there were still vast areas of forest that could be cleared. Consequently, measures to combat soil exhaustion and erosion were by no means always employed. Those who were more aware of the possible dangers of shifting cultivation were often unable to employ better methods because of lack of capital and/or the absence of the necessary technical knowledge. Added to this lack of capital and knowledge was the fact that people were often prevented by malnutrition and disease from achieving the amount of work that would be desirable. As a result of all this, the harvest was often modest, while the lack of good storage facilities meant that part of what was harvested was lost.

Tamer also pointed out that many *nordestinos* not only had a traditional outlook, but were even fatalistic and resigned. They often also had a poorly developed social instinct. The majority were strongly individualistic and they tended to be mistrustful of credit-giving institutions and cooperatives.

---

57 Alberto Tamer paid detailed attention to this in his *Transamazônica* (1971), particularly on pp. 123–130.

Alberto Tamer and others accordingly rightly remarked that one need not expect that people with physical disabilities, a lack of technical knowledge and the attitudes just described would suddenly behave in the Amazon region as modern, progressive farmers. Tamer therefore did not consider the *nordestinos* to be the best suited population group to realise a rapid and successful colonisation of the North, with its difficult natural environment.

The constantly inadequate government support

Disappointments and failures could be prevented by a proper supervision of the colonisation process. Up to 1970, however, the Brazilian government had never succeeded in providing large numbers of colonists with intensive and expert supervision. The successful realisation of large colonisation projects was naturally extremely difficult. The chance of success was present only if extensive preliminary studies were carried out and if plans were drawn up in advance, with all aspects of the colonisation process worked out in detail. In addition, a large and expert staff was required to supervise the whole process. By no means all these conditions had been satisfied in the past.

The colonisation process had, in fact, been largely spontaneous in the past while, where there had been official supervision, it had usually been very limited. The occupation of the lands which had been opened up by the Belém–Brasília highway had been chaotic in many respects and had taken place without any government support worth mentioning. Few provisions were made for the settlers. The government had also not taken sufficient care to ensure that those who occupied the land enjoyed security of tenure. A great many colonists became squatters and some of them were forced out again by *fazendeiros* who regarded them as intruders or were wishing to extend their properties (Glaser 1971, 27f.). All this largely explained why many preferred living in the shanty towns of the big cities to settlement along colonisation fronts, such as that along the Belém–Brasília highway.

In view of all this, it is not surprising that many people wondered immediately after the colonisation plans for the North were announced whether there would be sufficient interest in a pioneer existence and whether the government would be able during the coming years to provide the tens of thousands of colonists with adequate supervision. In other words, it was feared that there would be a repeat along the Transamazônica and other roads of what had occurred along the Belém–Brasília highway.

The less healthy environment

The pessimism in the early 1970s concerning the success of colonisation was also based upon the fact that the physically often weak *nordestinos* would have to go and live in a not immediately healthy environment. Malaria and other tropical diseases could make their lives very difficult and greatly discourage them. Naturally, many diseases could be prevented by appropriate government measures, but providing adequate medical facilities in a vast region was by no means a simple matter, particularly if the opening-up led in a short time to the settlement of thousands of people. Besides a lot of money, much specialised manpower was needed. It was, of course, also true that medical facilities would be of little effect if they were accessible only to certain population groups and if the population still had little understanding of the need for hygiene, as had more than once been observed, particularly among the poor *nordestinos*.

The problem of markets

Attention was naturally also drawn to the problem of markets. The question at once arose of whether there would be adequate markets in the still thinly populated Amazon region and the impoverished North East for the agricultural surpluses of the colonists' holdings and, if so, whether the high transport costs would result in an inadequate ability to compete. The distances to the more densely populated and more prosperous South East were still greater.

There was also the not unjustified fear that private traders would seize upon the difficult and expensive transport as an excuse to pay the farmers extra low prices in order to ensure themselves a respectable profit. Cooperatives might have been the solution in such a situation, but without supervision, advice and a feeling for community, it was difficult to get such organisations started. Cooperatives, accordingly, had hardly developed.

The nature of the soil

Not the least of the reasons for the reservations about the success of agricultural colonisation was the limited suitability of many of the soils for arable farming. Both earlier and more recent pedological investigations had led to the conclusion that the greater part of the *terra firme* (the higher land not subject to periodical flooding) consisted of soils of limited fertility, which might be rapidly lost after reclamation.[58]

According to Falesi, no less than 70% of the Amazon region consists of latosols, which have been formed mainly from Tertiary sediments. They are soils which are generally deep and permeable. Their profile shows them to be well aerated and to possess a good water circulation. The texture varies from sandy to very clayey, sometimes even with a clay content of more than 70%. Opposed to this, however, is a high acidity and a low chemical fertility (Falesi 1973, 4ff.). After reclamation the soils rapidly lose the limited amount of plant food which they contain. This is the result of a low retentive power and of exposure to higher temperatures, which lead to an accelerated burning up of the humus content. Consequently, the agricultural production capacity rapidly declines. Where these soils are occupied for shifting cultivation they are usually abandoned after two to four years (Meggers 1973, 22f.).[59]

58 See the publications by Sioli, Condurú and Falesi in the Bibliography. Harald Sioli referred in his "Ecologia da paisagem..." (1969b, 268) to a "pobreza extra-ordinaria dos solos da terra firme." He also pointed out in various publications that all the northern and many of the southern tributaries discharge nearly distilled water, which is indicative of an extremely low soil fertility.

59 As is well known, the dense forest growth is no indication of high fertility, since the forest lives by means of a branching surface root system on the humus which it produces itself. There is an almost closed cycle. Small losses are compensated because one or a few deep roots transport food from the deeper layers of the soil (Harald Sioli 1969b, 271).

Such soils are permanently suited to arable farming only if:

- trees or shrubs are planted on them. Because trees and shrubs protect the ground from extreme temperatures and rapid leaching, the soil fertility is maintained longer, while they also provide humus;
- lime and manure are applied. According to Sioli, the addition of artificial fertilisers is not sufficient, since the soils contain insufficient colloids to retain a large quantity of mineral substances, so that the latter would be rapidly leached out again. In Sioli's view, therefore, it is also necessary to use animal manure to supply the soil with colloids (Sioli 1969b, 275).

The *várzeas*, the low alluvial lands which are flooded during periods of high water levels and usually provided with a layer of silt, do generally form good agricultural land. The majority and the best of the *várzea* soils occur along the main river, which transports a large quantity of sediment from the Andes. Along the Amazon the *várzeas* actually cover a total area of about 60 000 square kilometres. Their exploitation for the cultivation of rapidly growing products could be intensified through improved accessibility. One problem, however, is that the construction of permanently usable roads in the flood plains is a difficult and expensive matter. The Transamazônica was therefore not planned in the immediate vicinity of the Amazon, but at a considerable distance from the river, so that it opened up mainly the poorer lands of the *terra firme* just described. The same was true of the road from Cuiabá to Santarém. It should incidentally be remarked in respect of the *várzea* soils that, in the view of agricultural experts, these do require some manure, at least if good yields are to remain assured (Falesi 1973, 32–35; Ministério do Interior 1971b, 21).

The agriculturally most productive soils are the *terra roxa* soils, which consist of the weathering products of basic rocks (basalt, diabase). The presence of these soils had been proved in various places, including the region of Altamira (on the Xingu), in Rondônia and Roirama. According to Falesi, the *terra roxa* soils certainly covered an area of 1.03 million hectares. Condurú, however, gave a figure of 2.5 million hectares and a study by the Banco da Amazônia mentioned an area of 2.3 million (Falesi 1973, 14; Condurú 1973, 5; Ministério do Interior 1971b, 18).

Large areas had not yet been covered by soil surveys in the early 1970s, so that the figures mentioned were obviously provisional, but enough was known to be able to state that the fertile *terra roxa* soils formed the exception rather than the rule. Soil investigations along the Transamazônica had already shown that these soils certainly did not occur everywhere south of the Amazon. It is incidentally also true of the *terra roxa* soils that they can be successfully permanently exploited only if the correct cultivation methods are employed and if manure is applied.

Earlier colonisation activity in the Amazon region: government supervision

We feel bound to conclude, on the basis of what has been stated in the preceding section, that the doubts which have been expressed since 1970 concerning the success of the colonisation plans were certainly not wholly unfounded. These doubts were further strengthened when it was noted that the colonisation which had taken place up to about 1970 in Maranhão and the Amazon region proper was not very extensive and also not very successful, even where it occurred under government supervision. The colonisation realised in the North up to 1970 had in fact contributed nothing to the solution of the socio-economic problems of the North East and provided the majority of colonists with only a very simple existence, as will appear from the examples below.

The colonisation in Maranhão[60]

In Maranhão, the state government made available 3 million hectares of land in 1961 to the SUDENE for colonisation purposes in an area where there had already been spontaneous settlement for some time. The area in question was situated near the locality of Alto Turi and Pindaré Mirim in the north west of the state, about 200 kilometres from São Luis. During the 1960s it was accessible only by a very poor road. The intention of this grant of land was to concentrate the migration from the North East more in certain areas of the state.

The SUDENE had already made a start with colonisation during the first years of its existence, but its activities had always remained very modest and one certainly cannot speak of a successful occupation.

According to a SUDENE publication, only 450 000 (4500 sq km) of the 3 million hectares were inhabited in about 1970. In the most southerly zone (1300 sq km), which possessed the best road network, some 3000 families had settled spontaneously a few years before and the number of large livestock holdings was increasing. An area of about 2700 sq km had been occupied spontaneously by about 8000 families, who were mainly engaged in arable farming, nearly always in the form of shifting cultivation. In the remaining area of 500 sq km, during the 1960s the SUDENE sponsored the settlement of about 1000 families, who lived dispersed in some 17 centres.

When the SUDENE began this colonisation, spontaneous settlement was already intensifying along highway BR-316, which was the principal traffic axis of the whole region and connected the places Teresina and Belém. Because of this settlement the SUDENE was unable to establish any further colonisation centres along the road, but had to found them on land situated farther from the road and still covered by forest. Each family obtained 50 hectares, incidentally without definitive title of ownership. In theory, there was proper supervision, but in practice the organisation and supervision were defective in many respects. This was mainly the result of the absence of clearly defined objectives, insufficient capital, the lack of experts in the field of colonisation on virgin land and of inadequate coordination between the different bodies involved in the colonisation process. In addition, insufficient preliminary studies had been made before beginning with the execution of the plan.

The colonists were in a somewhat better situation than the squatters, because they did not have to fear being driven from their land and because they did receive some support and supervision. Nevertheless, their existence was described as wretched. The average income from work on the agricultural holding in 1971 was only 72 % of the official regional minimum wage. The average annual income per family was 4133 cruzeiros

60 The following is based mainly on Tamer (1971, 142 and 238) and Apote *et al.* (1972, 13, 29–31).

(Tavares *et al.* 1972, 82 f.).[61] Sickness made life still more difficult. The predominant form of arable farming here was again mainly shifting cultivation, which was technically not very advanced and served only the local market. In fact, little was achieved of the intention set out in the SUDENE's first *Plano Diretor* to settle 6500 colonists' families in a three-year period.

A second potentially important colonisation zone was the area along the road from Santa Luzia to Assailândia, which penetrated into the transition forest (*matas pre-amazônicas*). The government of Maranhão decided in 1969 to reserve 540 000 hectares here for colonisation purposes, making provision both for family holdings and large livestock holdings, which could be established with the aid of taxation facilities. The intention of this reservation was to ensure a more organised and more concentrated occupation process. A short while before, however, detailed studies of the region had not yet been made, nor had concrete colonisation plans been worked out, while the government also lacked the necessary financial means. Consequently, it could in fact do little more than try to put some order into the spontaneous colonisation. According to a SUDENE study from the early 1970s, the area was at the time in danger of being occupied largely by extensive livestock holdings (Apote *et al.* 1972, 30). Here, too, the settlement of small farmers was on a modest scale and there was no supervision.

Colonisation along the Belém–Brasília highway

Along the Belém–Brasília highway, where the colonisation was uncontrolled and took place with minimal government support, many colonists made a living from the practice of simple shifting cultivation. After a few years of cultivation, therefore, they had to clear new areas of land. In so doing, many ran the risk of being driven off by big landowners because ownership rights had never been granted in many instances and the property titles had not been properly registered.

The land could be leased only on unfavourable terms. Generally half of the harvest had to be surrendered and the land could be cultivated for only one or a few years, after which it had to be handed over to the *fazendeiros* for livestock farming. As a result, the majority of arable farmers led a poor existence. The farm workers, who lived from their labour, had to be content with very low wages. Many had to contend with diseases. Educational facilities were inadequate.

In the north of the state of Goiás was to be found one of the few agricultural colonies established by the government before 1975. It was the settlement of Bernardo Sayão, which fell under the jurisdiction of the Instituto Nacional de Colonização e Reforma Agrária in the 1970s and was established at the beginning of the 1960s. 320 families were officially settled there in 1971 on *lotes* of 30 hectares. They suffered much disadvantage from the poor communications, because the road which connected with the Belém–Brasília highway was extremely bad. Nor was there a bridge over the river. There was no medical station, although malaria was very prevalent. The largest part of the land had not yet been demarcated. The changes in the official bodies supervising the colonisation during the preceding ten years had done little to encourage the rapid and successful development of the colony. About a half of the farmers lived predominantly from subsistence agriculture and some production for the local market (rice).

---

61 The amounts are given in cruzeiros at 1971 values. A cruzeiro was then worth about £ 0.07.

There were no cooperatives for dealing with the production surpluses, nor were there good storage facilities, so that a part of the harvest was lost. The average labourer's wage in 1971 was only 0.9 *salario minimo regional* (1867 cruzeiros at 1971 values). The average family income was 2.3 times the regional minimum wage (4770 cruzeiros at 1971 values) (Tamer 1971, 91 ff.; Tavares *et al.* 1972, 79–81).

It is not surprising that, in such circumstances, some of the farmers and agricultural labourers left again after a short period of time, often for the larger centres, where many tried to find a better living in the tertiary sector. Consequently, no strong bond was created between man and land.

Colonisation in the region around Altamira[62]

The state of things in 1970 in the area around the little town of Altamira, situated on the Xinguú, was not very different. During the 1960s, the government of the state of Pará had tried to attract colonists from the North East and to settle them in the neighbourhood of Altamira with the aim of expanding agriculture to meet local needs. The colonists received 100 hectares in provisional ownership and had to clear ⅛ of the forest within three years. 50 % of the land had to remain covered with forest. After these and certain other conditions had been met, definitive ownership rights could be obtained.

The final results were modest. In about 1970 a total of only 300 families from the North East had settled in the neighbourhood of Altamira. Some had come of their own accord, others on the initiative of the Pará government.

The soils in the region consist of *terra roxa* and are therefore fertile, but nevertheless the colonists did not lead a very flourishing existence. According to Tamer, they practised traditional shifting cultivation and produced chiefly maize, beans, rice and manioc, all of which were products used mainly for their own or local consumption. Livestock farming was of very little importance. Deterioration of the soil could already be observed in various places.

The communications with Altamira were poor and expensive. During the wet season the roads were even impassable, so that the colonists were compelled to transport the harvests partly by horse or mule. The marketing of the produce was greatly hindered by the long distances to the major urban centres, such as Belém.

Added to all this, was the nuisance of insects, which ate up part of the primitively stored harvest. Excessive rainfall sometimes diminished the yields, while production was also reduced by plant diseases and parasites. The majority of settlers did not have enough money to buy insecticides etc., which were very expensive, as well as being scarcely obtainable in Altamira.

In his not very encouraging account, Tamer also mentioned that the middlemen abused their position to pay low prices to the farmers. The majority of the latter led an impoverished existence, were primitively housed and troubled by disease. Because of the low income from their holdings they were compelled to rely wholly or in part on physical labour, but could not afford to employ hired labourers, although this would have been desirable for the further reclamation of the land.

62 Data derived mainly from Tamer (1971, 99–113).

Apart from *nordestinos*, a few dozen families from Paraná had also settled in Altamira after 1969. They had to contend with the same kind of problems as the *nordestinos*.

According to Tamer (1972), the situation described above arose from the circumstance that the colonists had received only land from the government, which in itself was totally inadequate, even though the land was of good quality. In Tamer's view, there should also have been supervision and all kinds of infrastructure should have been provided, such as roads, schools and small hospitals. Tamer considered that the district around Altamira furnished an example of the way in which colonisation in the Amazon region should most certainly not have been tackled.

The situation elsewhere

Tamer encountered a similar situation in agricultural colonies near Manaus, along the road from Manaus to Itacoatiara. Only the Japanese colonists formed a marked exception to the rather dark impression he formed (Tamer 1971, 114 ff.). It also seemed that the *nordestinos* who had recently settled voluntarily along the completed sections of road in Roirama would not find a much better living. They, too, practised shifting cultivation and enjoyed no government support.[63]

Lastly, up to shortly before 1975, the situation was also rather bleak in the agricultural colony of Iata, one of the few settlements established by the government in the territory of Rondônia. The colony lies not far from the little town of Guajará-Mirim. It was founded in about 1957 and contained some 600 families in 1970. Most of the settlers led a miserable, subsistence existence, because their holdings produced very little as a consequence of the progressive exhaustion of the soil, the small area of the holdings (25 ha), the primitive farming methods and the almost complete lack of government support. All colonists had, in fact, the status of occupier, as definitive property rights had not been granted. 61 % of the settlers were illiterate, 95 % of the families did not have sanitary facilities. There was no medical assistance. The majority lived in straw huts (Ministério da Agricultura 1971c, 13, 77–79).

Conclusions: The reaction of the Brazilian government to the criticisms of its colonisation policy

The above has shown that, for various reasons, the realisation of a successful, large-scale colonisation in the Amazon region was by no means a simple task. It has also shown that, up to 1970, the Brazilian government had not succeeded in helping large numbers of landless families to obtain a holding and in giving the colonists intensive supervision by providing facilities and granting extensive technical and other support. The doubts which were expressed when the colonisation plans for the Amazon region were announced in 1970 were therefore not without foundation.

In spite of all the criticism and all the doubts, the Brazilian government did not let itself be deflected from its plans. It clung to the view that it was necessary to integrate the Amazon region more into the national economy and that colonisation was one

63 *Opinião* 20 a 27 de agosto de 1973, p. 5 ("A corrida para Roraima").

means of achieving this. In order to rebut criticism, it repeatedly emphasised from the middle of 1970 that it did not intend to let colonisation proceed uncontrolled. It would be better supervised than before and would be carried out in an orderly manner. Spontaneous colonisation along the Transamazônica and other projected highways would not be permitted. A similar state of affairs to that along the Belém–Brasília highway would be avoided.

The Instituto Nacional de Colonização e Reforma Agrária (INCRA) was therefore created in July 1970 as a result of an administrative reorganisation. It was given the task of controlling and supervising colonisation in Brazil. Another task was to legalise the spontaneous occupation that had occurred in various parts of the country.

The INCRA from then on concentrated a great part of its activity on the Amazon region. In 1971, the total colonisation budget of the INCRA was 68.1 million cruzeiros, of which 20.3 million was used for colonisation programmes in North Brazil. One of its first activities was the drawing up of detailed plans (Panagides and Vande Lage 1973, 15).

The Brazilian government also repeatedly stressed from 1970 that the Amazon region still possessed good, but scarcely utilised, agricultural potential. Attention was drawn particularly to the extensive areas with fertile soils. In the popular publication *Uma nova marcha ao norte / Une nouvelle marche vers le Nord* (n. d., n. p.) reference was made to a "solo generoso, rico em materia orgânica, agrestável aos mais diversos tipos de culturas conforme levantamentos téchnicos já demonstraram." The more scientific publications and reports also contained passages full of optimism or tried to arouse it. One cannot avoid the impression, therefore, that the government was trying to push the problem of limited soil fertility into the background in the early 1970s by pointing regularly to the existence of areas of fertile soils.

One of the first measures taken by the government in advance of colonisation was the reservation of strips of land. It was initially determined that strips 10 kilometres in width should be reserved along both sides of the road from Cuiabá to Santarém and of the Transamazônica. The Decree of 1st April 1971 (No. 1164), however, declared all *terras devolutas* (state lands) in Amazônia Legal situated within a distance of 100 kilometres along both sides of all existing or proposed roads to be indispensable for national security and national development. They came under direct government control (Ministério da Agricultura 1971b, 25).

Proposals concerning the number of colonists were quickly made known. Up to 1975, within the framework of the Programa de Integração Nacional, a total of at least 100 000 families were to be settled in the whole Amazon region, in particular, along the Transamazônica and the Cuiabá–Santarém highway (Ministério da Agricultura n. d., *Desenvolvimento rural*, 14). The proposals envisaged 10 000 colonists in the first year, 20 000 in the second year, 30 000 in the third year and, finally, 40 000 in the fourth year (Condurú 1973, 19). The text of Decree 1106/70 refers to the settlement of 70 000 families during the period 1972–74 (Ministério da Agricultura 1972b, 19). Another official publication stated that the intention was to settle about 1 million colonist families (or some 5 million persons) in the North over a ten year period (*Uma nova marcha ao norte / Une nouvelle marche vers le Nord* n. d.).

These plans were immediately regarded as highly ambitious. The following chapter will show to what extent and in which areas the government succeeded in realising its plans. In it we give a short review of the state of affairs in the first half of the 1970s.

The progress of the colonisation sponsored by the INCRA

The zone along the Cuiabá-Santarém highway

No INCRA-sponsored colonisation had taken place within the sphere of influence of the Cuiabá–Santarém highway until 1975, although *nordestinos* had settled near Santarém in the years before and there had been an expansion of the number of large livestock holdings in the area north of Cuiabá. An FAO commission had recommended colonisation based on arable farming along and near this highway, as well as on the basis of forestry and livestock farming, possibly with financial support from the International Bank for Reconstruction and Development, but it was not known when this colonisation would begin nor what its character would be.[64]

Rondônia[65]

The territory was made more accessible in the years preceding 1970 through the building of a number of roads. The road to Porto Velho was completed in 1965. The region was also beginning to play a more important role nationally as a result of the growth in tin-mining. This greater accessibility, the economic growth and the good agricultural land which was present in various places led to increased voluntary migration, mainly from areas in the Centro-Sul, and to an increase in spontaneous colonisation along the principal roads (BR-319 and BR-364). This migration was strengthened when the existence of good *terra roxa* soils was proved in various places and the government suggested that Rondônia could become an important colonisation area for large population groups. During the period 1965–1974 the population of Rondônia grew from 97 000 to 143 000, mainly through voluntary migration.

The spontaneous occupation of large areas of land led to chaos and tensions in respect to property rights. The activities which the INCRA developed in Rondônia after

64 Apart from the area near Cuiabá and Santarém, the districts around Fordlândia, Belterra and Daniel de Carvalho, in particular, offered possibilities for further colonisation, because a more developed infrastructure already existed there (including the former Ford plantations and the hydro-electric power station near Curuá-Una). There had also been a large amount of spontaneous occupation in those areas. Near Belterra there were certainly 180 000 hectares of land available for colonisation. If this land was parcelled out in lotes of 100 hectares, however, it would nevertheless be necessary to settle some of the squatters outside the Belterra region (*Diagnostico perspectivo para o projeto de colonização ao longo da rodovia Cuiabá-Santarém* n. d., 147).

65 Data derived mainly from: Ministério da Agricultura (1971c; 1972a) and Arruda (1972).

1970 were therefore aimed at limiting this unorganised settlement and at supporting the officially permitted occupation of the land by such means as technical assistance, financial support and the granting of property rights. The INCRA hoped, through stimulating the colonisation process, to be able to satisfy the increased demand for agricultural products and to ensure the preservation of this economically and strategically important frontier region. According to plans drawn up in 1972, the INCRA proposed to settle about 8000 families in Rondônia by 1975. Although not all spontaneous migrants and settlers would be absorbed by then, it was hoped that this colonisation would help to restrict the unorganised occupation.

In 1970 and the following years the INCRA proceeded with the realisation of a few guided colonisation projects.[66] In the mid-1970s there were five recent projects, i. e. Gy Parana, Ouro Preto, Sidney Girão, Padre Adolfo Rohl and Paulo de Assis Ribeiro (Vilhena). Fig. 6 shows them to be situated along the two principal roads through Rondônia, i. e. BR-364 and BR-319.

Apart from settlements in these project areas, the INCRA had reception centres at Pimento Bueno and Vilhena. They were established to provide the migrants with advice and to direct them to the project areas.

Figure 6. General reference map of Rondônia

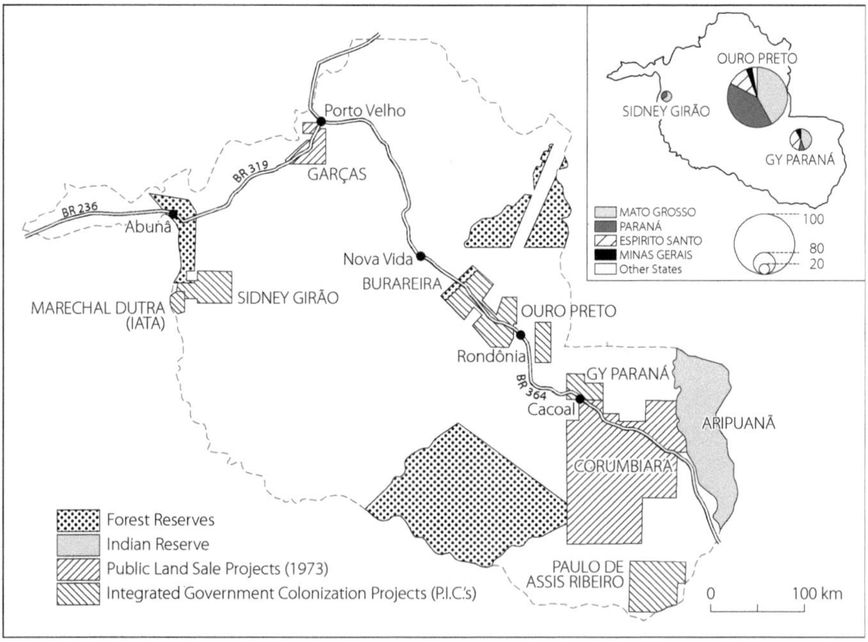

Source: Atlas de Rondônia (1975).

66 In addition, there were still a few projects in execution dating from the1960s or earlier. One of them was that of Presidente Dutra (Iata), where 976 colonists had been settled up to June 1976 and the settlement of a further 224 families was planned for 1977.

8,935 colonists had been settled in these five areas up to 1976, which meant that the integrated colonisation projects in Rondônia no longer lagged behind the programme which has since been realised along the Transamazônica, as they still did a few years previously. The distribution of the colonists was as follows:

Gy Paraná	2070	Padre Adolfo Rohl	1164
Ouro Preto	3564	Paulo de Assis Ribeiro	1732
Sidney Girão	405		

The colonisation in Gy Paraná was still at the preparatory stage at the end of 1972, but it was hoped to begin the settlement there in 1973 of 500 families whose movement had already been planned in 1972. The project area was situated near the Pimento Bueno reception centre on highway BR-364, about 500 km from the little town of Porto Velho (see Fig. 6).

Colonisation was further advanced in the oldest project zone – that of Ouro Preto. This zone, which had a total area of 226 000 hectares, was situated along highway BR-364, about 330 km from Porto Velho, between Rondônia and Ariquemes. Colonisation began here in August 1970. The target of the plans was the settlement of 2000 families, of whom 1079 had already been established in 1973. They had all come to Rondônia on their own initiative and originated mainly from the west and south east of Brazil. The settlers received grants of 100 hectares of land if they were engaged exclusively in arable farming and between 150 and 200 hectares if they were engaged mainly or exclusively in livestock farming. The soils were of good quality.

The colonisation zone of Sidney Girão was situated in the valley of the Rio Mamoré, 270 km S.S.W. of Porto Velho and 65 km from Guajará Mirim, close to the Bolivian frontier, on the road from Abunã to Guajará Mirim. The first colonists arrived in 1971 and only 210 families of a projected 500 had been settled by October 1972. The planned target for this area was 1500 families, settled on holdings of between 100 and 200 hectares. The total area of the colonisation zone was about 200 000 hectares. Many of the colonists up to mid-1973 originated from the neighbouring agricultural colony of Iata, which was established in 1957 near Guajará-Mirim. For various reasons, the majority of the approximately 600 families settled in this colony led a rather poor existence. The INCRA therefore decided to open the sponsored colonisation project of Sidney Girão to these people as well. 80 % of the heads of households resident in Iata were born in Ceará.

By far the greater part of the colonists came from the Centro-Sul (mainly Mato Grosso and Paraná), a very small minority came from the North East. It should be added that some of the colonists were already living in Rondônia as *posseiros*. Settlement had taken place on *lotes* and not in *agrovilas*.

As in the colonisation projects along the Transamazônica, the colonists were allocated 100 hectares of land, which they had to clear themselves and 50 hectares of which had to be maintained as *reserva florestal*. A limited number of grants of larger holdings had been made, which were devoted to cattle ranching. In Ouro Preto, for example, there were 200 *lotes*, each with an area of 200 hectares.

After clearing the land, the majority of colonists here, as along the Transamazônica, began the cultivation of a limited area of food crops, such as rice, maize and beans, both for home consumption and the market. No use was made of fertilisers. Rice was the most important crop in terms of area and here, too, it could be disposed of to the government at the official minimum price. To deal with these sales CIBRAZEM had two stores built in Gy Paraná and Ouro Preto.

The majority of farmers were also trying to turn to more commercial crops such as coffee, rubber and cocoa. Some farmers had gone further in this direction than others. The area of cultivated land, therefore, varied on each holding, but was generally limited here as well, i. e. on average less than 10 hectares. The growing of cocoa was on the increase, particularly since the Brazilian government had set itself the aim of making Rondônia the second cocoa-growing area of Brazil after South Bahia. The Burareiro project (Fig. 6) in fact also fitted into this policy. Its aim was to settle 200 small cocoa farmers from southern Bahia on holdings of 199 to 400 hectares. In addition, 240 holdings of 1000 hectares had been planned, for which farmers from other regions were also eligible. By mid-1976 the INCRA had already settled 332 families.[67]

The problems which occurred in the Rondônia colonisation projects were largely similar to those occurring along the Transamazônica. Here also, the division into parcels was not everywhere satisfactory, communications were defective, credit facilities and agricultural advice were not as good as they might be, there was an absence of local markets, crop rotations were inadequate, farm incomes were low and there were problems in the field of health care.

There were also differences. In Rondônia there were many more problems arising from claims upon the land than there were along the Transamazônica. They had been caused mainly by the failure to produce colonisation plans of any magnitude after the completion of the road from Cuiabá to Porto Velho. Many migrants then began to clear plots of land on their own initiative. The situation became even more chaotic because of the occurrence of all kinds of dubious practices referred to generally as *grilagem*.

These practices involved individuals or companies trying to gain control of large areas of land by the use of false deeds or other methods. Any *posseiros* living on the land were driven off, if necessary, with the help of private "police." Sometimes land was even acquired by driving off official colonists. The *grileiros* generally did not use the land to cultivate for their own subsistence, but to divide up and sell to people who wanted to start a small farm themselves and were waiting in vain for the government to meet their wishes. The *grileiros* themselves suffered little risk through these practices. It was the prospective farmer who might hear in the course of time from official sources that he had bought land from dishonest enterprises.

The main companies involved in *grilagem* were CALAMA and Gainsa-Guaporé-Agro-Industrial S.A. There were also several smaller ones.[68] CALAMA had managed to get its claims, which were based on a document from about 1915 and related to about one million hectares of land, recognised by the INCRA and had also succeeded in exercising control over a considerably larger area than the original claim. One of the areas controlled in the 1970s by CALAMA included the settlement of Vila Rondônia. More than 30 000 people lived in and near this town, as well as thousands of *posseiros*, some of whom regularly received a hint to leave the land.

CALAMA could go its way unhampered because it was supported by the INCRA and enjoyed the protection of the police. The latter even permitted the company to re-

67 Data supplied by the INCRA at Pôrto Velho.

68 The details which follow have been derived from Senna (1975, 77–80).

move unwanted settlers with its own well-paid *pistoleiros*. It need hardly be said that in such a situation there were fatalities from time to time.

The GAINSA was under the control of two large landowners. It did not enjoy the official recognition and support of the INCRA, but did have the protection of the magistrate in Porto Velho, as well as the support of the whole judiciary and police of Rondônia. In addition, the owners, known as the *Mafia dos Arantes*, had a hundred *pistoleiros* at their disposal. GAINSA operated mainly in the areas of Abuña, Nova Vida and Cacoal.

Officially, the INCRA had the task of stopping such practices as quickly as possible and ensuring that as many farmers as possible quickly came into legal possession of their own holdings. Apart from settling colonists in project areas, it had, where possible, to do this by legalising the property rights of *posseiros*, where they had taken possession and cleared the land. In practice, however, not enough was done. The INCRA worked slowly and inefficiently and its officials supported dishonest practices. The same was true of part of the judiciary, the police and the government. As a result, thousands of migrants led a marginal existence on land from which they might sooner or later be driven off. This situation was also exposed at the time by the North Brazilian bishops.[69]

Landownership problems

Undesirable situations as mentioned above occurred not only in Rondônia. In the mid-1970s, more or less all the land along the completed section of the Brasília–Manaus highway (from Brasília to the crossing with the Cuiabá–Santarém highway) seemed already to have fallen into the hands of *grileiros* and *posseiros*. In a great many places they had already started clearing the forest and were maintaining certain stretches of the road from personal interest, where it was already in a poor condition, although only recently completed. The government denied the existence of such unauthorised occupation, but was in fact unable to act effectively against it.[70]

In Acre there had been large, mainly illegal sales of public land to capitalists from the Centro-Sul and the atmosphere of violence and insecurity which accompanied the operation of *grileiros* had caused many farmers to migrate to Peru and Bolivia, where living conditions were more favourable. This had been happening particularly after 1970. It was estimated that some 40 000 people had emigrated to these two countries m the past few years.[71]

Grileiros also seemed already to have become active along the Transamazônica (in the area at a distance of more than 10 km from the road, i. e. outside the zone reserved by the INCRA for occupation by small farmers. Some pieces of land had already been sold several times. INCRA officials had also succeeded in acquiring land there.[72]

69 See "Pastoral da Terra" (1976).

70 "As rodovias e a integração." *Ultima Hora*, 8th August 1976.

71 *A Crítica*, 23 August 1976.

72 This has been revealed by information obtained verbally at Altamira. It was noted in the area near Humaitá by Müller *et al.* 1975, vol II, p. 639.

A similar development was feared along the Cuiabá–Sontarém highway, which was fully open to traffic in October 1976. It had already become a reality along the first section which came into use in 1972 (470 km).

While there were tensions between landowners and *posseiros* and conflicts between *posseiros* and *grileiros*, resulting in threats to the livelihood of the weaker population groups, the Indigenous population was also threatened by the illegal occupation of reserve lands. There was evidence that the Parque Indígena do Aripuaná along the road from Cuiabá to Porto Velho had been infiltrated by several thousand families who had obtained land there through the Companhia Colonizadora Itaporanga, established in São Paulo. This company had been operating in the area since 1972 and had already sold 1.2 million hectares of land in Rondônia. Apart from *posseiros* there were also *garimpeiros* (simple miners) living in the reserve. The Indigenous' service Fundação Nacional do Índio (FUNAI) had also given various companies permission to carry out mining surveys in the park. If even the reserves were no longer a secure territory, it was clear that the existence of the Indigenous was even more threatened outside them, not only by small-scale settlement, but also and, especially, by large land developers or speculators (Chimamovitz 1973).

Amazonas

In the state of Amazonas the INCRA had only one integrated colonisation project in progress in 1973, namely, in Bela Vista, on the Rio Negro, some 10 kilometres from Manaus. In mid-1973, a total of 246 colonist families (including 34 Japanese families) had been settled on parcels of land of between 50 and 100 hectares. The settlement of a further 100 families was expected shortly.

An important aim of the colonisation project was the better provisioning of the rapidly growing city of Manaus with vegetables, fruit, poultry, eggs etc. Apart from growing these products, some of the colonists were engaged in other forms of cultivation, such as pepper growing. The majority of the colonists were already living in the area as spontaneous occupants. An investigation by the IPEA showed that, in 1971, besides 110 colonist families, there were already about 1300 squatters living in the area. The INCRA was gradually settling them on the land legally. Once they had become official colonists, they also received supervision.

The IPEA observed in 1971 a quite considerable difference in prosperity among the colonists. The more successful farmers – the majority of them Japanese in origin – were engaged in horticulture, poultry farming and in growing permanent crops such as pepper and guaraná. In this "upper crust" the average income per worker was 4.1 times the official regional minimum wage. The poorer farmers, by contrast, were mainly engaged in traditional shifting cultivation, serving primarily the local market. The average income per worker in this group was equivalent to 1.2 times the regional minimum wage (Tavares *et al.* 1972, 84).

In mid-1973, the settlement of some 500 colonist families around Tabatinga, on the left bank of the Solimões, near the frontier with Colombia and Peru, was at the project stage. Here too, provision was made for holdings of about 100 hectares. It was hoped to be able to begin the execution of this project in 1974. The aim of the project was particularly to expand the production of food crops, both for the supply of an army unit stationed in Tabatinga and to feed the growing civil population. A further motive was the desire to increase the population density of the frontier zones of Amazônia in order to prevent possible infiltration by Peruvian *caboclos*.

Maranhão and Goiás

In Maranhão there was only one small colony under the supervision of the INCRA, namely that of Barra do Corda. Within the framework of the Programa de Integração National a total of 238 families had been settled here up to October 1972, as against a proposed settlement of 500 families during that year. The INCRA had also begun to legalise the settlement here of some 3500 squatter families (Ministério da Agricultura 1972a, 32).

In Goiás activity was limited to the previously mentioned colony of Bernardo Sayão, where colonists long had to contend with inadequate government supervision, so that many had hardly been able to rise above subsistence level. The INCRA hoped to be able to raise the level of prosperity through the provision of adequate supervision. Up to October 1972, 515 colonist families had been settled in Bernardo Sayão. It was hoped to be able to increase this number to 700 in 1973 (Ministério da Agricultura 1972a, 32 and 34).

Pará

In the state of Pará the INCRA was responsible for the small colonisation projects in Guamá and Monte Alegre, which began in about 1970.

In Monte Alegre 804 families were officially settled in 1971. There were also about 1400 families who had the status of "occupier." In May 1972, a total of 2505 *lotes* had been taken up by squatters and official colonists. 331 families had been settled in Guamá. A total of 532 *lotes* had been taken up here by official colonists and squatters in May 1972. The holdings in both projects had an area of 30 hectares.

In these two colonies also, the IPEA observed remarkable difference in prosperity in 1971. The more successful farmers consisted largely of Japanese, who were better educated, possessed more capital and enjoyed the support of the mother country. They often helped each other. This group concentrated to a large extent on pepper cultivation. The average income per worker in this "elite" was 10.3 times the official regional minimum wage in Guamá and 6.5 times in Monte Alegre. The group of less successful farmers depended mainly on traditional, subsistence agriculture. The average income per worker was only 0.9 times the official regional minimum wage (Tavares *et al.* 1972, 83-86; Arruda 1972, 30).

The Marabá-Altamira-Itaituba zone

Much more important than the colonisation activities of the INCRA in Guamá and Monte Alegre were the institute's activities in the zone of Marabá–Altamira–Itaituba, along the section of the Transamazônica that was completed in September 1972. This was the main area of supervised colonisation in the early 1970s, not only of the state of Para, but of the whole Amazon region.

The legal basis for the colonisation in this region was laid in Decree No. 67.557 and 68.443 of 12th November 1970 and 29th March 1971, respectively. In these decrees a *polígo-*

no in the area between Altamira and Itaituba was declared to be a region of social importance, thereby facilitating, if necessary, the expropriation of private property and the realisation of land reform and colonisation projects.[73] This *polígono* had an area of 64 516 square kilometres (see Fig. 7).

Figure 7. Areas in Amazônia Legal zoned for agrarian reform projects and colonisation

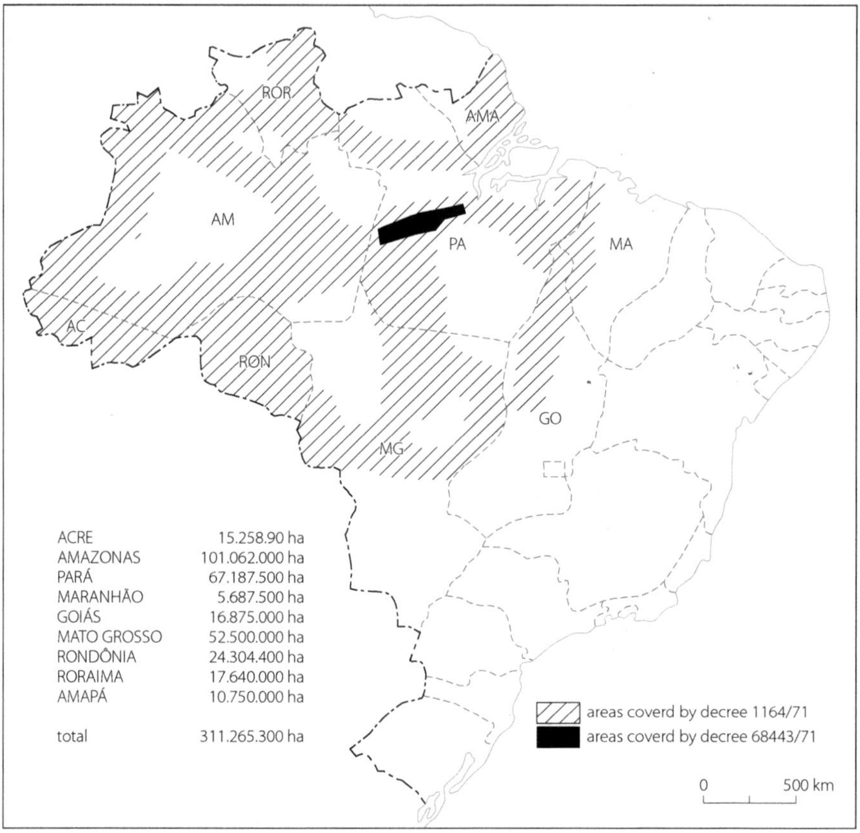

Source: Author's own elaboration.

The field of operations of the INCRA office established in Altamira extended 235 km to the west of that place, from where began the area under the jurisdiction of the INCRA office in Itaituba.[74] Within the zone of Altamira attention was particularly concentrated on the area 20–120 kilometres west of the town, where the soils largely consisted of fertile *terra roxa*. A detailed colonisation plan was drawn up for a part of this area which came to be called "Altamira I" and was in execution from 1971. The aim of the

73 The decrees laid down, that the land of those who could satisfactorily prove their ownership would not be expropriated and that they would receive support from the INCRA to improve their holdings (Ministério da Agricultura 1971b, 25).

74 The distance from Altamira to Itaituba is 490 km.

project was the settlement of 3000 families, the building of 66 *agrovilas* and the establishment of three larger settlements (*agrópolis*) (Ministério da Agricultura 1972b, 1).

In the zone which extended from 120 to 150 km west of Altamira no colonisation would take place for the time being. The forest here would remain a *reserva florestal*, because the land had proved through the nature of the soil and the topography to be less suited to arable farming. Colonists would be settled, on the other hand, on the land situated between kilometres 150 and 235. In August 1973 there were still only 80 families living here in self-built dwellings on land located on side roads. No *agrovilas* had yet been completed, although eight were under construction, where colonists would be settled at the end of 1973. The building of an *agrópolis* was also planned for this zone at kilometre 190 (Camargo 1973, 27).

In the area west of Altamira, the first colonists arrived in December 1970 and, in June 1971, the first *agrovila* was completed near kilometre 46 (measured from Altamira). In August 1973, a total of 18 *agrovilas* had been completed as a first stage. Eight of them were situated directly on the Transamazônica and ten on side roads. There was also a larger service centre (*agrópolis)* under construction about 45 kilometres west of Altamira, called Brasil Novo. A second was planned at about 90 kilometres from Altamira.

In mid-1973, a total of some 2400 colonist families was settled in the area up to 235 km west of Altamira. Apart from the *agrovilas*, they lived scattered along the Transamazônica (at intervals of from 500 to 1000 metres).

Colonisation activity east of Altamira was also modest in mid-1973. In the zone extending 240 km east of this town no side roads had yet been opened by August of that year and only a single *agrovila* had so far been built (18 km from Altamira). Nearly all the colonists lived dispersed along the highway and a total of only 400 families had so far been settled in this zone.

The field of operations of the INCRA Marabá office began 240 km east of Altamira.[75] In that area, too, only one *agrovila* (Coco Chato, approximately 40 km north of Marabá) was in existence and the majority of the settlers lived dispersed along the Transamazônica. No side roads had yet been built in mid-1973, although a start had been made on their construction. A total of 643 colonists had then been settled in the Marabá zone of operations. One *agropolis*, called Macapá, was under construction and a second would be built 63 km west of Marabá (Camargo 1973, 27 f.).

In the area of INCRA-Itatiuba, no side roads had yet been constructed mid-1973, nor had any *agrovilas* yet been built. Colonisation was still limited to the settlement of families in isolated dwellings along the main road. A total of some 600 *parceleiros* had been established. One *agrópolis* (Meritituba) was under construction in the neighbourhood of Itaituba, while preparations had also been made for the building of a still larger centre (*rurópolis*) near the crossing of the Transamazônica with the Cuiabá–Santarém highway (Camargo 1973, 28). In mid-1973 these centres were still inhabited almost exclusively by people employed by institutions concerned with colonisation and opening up the country, as well as people engaged in providing services for this group.

To summarise the foregoing, we may state that, in mid-1973, about 4000 colonist families had been settled in the Marabá–Altamira–Itaituba zone, 28 *agrovilas* had been completed or were under construction and seven larger centres were being built. By far the most important zone was the area west of Altamira. The above was the result

75 The distance from Altamira to Marabá is approximately 510 km.

of some two-and-a-half years of INCRA activity, at least if the settlement of the first colonists in late 1970 is taken as the starting point.

The following are the reasons why attention was concentrated in the first instance largely on the Altamira region:

- few problems were to be expected here in respect of property rights. The construction of the Transamazônica had opened up a large area of virgin land;
- the topography generally lent itself to arable farming. The terrain was predominantly gently undulating;
- fertile terra roxa soils occurred there;
- there had already been some colonisation in the vicinity of Altamira; the colonists already settled in the area would be able to benefit from the supervision of the INCRA;
- Altamira was a larger centre and consequently possessed some infrastructure, which facilitated the realisation of the colonisation plans, while the town would also later quite easily be able to perform a service function for the colonisation area, thanks to the infrastructure;
- no important concentrations of Indigenous were known near Altamira.

Conclusion

It appears from the broad review of the INCRA activities given in this chapter that progress up to the middle of 1973 was still quite modest. The ambitious plans drawn up in the latter part of 1970 and the early part of 1971 were still far from being realised. The target of 100 000 families settled in a period of four years would certainly not be achieved. Up to mid-1973 the INCRA had succeeded in settling no more than 1,300 families in Rondônia and 4000 families along the Transamazônica, although a large part of its activity was concentrated in these areas. One is justified, therefore, in speaking of a serious delay.

The principal colonisation zone was the area covered by Altamira I. In the next chapter the process of colonisation in this area will be analysed in greater detail, with the emphasis on answering the question of to what extent there was a well-organised and supervised colonisation here in mid-1973, providing a decent living to the population group concerned.

The other INCRA colonisation projects will not be discussed in greater detail, because they are less important and the INCRA adopted generally the same approach to colonisation in the various areas. Consequently, in our view, the following case study of the area near Altamira presents a sufficiently representative picture.

The Altamira I Colonisation Project

The colonisation process

The pattern of parcels

In mid-1973, in the area west of Altamira, the land extending on both sides of the Transamazônica had been, or was being, opened up by side roads built or being built, at five-kilometre intervals. The length of these side roads was initially 10 to 12 kilometres. Should the population grow, however, or if further colonists were settled, the roads could be extended. In any event, allowance was made for an extension to 20 kilometres.

The *glebas* situated between the side roads were divided into parcels (*lotes*) of 100 hectares. Along the main road these had a length of 400 metres and a depth of 2500 metres. Along the side roads the dimensions were 500 x 2000 metres (see Fig. 8). This regular parcel form was adhered to as much as possible.

In addition to a *lote* of 100 hectares, which could be selected by the colonist, the families also received a *lote urbano* of between 1500 and 3000 square metres, at least if they settled in an *agrovila*.[76] On the *lote urbano* was built the dwelling. The area around the dwelling could be regarded as farmyard, offering scope for the keeping of small livestock and small-scale gardening. The colonists not living in an *agrovila*, but in isolated houses along the Transamazônica, possessed only a single plot of land, of 100 hectares.

By mid-1973 an *agrovila* had been planned or already built on every *gleba*. In most instances, it was situated on a side road, but there were also a number of villages on the main road. At first, no more than 48 to 64 families were settled in these *agrovilas*, which meant that only the land at a distance of up to about 12 kilometres from the main road was given out, but since each *gleba* had a breadth of 5 kilometres and a depth of 20 kilometres from the main road, it contained about 100 parcels of 100 hectares and so colonisation could be continued within it through the granting of more land. This could be accompanied by an extension of the already existing *agrovila* or, if necessary, by the building of a second village or of isolated houses.

76 Small departures from these areas occurred as a result of differences in topography. They were generally of only a few hectares.

Figure 8. Pattern of parcels within a gleba of the Altamira I colonisation area

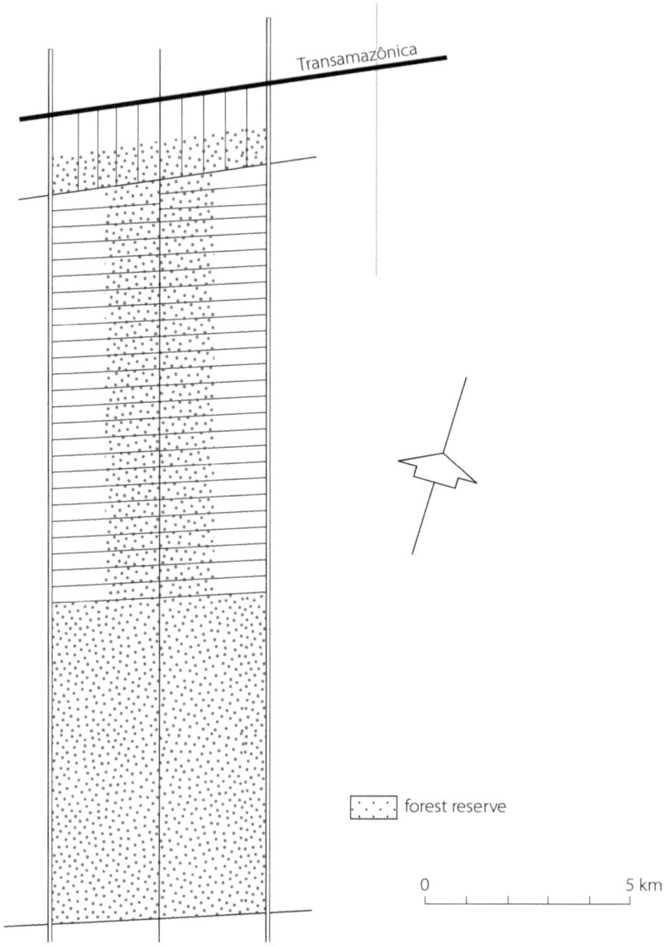

Source: INCRA (1972).

Almost immediately, problems also arose because insufficient account was taken in the planning of the parcel pattern of the nature of the soil and the terrain. There was consequently a considerable variation in the quality of the parcels, which caused a great deal of discontent, especially as the price for all the parcels was the same. The INCRA tried to solve the problems to which this had given rise partly by allocating more suitable parcels to the colonists, where necessary, but this sometimes meant that the colonist, living in the *agrovila*, found himself living farther from his land. Where the soil was very poor or the relief of the parcel made the land unusable, the parcel was not allocated, but maintained as forest. This did not always happen at the beginning, so that, in the mid-1970s, in some places one could see land that had been abandoned and reverted to forest. By 1976, the INCRA had also combined parcels which were unsuitable for arable farming into holdings of 200–300 hectares, where the colonists could carry on livestock farming.

Of the 100 hectares which were made available to each colonist only a half could be reclaimed. The other half had to remain *reserva florestal*. It was also laid down that reclamation had to take place in such a way that the remaining forest formed a continuous area (Ministério da Agricultura 1972b, 67). Figure 7 shows the way in which this was attempted. In the mid-1970s, the INCRA departed from its original standpoint that the *reserva florestal* of all parcels had to be so situated as to form a continuous stand of forest in each *gleba*. The forest reserve might be situated where the nature of the terrain made clearance undesirable or impossible.

The dwellings: facilities

Both the colonists along the road and the families concentrated in an *agrovila* would be accommodated in wooden houses with a floor area of 53.4 square metres. The dwellings contained a living room measuring 4.5 x 3 metres, two bedrooms each of 3 x 3.5 metres, a veranda of 6 x 1.5 metres, a kitchen of 2.5 x 3 metres and a wash-house constructed behind the dwelling. Because of the lack of mains water and sewerage, the toilet would be built at some metres distance from the house.

According to the plans, each *agrovilas* was provided with various basic facilities, such as a primary school, a pharmacy, a small building where a doctor could hold consultations, a cafe, and a shop for daily needs The shops would be supplied by the Companhia Brasileira de Alimentos (COBAL), a company responsible to the Ministry of Agriculture, which had to ensure that the shops contained the necessary articles at reasonable prices. In this way, the colonists were not placed at the mercy of private traders who might exploit their position of power to demand exorbitant prices.

For other facilities, larger centres, known as *agrópolis*, were planned. The INCRA assumed that these would have an initial population of 1500 to 3000 and that they would perform a service function for some 10 to 20 *agrovilas*. Apart from a number of government offices, they would include a small hospital, other permanent medical facilities, cooperative buildings, small agricultural industries and secondary (technical) schools. In the official plans the maximum distance between the *agrópolis* was 40 to 50 kilometres, but there would naturally often be departures from this figure because the density of colonisation would not everywhere be the same.

Some *agrópolis* were already under construction in mid-1973, such as Brasil Novo, 45 kilometres west of Altamira. In mid-1973 there were mainly government officials, concerned with the colonisation process, living here. There were various offices of the government bodies in charge of the settlement and supervision of the colonists, as well as a few small industries and service establishments. A motel had already been completed in the neighbourhood of the centre.[77]

Camargo christened the still larger service centres *rurópolis*. He proposed that these could be built at intervals of 140 to 280 kilometres and have a population of about 20 000. A number of *rurópolis* would be specially built, including the one planned near the intersection of the Transamazônica with the Cuiabá–Santarém highway. Further *rurópolis* would be created by the development of already existing centres. Not only Altamira, but also Marabá and Itaituba would assume a considerable service function

77 Settlements with central service facilities (*agrópolis*) were also proposed in the Rondônia colonisation areas (Ouro Preto and Sidney Girão).

in the near future as colonisation progressed and so they would emerge as *rurópolis* (Camargo 1973, 16 f., 21, 28). Measures to encourage this had already been taken.

This enlargement of function could already be clearly observed with Altamira. Until about 1970 it had been a very modest, sleepy little town on the Xingu. It consisted almost entirely of low, ramshackle little huts and houses, built along a few dusty and unmade north-south and east-west streets. The "urban" population of the municipality of Altamira was then only 5741. It lived chiefly from shifting cultivation, the hunting of certain kinds of animals, from gathering and from a little trade. It was a village without many social contrasts. In fact, everyone was poor. There was no electricity, sewerage or mains water.

Following the construction of the Transamazônica, however, the little town woke up. The simple commercial sector was greatly expanded. The number of cafés, bars and little restaurants became many times greater. A new cottage hospital was built. Electricity and water mains were laid. Several dozen taxis livened up the street picture. In mid-1973, preparations had already been made to provide some of the dusty and uneven streets with proper drainage and an asphalt surface. There was an air service to Belém, Itaituba, Santarém and Manaus three times weekly by the mid-1970s.

A distinction could now be made between the population of the *Cidade Nova* and that of the the *Cidade Velha*. The latter was the old part of the town, while the former had its origin in the establishment of government departments and the settlement of officials concerned with the colonisation process.

The situation outside Altamira was different in the mid 1970s. Many side roads of the Transamazônica were of poor quality, so that they were almost impassable, particularly during the wet season. Many parcels were consequently difficult to reach, there were problems in gathering and transporting the harvest and the colonists were isolated. This isolation led, *inter alia*, to problems with food supply, especially during the wet season.

Photo 5. The town square of Altamira

Photo 6. One of the main streets of Altamira, mid 1973

Photo 7. Another of the streets of Altamira, mid 1973

Photo 8. The exit road from the fast-growing Altamira was improved in mid-1973

Land use

Under the original colonisation plan, the INCRA would reclaim a few hectares of land for each colonist, so that they could begin farming immediately. At first, the INCRA carried out this intention, but very soon it ceased to do so because of organisational problems. Consequently, the colonists received 100 hectares of forest land and they had to carry out the reclamation entirely themselves.

Without exception, the colonists began to clear part of the forest with the aid of simple equipment, such as an axe and machete; methods which were characteristic of shifting cultivation. Some of the trees were felled and the timber, after it had dried sufficiently, was then burnt. As a result, much of the land had the chaotic and "dirty" appearance characteristic of recently cleared forest plots. A number of, usually dead, trees remained standing, the plot still contained tree stumps or other tree remains and the crops were planted among them.[78] In general, clearance proceeded slowly, because the colonists had no money to pay for hired labour, nor did they wish to take up large loans to finance clearing. They had in fact to fall back mainly on the available family labour, but this was already largely needed for cultivating the few hectares of cleared land.

The some 1400 colonists who settled in the INCRA-Altamira area during 1971 had reclaimed, on average, 10 hectares of land by 1973. Those colonists who did not arrive until 1972 had, in general, reclaimed no more than two or three hectares for cultivation. There were colonists who reclaimed larger areas, but their numbers were small.

78 The use potential of the arable land was therefore estimated at 70 % for the first year, but by the third year the proportion had risen to 90 %.

Photo 9. A recent reclamation

Photo 10. One of the agrovilas under construction near Altamira

Photo 11. A 'street' in one of the agrovilas

Photo 12. A colonist house along the Transmazônica near Altamira

The total area of cultivated land could therefore be estimated in 1973 at about 16 000 hectares, which meant that it had not yet reached the extent originally anticipated. According to the official plans, the total area in the first year should have been about 12 000 hectares and as much as 18 000 hectares in the second year. The target for the third year was a cultivated area of 24 000 hectares and 33 000 hectares for the fifth year. These figures were based on assumed averages per colonist of 4, 6, 8 and 11 hectares, respectively (Ministério da Agricultura 1972b, 163).[79] The total area of land brought into cultivation in the Altamira zone was estimated in mid-1976 at no more than 22–25 000 hectares. The majority of colonists had cleared less than 10 hectares.

The colonists did not use fertiliser and practised a form of agriculture that bore the characteristics of shifting cultivation. This had the approval of the INCRA, which even assumed, in drawing up its colonisation plans, that the colonists would practise such a form of farming. They assumed this for the following reasons:

- the types of farming that would make possible a permanent and more intensive use of the humid tropical forest soils were only poorly developed in Brazil, certainly as far as family holdings were concerned;
- the majority of farmers who offered themselves as candidates for colonisation did not possess much agricultural training. Those who could be recruited in the North East, the Amazon region or elsewhere in Brazil were not capable in their new environment of much more than shifting cultivation;
- it is extremely difficult to change farming traditions radically in a short time. INCRA experts believed, therefore, that the colonists had to arrive at better production techniques by gradual means;
- it was difficult to realise the necessary conditions for the application of more perfected agricultural methods in the short term. Such methods required the availability of fertilisers, machines etc., which meant that the colonists had to borrow more money, that they had to receive more intensive technical training and that a cheap and plentiful supply of fertilisers had to be made available.

The latter was certainly not the least important problem, since no artificial fertiliser was yet being produced in Northern Brazil. Everything had to be imported from elsewhere, so that the use of artificial fertiliser was an expensive matter at the time and justified only for the cultivation of high value crops. Lime, for the improvement of acid soils, was also insufficiently used for the same reason. Its price was ten times as high in some parts of the North as in the South East.[80]

Although they were free within certain limits to grow what they wished, nearly all colonists produced mainly rice, beans, manioc and maize, for which the natural environment was generally not unfavourable. The emphasis was also on these crops in the colonisation areas of Rondônia, with rice being by far the most important.

Initially, the colonists did not, in fact, have many other possibilities, because numerous other products could not yet be grown properly on the recently cleared plots, with their many tree stumps. A further point is that the colonist was generally already more or less familiar with the crops we have named and they did not make too many demands on his technical capabilities. These crops were also able to provide a major

79 There are two reasons for the failure to achieve the expected figures: a) it was assumed that 3000 colonists would be present at each date, which was unrealistic because settlement took place gradually; b) it was assumed that the colonist would already be able to cultivate four hectares in the first year because of the support of the INCRA, but the new settlers did not have more than two hectares available.

80 North Brazil accordingly consumed in 1971 only 0.2 % of all the artificial fertiliser used in the country (Condurú 1973, 15 and 17).

part of the colonist's primary subsistence requirements and to supply him quickly with some income (Ministério da Agricultura 1972b, 163).

In 1973, therefore, the farming was still characterised by the production of commonly used food crops. The lack of large markets at not too great a distance acted as an important brake on the expansion of the range of crops and the colonists complained that they could not dispose of certain production surpluses, such as those of bananas, other fruits and manioc. The situation was more favourable only for rice, because the Companhia Brasileira de Alimentos (COBAL) had agreed to buy up the surpluses.[81] In doing so, it paid at least the minimum price, but often a higher one.[82] Other crops were not bought up or only to a more limited extent. In view of this situation, there was not yet too great a tendency for the colonists to become rapidly commercially orientated.

In mid-1976 an estimated 70–75 % of the cultivated land was still planted with rice (18 630 ha), approx. 10 % with maize and beans, and approx. 10 % with more commercial crops.[83] Many of the plantations had not yet reached the productive phase.

It was not the INCRA's intention, however, that the farmers should continue to produce mainly simple food crops which could also be consumed on the farm. The emphasis would be changed gradually to true cash crops, which was indeed also the aim in other colonisation areas, such as those in Rondônia. The INCRA was thinking, therefore, not so much of extensive commercial production of simple food crops such as rice, because it was doubted whether such commodities could be produced cheaply enough in the North to compete with the products of the North East and South East, but had much more in mind high value commercial crops, such as sugar cane, pepper, soya, cocoa, rubber, cotton, tobacco, groundnuts, mallow and fruits such as pineapples, bananas, citrus and guaraná. Accordingly, it also encouraged the planting of these products. Various colonists had already begun growing different crops, while the INCRA and other government bodies were engaged in making available increased quantities of seeds and young plants.

In the short term, sugar cane was expected to be the most important crop. In 1972, the government had already planted 20 000 sugar cane seedlings on an area of 185 hectares with the aim of multiplying the cane to provide sufficient seedlings to plant an area of 1000 hectares (*Relatório anual de atividades 1972* 1973, 93). About 130 colonists, who incidentally also produced food crops, had been involved in the scheme. There were also colonists who had planted some cane on their own initiative.

It would soon be possible to process the sugar cane locally, since a sugar factory was already being built near the present cane fields, about 9 kilometres west of Altamira. The work was making relatively slow progress, because everything had to be brought in from elsewhere, but it was hoped in 1973 that the factory would be completed during the course of 1974. The production capacity would then be 500 000 bags per year. In 1976 the factory was processing sugar-cane into sugar and alcohol. Panagides wrote

81 If the harvests were good there were easily production surpluses. The rice yield could reach 1500 kg per hectare, 1000 kg milled. A family required only 270 kg per annum, however, for its own consumption. The harvest of brown beans was estimated at 800 kg per hectare, while the average family consumed 180 kg per annum (Ministério da Agricultura 1972b, 184).

82 This minimum price was 21 cruzeiros per bag.

83 The main cash crops are sugar cane, cocoa and pepper, occupying in 1975–766, according to the INCRA, 1256, 905 and 461 ha, respectively. Some 150 farmers grew sugar-cane, about 185 cocoa and about 400 pepper.

in 1973 that insufficient studies had yet been made to discover which crops best lent themselves to commercial production along the Transamazônica, but that the government nevertheless wished to show some quick results from its colonisation policy. It was therefore encouraging sugar production and had proceeded to build a processing factory (Panagides and Vande Lage 1973, 17).

Photo 13. Sugar cane field near the sugar factory under construction, mid 1973

Photo 14. Sale of pepper at one of the stops on the Transmazônica

No rubber trees had yet been planted, but cocoa and pepper were among the typical commercial crops already in production in 1973. Cocoa plants were introduced in 1973 and about 100 colonists had already planted this crop in that year. Pepper had also recently been introduced. There was considerable optimism with regard to this crop since the Japanese had begun growing it in the Amazon region during the 1940s and since it had appeared that it could yield very high returns per hectare. Pepper could even be one of the most lucrative crops. Incidentally, the success of the Japanese was due mainly to the great care which they devoted to the crop and to the use of fertiliser. Since many colonists had a low level of technical ability in agriculture, it was therefore by no means certain that the enthusiasm with which some of the Brazilian colonists took up the crop – or would shortly do so – would eventually result in pepper growing on a large enough scale to provide many farmers with a reasonable standard of living. It is noteworthy in this connection that the INCRA assumed that only about 10 % of the farmers in the Altamira I colonisation zone would be engaged in the exacting cultivation of pepper (Ministério da Agricultura 1972b, 164).

There was no incipient fruit growing or horticulture as yet in mid-1973. Many colonists did have a few banana trees, but they were unable to dispose of the surpluses, so that the fruit was used mainly for home consumption. Fruit growing and horticulture on any scale were not to be expected until food conserving industries were established. Several colonists had shown themselves in favour of this. They criticised the government's attention to wood-working industries and large-scale livestock holdings, which were of no use to the small arable holdings of the colonists.

Apart from the absence of a nearby market, a number of other factors hindered the rapid expansion of the commercial plantations, such as the delay of a few years before the trees and shrubs yielded a harvest, the absence until about 1974 of plentiful supplies of seeds and plants, the reluctance of the Banco do Brasil to advance long-term credits, the limited farming experience of many colonists and the late and inadequate advice supplied by the experts, who had first themselves to gain the necessary experience of local production conditions (Wesche 1974, 112; Kohlhepp 1976a, 197).

The farming practice of the colonists was almost wholly directed towards arable production. Cattle farming played an insignificant part. The colonists had little or no experience or interest in this field and it was not being propagated by the INCRA. The following were the reasons for the INCRA's attitude in this respect (Kohlhepp 1976a, 201):

- the soils in the Altamira zone were of good quality and lent themselves well to the production of arable crops. Livestock farming, on the other hand, could better be practised on the poorer quality soils, which occurred in numerous places in the Amazon region;
- cattle farming demanded more capital and provided relatively little employment;
- cattle farming yielded better returns on large holdings;
- the colonists who had already been settled or were waiting to be settled had little or no experience of cattle farming.

Very few colonists at that time possessed cattle.[84] Of the 2800 colonist families who had been settled in the field of operations of the INCRA-Altamira in mid-1973, no more than about 100 owned cattle, with a total of no more than 700 head. They held on average only a few animals, mainly zebu, which served both for milk and meat production. Livestock farming was limited mainly to the keeping of a few pigs or chickens, principally for subsistence. The breeds were those that had been traditionally raised in the region. There was no question of the introduction of highly productive cattle races from elsewhere. In the view of the INCRA, cattle farming was better practised by larger holdings on the poorer soils.

Farming techniques

Farming practice was still characterised in the mid-1970s by simplicity. In order to produce simple food crops and, eventually, typical commercial crops, the colonists had, without exception, adopted methods that were characteristic of shifting cultivation. No fertiliser was applied to the land, which was not surprising in view of the existing agricultural traditions in Brazil, the lack of knowledge of many of the colonists and the absence of fertiliser factories in northern Brazil. Only a few colonists were beginning to use very small quantities of artificial fertiliser for demanding commercial crops. There was hardly any livestock farming and those who kept cattle had so few animals that no large-scale production of manure was possible. Animal manure was therefore not used to maintain soil fertility. Insecticides were used, but by only a very few colonists and on a modest scale, since they also had to be brought in from elsewhere and were consequently expensive.

There was no mechanisation whatsoever. The forest was cleared with simple tools, such as axe and machete, while burning was an important additional aid. The methods used resulted in badly cleared "dirty" land, with tree stumps, remains of roots etc., so that the use of machines to work the land was impossible during the early years.[85] The land was cultivated only with the hoe.

Nor indeed did the colonists yet have the use of tractors or agricultural machinery for other purposes. They would have to buy them, but the majority were not yet able to do so. In the most favourable instances they had available a power saw, simple threshing machinery and an insecticide spray.

The colonist had consequently to rely mainly on manual labour, that of himself and of members of his family, for the reclamation of more land. It was to be expected, therefore, that further reclamation would progress slowly, unless colonists would shortly be able to bring in machinery or make use of paid labour on a larger scale. This was, of course, possible only if they obtained a sufficient income from the land already in cultivation or if they obtained bank credits for the purpose. In the light of developments until then, the former was not very likely in the immediate future, while colonists with modest farm incomes would obviously not be readily inclined to borrow

84 This also applies to Rondônia. In Ouro Preto only 40 of the 1000 families settled in 1972 had a livestock holding.

85 An exception was the land around the sugar factory (at the time under construction), which was intended for the production of sugar cane cuttings. This had been cleared by machinery and almost entirely freed of tree stumps and root fragments.

large sums of money, apart from the question of whether these could generally be obtained at all. It was most likely that many would try to reclaim the land mainly through their own physical labour.

This meant that it would become more difficult to increase the area of cultivated land as the holdings became larger. According to calculations made by the INCRA, the cultivation of 4 hectares of land with rice, manioc, maize and beans required about 295 man days per annum.[86] If it was assumed that each family had available 2.5 workers and that it was possible to work on the land for approximately 200 days a year, each family would not be able to cultivate more than 6–7 hectares. Consequently, mechanisation and paid labour would be needed to achieve further reclamation. The fact that colonists had to rely mainly on their own labour incidentally also explains why the tempo of reclamation was rather low in the early 1970s.

The agricultural advisory work of the ACAR-PA

The Brazilian government aimed to raise the level of farming skill of the colonists in order to create favourable conditions for a greater commercial bias in arable farming. The government also intended to assist the colonists in the cultivation of food crops that were still grown by traditional methods.

The Associação de crédito e assistencia rural do estado do Pará (ACAR-PA) was brought in to realise these aims.[87] This body, which had the task of providing agricultural advice in the state of Pará, was given ample funds within the framework of the Programa de Integração Nacional, which enabled it to recruit more staff during the course of 1971 and acquire the necessary material to work along the Transamazônica.

At the end of 1972, the ACAR-PA had a total of 33 experts and 12 administrative staff working on the Transamazônica.[88] In 1975 it had 73 people in its service along this road with a qualification in economics or agricultural science. 59 of these were educated to secondary school standard and 14 to an advanced level.[89] Activity was concentrated in the zones of Altamira, Marabá, Itaituba and Santarém. In these places, ACAR-PA had established four *entros polarizadores* to enable it to carry out its work.

Advice was given for free. It concerned both arable and livestock farming, as well as nutrition, hygiene, health and housing. The agricultural advice related mainly to cultivation methods for food crops, production methods for commercial crops, such as sugar cane, pepper and cocoa, and to ways of conserving the soil. Advice in the field of nutrition related particularly to the composition of the daily menu, while that on

86 The cultivation of 1 hectare of rice required approximately 56.5 man-days, that of 1 hectare of beans 21 man-days, 1 hectare of maize 32.5 and 1 hectare of manioc 51 (Ministério da Agricultura 1972b, 165). The estimate of 295 man-days for 4 hectares was based on the assumption that part of the land would produce several harvests per year.

87 The Instituto Nacional de Pesquisas e Expermentação Agropecuaria do Norte only carried out agricultural and pedological research; it did not provide advice.

88 The experts included seven agricultural engineers, 14 agricultural technicians with secondary education, one doctor, three social workers, seven workers with secondary education to give advice in domestic science and related fields and one nursing sister. At the end of 1972, the team of 45 people accounted for 26% of the total personnel of ACAR-PA (*Relatório anual de atividades* 1972 1973, 23).

89 Agricultural advisers of the CEPLAC were also active along the Transamazônica,but they limited themselves to giving advice about cocoa and distributing seeds for this crop.

health and hygiene drew attention to the dangers of drinking unboiled or unfiltered water and to the necessity for building and using toilets. Advice began after the colonists had established themselves on their holdings. They did not receive any education before they moved.

The advice programme approved by the government ran from 1971 up to the end of December 1974. In mid-1973 it was not yet known what would happen after that date. ACAR-PA took the view that there was a permanent need for agricultural advice, although its intensity could be gradually reduced as the colonists gained more experience. Much would obviously depend upon the money and the manpower that the service had at its disposal. It was, therefore, by no means impossible that ACAR-PA would be forced to move its team largely to new colonisation zones in the course of time or to let its experts drift away.

ACAR-PA was dealing generally with farmers who were more receptive to ideas of farming improvement than the average country dwellers of North or North East Brazil. Nevertheless, its task was by no means an easy one. There were various reasons for this:

- the level of general education and farming knowledge of the majority of the colonists was low, particularly among the nordestinos;
- good farming practice and a satisfactory farm income depended not only on the nature and intensity of the agricultural advice, but also on numerous other circumstances, such as the availability of markets. The conditions of production during the previous years had been by no means favourable and this limited the effectiveness of the agricultural advice;
- many colonists lived scattered along the Transamazônica or in *agrovilas* along the side roads, which were difficult to access, particularly during the rainy season. These circumstances meant that the advisory service required a lot of personnel;
- the ACAR-PA possessed only limited means, as was indeed the case with many government services.

At first, the ACAR-PA enjoyed a great deal of confidence. The service had a high reputation among the colonists. This situation changed during the course of 1973, however, and this certainly did not make the task of ACAR-PA any easier. The reason was the failure of the greater part of the rice harvest on the holdings of a large majority of the colonists in the first half of 1973. At the end of 1972, ACAR-PA introduced a variety of rice that promised very high yields. Initially, the farmers were greatly in favour of the crop and some were unreservedly enthusiastic, but when the ears were due to form in May, the optimism changed to deep disappointment. Very few grains formed and the majority of colonists obtained very low yields. As a consequence, a lot of farmers had to tighten their belts, got further into debt, and did not have sufficient resources for the harvest of the following year to have a good chance of success. To add to their difficulties, the brown bean harvest also failed because of unfavourable weather conditions. Consequently, the situation was much less favourable in 1973 than in 1972, when the Altamira region produced 150 000 bags of rice and 35 000 bags of beans, which could have supplied 15 % of the Belém market, if required (*Boletim Informativo* 406, 27 December 1972). In September 1973 it was not yet known whether the government would come to the aid of the colonists and, if so, in what manner and to what extent. For many colonists this help probably would come at a time when they already had several difficult months behind them. If ACAR-PA was to regain the confidence it once enjoyed, the government had to pay reasonable compensation.

The shattered confidence could lead to the accelerated creation of cooperatives. These did not yet exist in mid-1973. Most of the colonists had only recently been settled on their holdings, so it was understandable that they had not yet passed beyond the stage of rather vague plans.

Accommodation for the storage of the harvest

Apart from ACAR-PA, the Brazilian government also made use of the services of the Companhia Brasileira de Armazenamento (CIBRAZEM) for the construction of storage accommodation, thus enabling some of the rice bought up by the COBAL to be stored locally. With a fund of 2.36 million cruzeiros, made available within the framework of the Programa de Integração Nacional, CIBRAZEM built, in 1972, three metal storehouses, each with a capacity of 3600 tons, in Imperatriz, Marabá and Brasil Novo, respectively. A similar store had already been constructed earlier in Altamira. In 1976 a total of seven stores with a combined capacity of 350 000 bags were completed in the region of Marabá–Altamira–Itaituba–Santarém, three of them in the area near Altamira. These made it possible to buy up surpluses of the principal product (rice) and put them into store. The government paid the minimum price when it bought the crop. If the farmer succeeded in selling his harvest to private dealers he paid only storage costs.

The plan was to bring the total number of stores along the Transamazônica to eleven, because the storage space for rice was not yet sufficient during years of good harvests, especially since the area of cropland was continuing to expand. Consequently part of the harvest had to be stored in a primitive manner, which resulted in losses. The transport was delayed by bad roads and transport costs had risen as a result of increased fuel prices.

CIBRAZEM had also already built a number of smaller storehouses of combustible materials (*Relatório anual 1972* 1973, 5 and 12).

The granting of credit

Although its name suggests that ACAR-PA granted credits, this was not, in fact, the case. The farmers had to rely wholly on the facilities of the Banco do Brasil to obtain business credits, although ACAR-PA did offer advice and make applications for credit on the colonists' behalf.[90] When ACAR-PA supported a request for credit, the Banco do Brasil, in fact, almost automatically granted the request.

In order to be able to offer its services effectively, the Banco do Brasil had opened offices in the larger centres along the Transamazônica, such as Altamira, Itaituba and Marabá, or was planning to do so shortly. In Altamira, which was the service centre for the most important colonisation zone of the INCRA, the bank possessed a modern office, which was one of the most striking buildings of the little town.

The credit facilities offered to the colonists were very favourable by Brazilian standards, partly as a result of the special measures promulgated in 1971 to stimulate the agricultural sector in the North East and North (PROTERRA). No interest was due if

90 This bank also granted business credit to non-colonists.

the credit was granted for the purchase of *insumos*, i. e. materials such as seeds, fertiliser and insecticides. In other cases, the interest was 7 %, since the government accepted responsibility for 5 % (Carneiro 1972, 7). Consequently, the interest rate owed was lower than the rate of inflation.

The repayment periods for the loans varied according to the purpose for which the money was required. Credits for rapidly growing crops had normally be repaid within one year. For tree crops, such as cocoa, however, which did not yield an income until after several years, credits with a currency of 12 years were possible and repayments generally did not need to begin before a number of years. Loans could be made for very different purposes, such as the clearance of forest, the purchase of tools or machinery, the laying down of pastures, the purchase of seedlings etc.[91]

Many colonists made use of the credit facilities. They had, in general, little or no capital and so were forced to borrow money. The Altamira office of the Banco do Brasil was consequently quite busy and waiting periods of 30 to 40 days sometimes occurred before loans came through. The farmers were aware of these long delays and tried to make their applications as early as possible. Nevertheless, the slow processing of their applications sometimes created problems for them. Another complication was that the issue of the property deeds by the INCRA was not always quick enough.

The Banco was extremely cautious and granted particularly short-term loans, mainly to finance rice-growing and clearance operations (Wesche 1974, 112).

It was also possible for the colonists to borrow money, where necessary, from a special INCRA fund in order to be able to provide temporarily for their subsistence during the early stages.

Incidentally, not everyone was in favour of the quite generous credit facilities. Some people feared that the farmers would incur too many debts and not be able to meet their obligations, which might result in the forced sale of their holdings. Some inhabitants of Altamira, therefore, who were concerned with the well-being of the colonists and somewhat anxious about their future, advised them to take up as little credit as possible and to try to expand the holding gradually from their own resources. There was also a certain fear among the colonists of falling too much into debt. In mid-1973, however, it was still too difficult to judge to what extent the Brazilian government's credit facilities were having undesirable side-effects.

The obligations to the INCRA

Besides financial obligations to the Banco do Brasil, the colonists had debts to the INCRA. The Brazilian government originally took the view that the colonist should not receive his land, the dwelling and his equipment free, but should pay for them. This seemed better from the educational point of view, while the obligation to repay a portion of the costs might lead to a stronger tie with the holding, thereby reducing the tendency to move away as soon as there was any set-back. This was by no means unnecessary in a country like Brazil, where the ties between the land and the people who cultivated it were often rather weak. A further important advantage of the requirement to repay was that the government received money from which further colonisation could be financed.

91 8 year credits were available for reclamation with repayments beginning after three years.

The colonists had to pay approximately 4000–7000 cruzeiros for the land they received from the INCRA.[92] They also owed about 4000–7000 cruzeiros for the house that they occupied.[93] These sums had to be repaid within a maximum period of 20 years, beginning after the third year.

The colonist further received from the INCRA a set of implements, including a hoe, axes, machetes, a scythe and a dibber, to the value of 153 cruzeiros. Lastly, he received a sum equivalent to six months legal minimum wage, in order to be able to provide subsistence for himself and his family. The minimum wage in 1973 was 240 cruzeiros per month.

The value of the tools had to be repaid within three years, beginning after one to two months, as did the subsistence payment (in instalments of 30, 30 and 40 %) (Ministério da Agricultura 1972b, 206). After four years, therefore, the colonist had repaid these debts, while he also enjoyed full ownership of the land and house after a maximum of 23 years.

He received a declaration of authorisation at the time he was settled, which gave him the status of legal occupier. After two years, he signed a deed of conveyance for the house and the land.

The selection of the colonists

The people who wished to be selected for settlement on a holding had to satisfy a number of conditions which did not apply exclusively to the Amazon region, but were also used for colonisation projects elsewhere. To sum up the conditions, the colonists:

- had to be at least 18 years old and not older than 60 years;
- they had to have done their military service;
- they must not have any serious physical disabilities or illnesses;
- they had to be of good character;
- they had to have farming experience;
- they must not enjoy considerable sources of private income.

There was a preference for married colonists with wide agricultural experience, aged between 25 and 45 years and with children who were already able to give some help on the holding. Such families were most easily able to score the necessary number of points at the selection stage. Families with many children were given precedence over those with few, at least if the other circumstances were the same. Illiterates were not excluded, although the ability to read and write increased the chances of being selected.[94] The possession of initial capital was not a prerequisite.

In fact, the requirements placed on the candidates were not severe and the selection was not rigorous. Those who could satisfy a few elementary conditions already stood a good chance of being selected. This explained why by no means all the colonists adhered to the procedure originally desired by the INCRA. At first, the latter selected the candidates through the agency of its regional offices, which took the responsibil-

92 Inclusive of land surveying costs.

93 1 cruzeiro was worth approximately £ 0.077 in mid-1973.

94 At the end of 1971, 1118 colonists had been selected for the project. 74 % of these could read and write, 1 % had enjoyed full primary education and 25 % were illiterate (Ministério da Agricultura 1972b, 202).

ity for sending the colonists on to the Amazon region. Various problems arose from this procedure, as a result of which, after some time, many candidates moved to the Amazon region on their own initiative before reporting to one of the INCRA regional offices. Provided a person satisfied a few minimum conditions and possessed the necessary papers (which he could easily ascertain for himself after some inquiry), he had a good chance of being eligible for a holding, either immediately or after a short space of time.[95]

It has already been remarked that the plans for the opening up and colonisation of the Amazon region took concrete shape after the North East had again been struck by an abnormal drought in 1970. The government then emphasised that the foremost aim of the colonisation was to provide a better livelihood for *nordestinos*. In later publications, however, the government linked the colonisation less strongly to the problems of the North East. For the Altamira I project it was clearly stated that the colonists should be recruited from all areas with serious social tensions. Emphasis was also placed on the desirability of recruiting colonists from the more developed southern regions in order to raise the level of farming skill of the colonist population. In the detailed plan for Altamira I the desirable ratio between colonists from the North East and other problem areas and farmers from the more developed South and South East, was put at three to one (Ministério da Agricultura 1972b, 203; 1972c, 12).

Table 5 illustrates the regions of origin of the colonists who had been settled in the zones of Altamira, Itaituba and Marabá at the beginning of 1973. This summary shows clearly that, in practice, the colonists came from all parts of the country. It also appears that the North East (including the Meio Norte region) accounted for only 44.2% of the total colonist population, with the states of Ceará and Rio Grande do Norte providing by far the greatest number of families.

A further remarkable feature was the considerable share of the "North." Apart from seven colonists in the Altamira zone, the colonists in question all originated from the state of Pará. A large number of them were already living in the area, because they had moved there of their own accord or on the initiative of the government of Pará. These families had been resettled and now all occupied land legally.[96] The remainder were people who had moved to the colonisation zones from other, relatively nearby, parts of the state of Pará.

In the early 1970s there was some change in the origin of the colonists. At the end of 1971, 900 colonist families had been settled by the INCRA in the zone of Altamira and 218 were awaiting settlement. 57.7% of these 1118 families came from the North East and Meio Norte while, according to Table 5, the share of these two areas had fallen to only 47% in 1973 (Ministério da Agricultura 1972b, 202).[97]

The colonists from other parts of Brazil, particularly those from the South East, proved in general to be better equipped to deal with the difficulties of the Amazon region than were the *nordestinos*, partly because they had a better agricultural and gener-

95 If this, nevertheless, did not eventually happen, the applicant generally succeeded in finding employment somewhere as a labourer. A number of Brazilians also migrated in the early 1970s to the Amazon region with the sole intention of finding paid employment in the colonisation zones.

96 In the Altamira area about 100 families were involved.

97 In addition, 16.7% from Pará, 7.5% from Minas Gerais, 4.4% from Rio Grande do Sul, 5% from São Paulo and 8.7% from the remaining states.

al education and because many also brought some capital with them. The enthusiasm for colonisation in the North East, on the other hand, was not so great as had originally been expected.

Table 5. Colonist families settled at the beginning of 1973 in the colonisation zones of Altamira, Itaituba and Marabá, by area of origin[98]

Zone	Total number of colonists	Division of the colonists by area of origin					
		South	South East	Meio Norte	North East	North	West
Altamira	2559	543	147	335	862	566	106
Itaituba	571	109	37	4	136	264	21
Marabá (Itupiranga)	643	3	34	262	71	114	159
Total	3773	655	218	601	1069	944	286

Many *nordestinos* found themselves in a much weaker position compared with the colonists from the South and South East, because of a number of circumstances already described. In addition, the relatively limited interest among the *nordestinos* for the colonisation projects in the Amazon region may also be attributed to the fact that they were less ambitious and that more attention was being devoted in the early 1970s to solving the rural problems of the North East itself.

Consequently, in the early 1970s, the INCRA showed a certain preference for colonists from the South and South East, who were more likely than the *nordestinos* to make a success of colonisation. In mid-1973, the early arrival was expected in Altamira of some 600 colonists, the majority of them from the more developed part of the country.

A provisional assessment

More intensive government supervision than before

It has appeared from the above account that the Brazilian government did attempt to supervise the colonisation process. The principal measures, already referred to, may be briefly summarised once more:

- the reservation of land along the roads through the Amazon region to enable the land to be occupied in an orderly fashion;
- the building of side roads to open up the land along the Transamazônica;

98 The figures have been provided by the INCRA and relate to the place of origin of the colonist. The state of origin is naturally by no means always the state where a colonist was born. The Table defines as the South: Rio Grande do Sul, Santa Catarina and Paraná; as the South East: São Paulo, Rio de Janeiro, Guanabara, Esperito Santo and Minas Gerais; as Meio Norte: Maranhão and Piauí; as the North East: Ceará, Rio Grande do Norte, Paraíba, Pernambuco, Alagoas, Sergipe and Bahia; as the North: Pará, Amazonas, Amapá, Roraima, Rondônia and Acre; as the West: Mato Grosso, Goiás and the Distrito Federal.

- a planned subdivision of the land and systematic land grants to the colonists;
- the selection of colonists;
- the building of *agrovilas,* including a school and a store, among other facilities, and the building of larger service centres;
- the building of houses for the colonists, including those living scattered along the Transamazônica;
- the provisioning of the shops in the *agrovilas* and other centres;
- the propagation of seeds and young plants to assist the dissemination of the various crops;
- the provision of an agricultural advisory service;
- the provision of loans for subsistence and for the purchase of simple tools;
- the making available of credit facilities;
- the buying up and removal of certain production surpluses;
- the building of storehouses to hold the harvest.

To these may be added the following:

- the provision of medical facilities, particularly in the larger centres along the Transamazônica;
- the training of labour for various jobs, both agricultural and non-agricultural, by means of special courses (including the use of power saws).

Although it may be noted, therefore, that the government supervised the colonisation process and did so more intensively than before, it was still by no means possible to speak of a successful colonisation. The colonisation process during the preceding years showed a number of obvious faults and shortcomings. These were partly the result of inadequate planning and partly of plans being carried out incompletely or too late. A number of unforeseen unfavourable circumstances also arose, as may appear from the following provisional assessment of what had been achieved up to the middle of 1973.

Unsatisfactory settlement forms; late and inadequate provision of facilities

A debatable aspect of the planning was the fact that a large proportion of the farmers were settled in *agrovilas.* Although there were most certainly arguments in favour of a concentrated form of settlement, there were also very serious disadvantages to the colonists from such a form of settlement. The farmers lived several kilometres from their land, sometimes as much as five to eight while, at certain times of the year, they needed to visit it frequently. Moreover, they did not own any means of transport, not even bicycles, and these would be difficult or impossible to use in any event, because of the poor quality of the side roads.

The consequence of this situation was that a considerable number of colonists were forced to go and live on their *lote* during the busy season of the year, under a simple canopy (*tapiris*) constructed of wood, leaves and other materials. If they lived there alone, the bond was broken with the family that remained behind in the *agrovila,* while they also had to provide completely for themselves or be regularly supplied with food. If they took their families with them, they were faced with another set of practical domestic problems and the children no longer attended school. Among some of the *nordestinos*, in particular, the children were readily kept away from school.

Because of this state of affairs, a great many *agrovilas* were, in fact, inhabited largely only at the weekends during the farming season. During the week many houses were closed up.

Living on the land incidentally had another advantage. There were difficulties in keeping free range small livestock (poultry) in the *agrovila*. People could keep livestock on the *lote urbano* only if they provided fencing, but such measures were not needed out on the land.

In 1973, the normal situation was that the colonists lived outside the *agrovilas* in self-built structures or built their homes in the village themselves.[99] Only during the first two years did the INCRA build houses. The majority of the colonists found the simple wooden houses of the INCRA, which were said to let in the rain and to be quite poor in other respects, too expensive. As a result of this unforeseen development the INCRA decided as early as 1973 to build no further new *agrovilas* and to permit the colonists to live on their land. In the villages there then lived only those colonists who wished to live there of their own accord. Newcomers were settled there only if they expressed a preference to do so. In several *agrovilas* the colonists had rented out some of the houses to labourers.

It was not to be expected that the limited range of facilities existing in the villages would be increased to any extent, since many colonists were showing a preference for living on their land.

Problems also arose for a great many colonists because the INCRA or other bodies did not always succeed in providing the promised facilities in time for the colonists to obtain immediate benefit from them. During the early 1970s colonists had arrived to find that their *agrovilas* or houses were not completely ready for them. Some of these were families who had been selected through the regional INCRA offices. The latter were by no means always sufficiently familiar with the many problems facing the executive organs of the INCRA in the Amazon region and so could not properly judge how many colonists they should send out. The regional offices were also sometimes under pressure. After selection had taken place, a great many colonists had given up their work and sold their possessions, and were more or less compelled to set out for the Amazon region. They could not wait if there were delays in the building of the villages. A further point was that it was also necessary to leave by a certain date in order to be able to clear some of the forest in good time and prepare the ground before the beginning of the farming season.[100] Some of the problems were caused by the fact that, in addition to the officially selected colonists, other candidates were arriving on their own initiative. They naturally also wished to be settled as soon as possible.

In order to understand the problems which had arisen, it should be remembered that the Brazilian government wished to show quick and spectacular results from its colonisation activity, so that, at the beginning, it made a great deal of propaganda and urged the INCRA regional bodies to proceed quickly in selecting and sending out

99 In June 1973, 2550 families had been settled in the area of Altaraira, but only 2065 houses had been completed. In the area of Marabá and Itaituba the situation was still more unfavourable (Arruda 1973, 33).

100 The most favourable period to arrive was May–August, enabling part of the land to be prepared for cultivation before December. The agricultural season proper lasts from December to June.

colonists. The offices in Belém and Altamira were not willing to admit immediately in response to this that it was, in fact, impossible to absorb and settle satisfactorily large numbers of colonists in a short time.[101]

In 1973, the operation was carried out with rather less haste. Up to September of that year, INCRA-Altamira was able to prevent colonists arriving in large numbers. There may also have been a diminution of interest in the country for a pioneer life along the Transamazônica.

The failure to provide facilities in time meant that some of the colonists arrived late and so had difficulty in clearing sufficient land in time, or it meant that the colonists had to go and live in *tapiris*. In mid-1973, a number of colonist families were living in primitive accommodation of this kind, some of them along small jungle tracks. This was the situation in the zone 150 kilometres west of Altamira, for example.

Delays in the building and handing over of houses had, incidentally also already resulted in some of the colonists building their own homes in consultation with the INCRA.

Nor were the facilities in the *agrovilas* by any means everywhere ready in time. In a great many villages, which had already been inhabited by colonists for a considerable time, people still did not have the use of *privadas*, shown in the building plans, which was not very conducive to hygiene. The INCRA promised to build these as soon as possible, but it had insufficient money or suitable labour or it had more important facilities to provide. The colonists could naturally build themselves simple *privadas*, especially since the ACAR-PA distributed leaflets setting out clearly the various construction possibilities, but many colonists considered that the INCRA should do this. In addition, by no means everybody saw the necessity of privies. Many families also previously lived without a *privada* and those who lived outside the *agrovila*, on the land, also had to manage without one.

Another area where the executive bodies failed up to mid-1973 was in the provision of a piped water-supply. In some *agrovilas* immediately adjoining the Transamazônica, the Fundação Serviço Especial de Saúd had provided a water-supply network, but in the *agrovilas* situated along the side roads in the Altamira I colonisation zone this was not the case. Here, the authorities had limited themselves to the sinking of simple wells. Where not even this had been done, the colonists had to drink spring or river water.

Only the *agrópolis* of Brasil Novo had a mains electricity supply.

Lastly, there were delays in the field of educational supplies. The INCRA built simple schools, both in the *agrovilas* and elsewhere for the needs of the scattered population, but the location of some of them was not ideal and not everywhere had they been completed in time or provided with the furniture and the school materials needed to enable the schools to function properly. The provision of these items was the responsibility of the Ministry of Education.

There was a lack of doctors and other medical personnel and the often inaccessible *agrovilas* were seldom if ever visited by a doctor. In order to improve health care, the Brazilian government had provided various new medical facilities along the Transamazônica and expanded or improved existing ones by 1973. These facilities varied

101 Alberto Tamer phrased his criticism as follows: "O INCRA logo a inicio das obras de entrada transferiu sem qualquer planejamento centenas de familias para Altamira, talvez com o objetivo de demostrar realizações" (1971, 99).

from simple stations with one doctor to small hospitals with a few dozen beds. They were concentrated mainly in the larger centres, such as Altamira, Marabá and Itaituba. Anyone requiring medical care was compelled to travel to one of the larger centres, more or less far away, hoping that rapid and adequate help would be available. Nevertheless, the health situation was certainly not without its problems. Malaria was prevalent. An unexpected hindrance for many colonists was a species of mosquito which occurred in large numbers at several places during the rainy season along the Transamazônica.[102] With their bites the *borrachudos* had already caused a great many cases of illness, as well as undermining people's resistance. A number of children had already spent some time in hospital as a result of these mosquito plagues. The use of mosquito nets could have prevented a great deal of misery, but many colonists had no experience with them, while their housing was not always suitable for their use. Many people also found them too great a luxury.[103] A further point, already mentioned, was that the great majority of colonists did not have a piped water supply in their houses and sanitary provisions (*privadas*) were still inadequate or completely lacking. According to local experts, infant mortality was still high, but precise figures could not be obtained.

This medical provision served not only for the colonists, but also for the road builders and the Indigenous population. There were also mobile units at work and a start had been made on immunising the workers and the colonists against various diseases.

The shortcomings noted here were partly a result of the circumstance that a number of government bodies were involved in the work. First class coordination was required, but this could not always easily be achieved. The failures could also be attributed to the lack of experience, finance and manpower. Panagides wrote that the INCRA staff in Altamira in 1972 consisted of no more than 80 people and that there was a turnover during that year of 90 % (Panagides and Vande Lage 1973, 19). The great distances to the important urban centres undoubtedly also formed a serious handicap.

Limited investments

Criticism can also be made of the fact that the government ultimately invested very little per family in the colonisation project, as appears from the following points:

- far too little money was allowed for the construction of a number of good secondary feeder roads. The Transamazônica was of very good quality by Brazilian standards and traffic could move quite quickly along it, but the side roads were downright bad. Their quality was even such that they were almost or entirely unusable during the rainy season, with the result that it was difficult or impossible to bring in and dispose of part of the harvest and the colonists had difficulty in reaching their land (bicycles were out of the question). This situation also made it difficult for doctors to reach the villages and there were often delays in the supply of articles to meet the basic necessities of life. Many agrovilas were isolated for months during the rainy

102 The increase of these mosquitoes may have been assisted by the existence of large expanses of stagnant water on both sides of the Transamazônica, as a consequence of the fact that this highway had interrupted the natural drainage in a number of places.

103 Something was being done about expanding these. In 1977, for example, a small 100-bed hospital was under construction.

season and some farmers had to walk tens of kilometres to buy certain provisions in Altamira. Some bodies were buried on the land because of the lack of transport to Altamira;
- the wooden dwellings in which the colonists were housed were extremely simple and would probably already have largely perished or fallen into disrepair before they had been paid off;
- the road surface in the agrovilas was of very poor quality;
- the facilities in the villages were limited to the barest essentials. There was electricity only in the already existing small towns and in the agrópolis of Brasil Novo. The *agrovilas* had no electricity supply. Only those centres situated along the main road had a piped water supply. The little schools were extremely simple and, because of the low salaries, they were by no means all staffed with trained teachers. Where provision had been made for a doctor, who was presumed to visit the *agrovilas* occasionally, such provision was limited to a very simple wooden building. Most of the *agrovilas* did not yet have a church. The INCRA had built an "ecumenical temple" in only four villages, although churches were under construction in a few villages;
- the farmers were provided with very limited farming equipment. They received only a few tools, so that reclamation was very crude, as was also usually the case elsewhere where shifting cultivation was practised.

The total investment in the Altamira I project, intended for 3000 colonists, was estimated in 1972 at 78 824 million cruzeiros. This sum included the value of the land and the houses and the costs of educational and health facilities. This meant an investment per colonist of 26 275 cruzeiros (worth at that time nearly £ 1630), of which 15 284 cruzeiros had to be repaid.[104] The investments were therefore quite modest. On the other hand, the Brazilian government did spend large sums on the construction of new roads to open up the country, such as the Perimetral Norte. The government evidently wanted to open up a large part of the Amazon region as quickly as possible and found it less attractive to use the available money to ensure the proper development of a relatively small area. The enormous sums of money being invested in the ambitious roads programme might also have been used for the building of good side roads, for mechanised help in the clearance of forest and for various other kinds of support.

The problem of markets

A serious problem was the lack of nearby markets and local processing industries, the only exception being the sugar factories. In mid-1973, there were only a few of these along the Transamazônica, because there were no large population concentrations along this highway. The nearest large urban centre was Belém but, because of the absence of direct links, the distance between Altamira and Belém was still about 1460 kilometres. In Belém, however, the farmers of Altamira had to compete with the products brought in from elsewhere, including those from areas situated along the Belém–Brasília highway. In view of the high transport costs, such competition was by no means easy. In other places, such as Manaus, the situation was not much more

104 The costs of education, health care and road construction did not have to be repaid (Kleinpenning 1977, 14).

favourable. The markets in the Centro-Sul and abroad were too far away. The farmers would therefore have to concentrate on high-grade products, while the government would have to provide support by such means as establishing local food-processing and conservation industries. The future would show what the outcome would be. In the mid-1970s agriculture was still very much adapted to the production of simple food crops, partly for home consumption, and rice was by far the most important of these.

As a result of this still low degree of commercial orientation little had come of the planned crop rotation schemes on the majority of the holdings. This might mean that the colonists would eventually be compelled to clear fresh areas of land and let the cropped areas rest.

Disappointed colonists

The circumstances described above were part of the reason why there was little optimism or satisfaction among the majority of colonists in mid-1973. A great many colonists were disappointed or even embittered. Many had lost confidence in ACAR-PA, which had supplied the wrong seed, and in the INCRA, which had promised more than it could achieve. Only a small proportion of the colonists had so far been able to achieve a certain level of prosperity. For the great majority, however, the farm income had been very modest as a result of the still small area of cultivated land, the crude farming practices, the limited markets and the occurrence of poor harvests. Even if they were better off than where they came from, they do not earn very much more than the official minimum wage, which, for the majority of families, was no more than a hunger wage. According to the INCRA, 10–15 % of the colonists had left again as a result of sickness or other circumstances.[105] Experts in Altamira, who had no official connection with the INCRA, remarked that these percentages meant relatively little. A great many colonists would have preferred to return to their place of origin. Those who lived along the side roads, in particular, had a difficult life. The fact that they stayed on was sometimes the result of divisions within the family, but very often solely of the fact that they had incurred debts through accepting a house, land, equipment and a few months' wages from the INCRA. Perticularly those whose harvests failed were finding things very difficult in mid-1973.

Many inhabitants of Altamira foresaw a relatively sombre future for the colonists. They feared that the 1973–1974 rainy season would be even more serious for many people than the previous one, because they had passed through difficult times and had little resistance left. In late 1973, the Northern bishops had already expressed their grave concern about the fate of the colonist population.

By the end of 1975 the situation along the Transamazônica had not improved. Taking the Altamira project as an example, a total of 4125 colonists had been settled there between the commencement of the scheme and the end of 1975. But no fewer than 1125 had left again, i. e. about 27 %, particularly after 1973. There were similar re-emigration rates in the Marabá and Itaituba zones.

---

105 Alberto Tamer also referred in the second edition of his *Transamazônica* to this emigration of colonists. He stated: "os primeiros resultados estão sendo altamente negativos, con dezenas de colonos retornando para suas terras" (1971, 99).

Potential farm incomes; the reality

Many colonists, therefore, found themselves in difficult circumstances. In 1972, however, the Brazilian government stated in a popular publication that the colonist could expect to enjoy an income of 12 000–15 000 cruzeiros within a year, or considerably more than the official minimum wage (*Uma nova marcha ao norte / Une nouvelle marche vers le Nord* n. d.). In calculating potential farm incomes the INCRA had taken as its starting point two different cultivation schemes. The first scheme assumed that the farmers grew rice, beans, maize, manioc, cotton, castor oil plant, tobacco, pepper and cocoa. The second scheme was largely the same as the first, except that groundnuts, soya and guaraná were grown instead of the last three crops. In both instances, a cultivated area was assumed of 11 hectares.

According to calculations made by the INCRA in 1972, following the first cultivation scheme could yield a total gross income of 15 623 cruzeiros, while expenses, inclusive of labour, would be 8288 cruzeiros, giving a net income for the farmer of 7335 cruzeiros. 764 cruzeiros should be deducted from this sum, being 1/20 of the investment due to be repaid, so that the net income for consumption would then be 6571 cruzeiros. This was an average of 548 cruzeiros per month or 219 cruzeiros per worker, assuming 2.5 workers on a holding. These monthly sums were then higher than the legal minimum wage, which was only 172.8 cruzeiros at the time the calculation was made.

The above sum of 6571 cruzeiros would be the net income available for consumption. The net farm income, however, would be greater, since the farmer also earned 764 cruzeiros towards repayment of his debt, 1210 cruzeiros by not making use of paid labour and 780 cruzeiros because he did not sell part of his farm output, but consumed it himself. The *rendimento real* would therefore amount to 9325 cruzeiros.

The sums involved in the second cultivation scheme were somewhat higher. The gross income was estimated at 15 911 cruzeiros and the exploitation costs, including labour, at 7497 cruzeiros, giving a net income of 8414 cruzeiros. The disposable income, after compulsory deduction of 764 cruzeiros for debt repayment, was 7650 cruzeiros or 637 cruzeiros per month (255 cruzeiros per worker). The *rendimento real* in this instance would be 10 246 cruzeiros (Kleinpenning 1977, 16 and 19).

The Brazilian government concluded on the basis of these calculations by the INCRA that there was a better life in store for the colonists. In our view, however, too rosy a picture was painted of the initial phase. It was assumed that the farmers had available 11 hectares of land, but most of them did not do so for several years (officially five). The INCRA also assumed that the farmers produced a number of high-grade commercial crops, that the marketing conditions for the produce were normal and that the farmers obtained normal yields. There was certainly no question of the latter, at least in 1973. The observation that one could obtain an income above the minimum wage was not very realistic, since the legal minimum wage was extremely low. It was, in fact, not much more than a hunger wage. After the poor harvests of 1973 the majority of colonists did not earn even this amount. Only in the longer term was there possibly a prospect of greater prosperity.

Expansion of employment

As well as being optimistic about the income per holding and per worker, the Brazilian government cherished good expectations of the profitability of the investments it was required to make in the Altamira I project. Assuming a total investment per colonist family of 26 275 cruzeiros and an average work force of 2.5 persons per holding, this gave a figure of 10 500 cruzeiros needed to create one job in the agricultural sector. It should be remembered, however, according to the INCRA, that this one job, through multiplier effects, created four other "indirect" jobs. In other words, the capital necessary to provide a living for 3000 colonist families created a total of a further 30 000 indirect jobs (Kleinpenning 1977, 32). If the total investment of 78 824 038 cruzeiros was divided by the total number of jobs, it would appear that the creation of one job by the INCRA ultimately required an investment of only about 2100 cruzeiros. This was very low in comparison with the investments often required in other sectors.

To place these positive conclusions in perspective, however, the following should be noted:

- the assumption that one job created in agriculture created four other jobs elsewhere was somewhat optimistic, certainly when the colonists continued to concentrate on the production of simple food crops;
- in order to create "indirect" jobs, further investments would naturally be required by private concerns or other government bodies;
- it was not only the volume of employment that was important. There was also the question of quality, i. e. of the income yielded by the employment.

The danger of soil exhaustion

If the situation in mid-1973 gave cause to view the future with some concern, such concern was further justified when it was also realised that the farming methods employed were rather crude. The detailed colonisation plan originally drawn up for Altamira I recommended that no fertilisers should be used during the early years, but that advantage should be taken of the natural soil fertility (Ministério da Agricultura 1972b, 18).[106] The colonists were therefore working the land at the time in the traditional manner. They were using the reclamation methods associated with shifting cultivation, not applying fertilisers and this usually resulted in an appreciable deterioration in the condition of the soil over a period of three to four years.[107]

In mid-1973 it was not yet clear how it was intended to prevent or solve these problems. Would the farmers simply let the reclaimed land lie fallow when yields declined and would they then take another part of their land into cultivation? Or would they try to plant tree and shrub crops as soon as possible in order to limit soil exhaustion?

---

106 Advantage was also taken of the natural fertility in the Rondônia colonisation area and no use was made of fertilisers.

107 Thanks to the fact that the INCRA had so far restricted colonisation near Altamira to the zones with fertile terra roxa soils, the IPEAN experts believed that arable farming could be practised for a longer period before marked degradation of the soil occurred. They had in mind a period of 10–12 years, which nevertheless meant that problems would arise in a relatively short time.

Or would they try to introduce a crop rotation in which legumes and green manures played an important part? Much would depend upon the support and advice provided by the INCRA and other government bodies, and upon the speed and the degree to which farming was able to take on a commercial character.

It must be concluded in this connection that the Brazilian government acted with rather too much haste.[108] It had settled colonists on soils that it knew might be relatively quickly exhausted if simple agricultural methods were employed, while there might be no positive or real possibility in the near future of maintaining the soil fertility.

It was, in fact, by no means unlikely that the farmers would be compelled to practise shifting cultivation permanently, which would mean that, with a 20-year rest period, only 5 hectares of the holding could be exploited annually (including the *reserva florestal*).

Conclusion

To briefly summarise the above, we may state that the colonists in the Altamira area had to contend with a number of serious problems and that, in mid-1970s, one could hardly speak of a well-prepared and intensively supervised colonisation. The majority of colonists still enjoyed little prosperity. One should speak rather of a greater dispersal of poverty and hardship than of a remarkable socio-economic advance. The colonisation was still modest in extent and, partly for this reason, had so far scarcely contributed towards the reduction of the many serious problems in the North East. It was questionable, moreover, whether tens of thousands of *nordestinos* would be prepared to emigrate to the Amazon region, even if there was more government propaganda to encourage them to do so. It was still difficult to judge how the process of colonisation would develop in the near future, but there was certainly no reason for unlimited optimism.

Various countries, including the Andean states, had tried during the decades before 1970 to make their thinly populated regions more accessible and to encourage colonisation there, with the aim of relieving population pressure in other parts of their territories. Analysis of these attempts shows that the results have nearly always been modest. The fact is that well-prepared and properly supervised colonisation projects demand a lot of capital and know-how, which developing countries lack, while there are generally all kinds of other problems which hinder the colonisation work still further. Sponsored colonisation projects therefore nearly always progress very slowly in these countries. The alternative is not to control the colonisation process, but then the enthusiasm for a pioneer existence often fades, while those who do venture upon such a course are frequently faced with so many difficulties that they cannot solve them unaided. These colonists, therefore, often remain poor.

Brazil felt obliged to opt for sponsored colonisation for the occupation of the vast North but, due to hasty planning, limited government investment, insufficient deployment of manpower, lack of experience of many officials (partly as a result of a high turnover), inefficient organisation, insufficient coordination of the work of the various government bodies, as well as various unexpected obstacles, the results up to the mid-1970s were unsatisfactory.

108 Panagides reached a similar conclusion (Panagides and Vande Lage 1973, 16).

If the situation described in this chapter was to be improved, in any event, more capital and more manpower would have to be invested in the preparation and execution of the colonisation projects. It would have been no easy task to find large numbers of capable officials prepared to assist in the realisation of the colonisation process in the Amazon region, but it seems to us that it would have been less of a problem to invest more capital. As long as the government was willing to continue with the building of great highways, such as the Perimetral Norte, the need for which was still debatable, lack of money formed no excuse.

The following were the minimum requirements for more satisfactory results:

- the construction of good side roads, usable at all seasons of the year;
- the making of more generous provisions in the fields of housing, education and health; the necessary facilities needed also to be completed in time;
- the development and dissemination of farming techniques to assure the maintenance of soil fertility;
- the creation of conditions that would allow farming to become strongly commercial in character;
- the encouragement of mutual cooperation among the colonists (creation of cooperatives and associations of workers).

We have concentrated so far on the more qualitative aspects of the colonisation, without considering the size of the programme so far realised up to the present. Turning to the number of colonists settled, we find that, despite of all the efforts of the government bodies, nothing had come in practice of the plan to settle at least 100 000 families along the Transamazônica by 1975. In January 1974 a total of only 4697 families had been settled in the zones of Altamira, Itaituba and Maraba. Since then, because of a change in government policy which will be discussed later, the process of settlement had gone even more slowly, so that, by the end of 1975 no more than some 6000 to 6500 families had been settled, with the Altamira area taking more than 3000.

A total of 29 *agrovilas* had been completed, one of which was situated near Marabá and all the rest in the zone 20–120 km west of the little town of Altamira. In the area of Marabá and Itaituba nearly all the colonists had been settled on their actual holdings, which stretched away from the Transamazônica while, in the zone of Altamira, many colonists had moved on to their land of their own accord. In practice, therefore, dispersion had become the dominant form of settlement. In the *agrovilas* there were no more than about 1500, often not permanently inhabited, houses.

The number of *agrópolis* remained limited to two, i. e. Brasil Novo (45 km west of Altamira) and Miritituba (near Itaituba). The latter, however, contained little more than the barracks of government officials. Only in Brasil Novo had a considerable part of the originally planned facilities been realised. A similar situation existed in respect of the first stage of the *rurópolis* of Presidente Medici, situated near the crossing of the Transamazônica with the road from Cuiabá to Santarém. It had a population of about 2000.

It is also clear from the numbers of colonists quoted above that, in fact, nothing had come of the plans to make an important contribution towards relieving the socio-economic problems of the North East. Ultimately, only a relatively small proportion of the colonists came from the North East. From the beginning, the INCRA had also admitted colonists from other regions and had even done so increasingly since

1972. It was the INCRA's original intention in settling experienced farmers from the South East to give the colonists from other regions the opportunity to become familiar with better farming methods. At a somewhat later stage, however, the INCRA also settled many non-*nordestinos* simply because large numbers of prospective colonists were arriving from all parts of the country and because it hoped that better results might be achieved with non-*nordestinos*. The INCRA made this departure from the original plans acceptable by pointing out, *inter alia*, that in this way various problems of the *entro-Sul*, such as minifundism, could be reduced.

According to data from mid-1973, about 40 % of the colonists in the zone of Altamira originated from the northeastern states (inc. Maranhão) and 26 % from the three southern states. A not inconsiderable proportion originated from the North (19 %). There were certain differences between the projects as far as the origin of the colonists was concerned. In the Marabá area, for example, more than 50 % of the colonists were *nordestinos*, but in the zone of Itaituba they made up only 25 %.[109]

The most successful colonists generally came from the Centro-Sul. Both because of their greater knowledge and experience and the possibility of taking over the holdings of other colonists, many of them had been able in the course of time to settle on parcels which were more accessible or had lower relief and better soils. According to Wesche, they had also already become more commercially orientated than the other farmers and were beginning to use insecticides, artificial fertilisers and other inputs in the process. Because they often lived more or less together in particular *glebas* the influence which these more successful colonists had been able to exercise on the others remained below expectation. Particularly in the area west of Altamira lived relatively many farmers from the Centro-Sul (inc. those of Japanese origin) (Wesche 1974, 112). Accordingly, the commercial orientation was relatively strongest there.

109 Data supplied by the INCRA (personal communication).

The plans for encouraging medium-sized farms[108]

The activities concerned with the occupation of the land near the great strategic highways were no longer limited to the settlement of colonists on 100-hectare holdings from 1973. The government also began to sell land along these roads to private individuals and corporate bodies. The aim was to encourage the growth of the number of medium-sized holdings, so that there would eventually be a varied agrarian structure. This activity was designated as the "second stage" in the colonisation process.

By "medium-sized" was meant *lotes* of up to a maximum area of 3000 hectares.[111] These parcels could be obtained through *concurrencia pública*, which involved applicants in first paying 3 % of the statutory minimum price and then making an offer. At the same time, a detailed plan had to be submitted of the proposed type of farming, particularly the techniques to be used and the cultivation scheme. The applicants had also be able to show that they possessed sufficient farming experience, capital or means of obtaining credit in order to be able to realise their proposals. The plans had to be carried out within five years of signing the deed of purchase. The accumulation of properties was illegal.

Both the monetary bid and the submitted farming plan were of great importance in determining an applicant's chances of being allowed to buy the desired piece of land and applicants therefore often had their plans drawn up by agricultural engineers. In mid-1973, the Brazilian government had definitively already reserved 2 million hectares of land for public sale. Three *glebas* had been demarcated in the state of Pará and two in Rondônia.

The names of the *glebas* in Pará were Aratataú, Uruará and Anapú and they were situated along the Transamazônica, between Marabá and Itaituba. They had a combined area of 1.41 million hectares. The names of the *glebas* in the territory of Rondônia were Corumbiara and Garças. The former was situated along highway BR-364, between Cuiabá and Porto Velho, and the latter near highway BR-319, between Porto Velho and Abunã (see Fig. 5). They had a combined area of about 0.6 million hectares.

The first *concurrencia pública* was held in the spring of 1973 and had been completed by the end of August of that year. A second *concurrencia pública*, beginning in the same month, was held to dispose of the land still remaining. In 1976 almost all the land in the *glebas* had been sold. Further areas, however, had already been reserved, which shows that the government wished to continue its policy. The majority of purchasers so

110 This chapter is based on information gained in Belém and Altamira, as well as upon the publication by Ministerio da agricultura (1973a).

111 In Rondônia the areas ranged in size from 800 to 2000 hectares. Along the Transamazônica, the largest of the parcels were 3000 hectares, their dimensions being 4 x 7.5 km (Ministerio da agricultura 1973a, 11–12).

far came from the Centro-Sul and proposed to take up cattle ranching. The maximum area available to them for this purpose was 1500 hectares, because half of the land had to remain *reserva florestal*.

The *glebas* near the Transamazônica were still very inaccessible, so that applicants were forced to gain an impression of the situation and topography of the land on offer by way of nearly impassable jungle tracks or from an inspection flight by aeroplane. Since the results of such an inspection were limited, a great many applicants eventually made their bids without having seen the land. The course of events was no different as far as certain parts of the *glebas* for sale in Rondônia were concerned.

In mid-1973 the INCRA had not progressed further than putting up the land for offer and selling some of the parcels. Roads were still to be built to open up the land and not until then would it be possible to establish holdings. The INCRA would not concern itself with this, which would be a matter for those who had bought the land or were about to do so.

The advantages of granting land in this way are clear. It enabled the Brazilian government to involve private enterprise and so limit its own intervention. By offering fairly large parcels it ensured that the holdings had a strong commercial basis and also accelerated the occupation of the Amazon region. While there were also social motives behind the granting of the 100-hectare parcels, the sale of the medium-sized holdings was governed only by economic motives.

The dangers of such a land sale policy, however, are equally clear. There was the possibility that it would eventually lead again, by legal or illegal means, to the creation of very large holdings. Although the government had expressly laid down that an applicant was allowed to bid for only one parcel and that, after a bid had been accepted, he was not eligible to participate in any further land sales, this did not prevent adjoining parcels belonging to several owners being later combined into a single holding. Moreover, if the policy was continued, large areas of land would fall into the hands of a relatively few people. The future would show what the positive and negative consequences of the new government policy were in practice.

The federal government was incidentally not acting alone in this. A few years earlier, the government of the state of Piauí had the plan of offering areas of land of 10 000 hectares for sale to interested entrepreneurs. The land in question was near the Parnaiba delta, in the Teresina district and in areas near the Transamazônica. The state government also wanted to develop the southern part of Piauí through the agency of a development company. In that area there were about 1 million hectares of land that were still almost unused and which would be made more accessible through the improvement of highway BR230 ("Transamazônica acelera o ritmo," *Rodovia* 291 1971, 44–50, especially p. 49).

The development measures of the period from 1974 to 1976

The road building programme

Whereas an attempt was made at the beginning of the 1970s to construct a few very important roads to open up the territory in a short time, the road building programme after 1974 showed far fewer signs of being a forced effort. The lack of adequate resources and a less rapidly developing economy were the principal reasons for this.[112] The Perimetral Norte, which was due to be completed by the end of 1977, had only reached the stage of construction in mid-1976 where it was certain that the original deadline could no longer be achieved. The government also proceeded more easily in respect of the other roads. The Cuiabá-Santarém highway was not finally officially opened to traffic until October 1976, although it was originally planned to be opened in 1974 (*Boletim Informativo Embaixada do Brasil 21*, October 1976).

This lower rate of road-building activity did not mean that the government had gone back on its intention to integrate the Amazon region more into the national economy and society in a short time. In the second development plan, drawn up for the period 1975–1979, it was emphatically stated that the infrastructure provided during the preceding years and the results of all the research that had been undertaken had to be used to achieve as soon as possible a more intensive exploitation of the Amazon region in accordance with the basic objective of the development plan, which was the achievement of a rapid growth of the gross national product (Presidencia de la Republica/Minsterio do interior 1974, 65).

Development of a modern, large-scale agriculture and forest exploitation

As far as Amazônia was concerned, the increase in the gross national product would have to be achieved mainly through the development of the primary sector, with an orientation both on export and the home market. The area was planned through a considerable expansion of the area of grassland in the southern part of Amazônia Legal and a significant improvement in the quality of the livestock, to develop by the end of the 1970s into one of the major meat-producing regions, able to meet the growing

112 In 1975 the GNP grew by only 4 %.

needs of a rapidly growing world population. To this end, the realisation of the cattle ranching projects already in progress had to be accelerated and new ones initiated.[113]

No less ambitious were the plans to expand the plantations of tropical trees and shrubs. Among the important projects were the expansion of rubber and cocoa production. The aim of the national programme to encourage the growing of rubber was to make Brazil self-sufficient at an early date, both through the exploitation of the wild product and the planting of rubber trees. An important condition for this seems to have been realised. Goodyear had recently discovered on its Brazilian plantation that the dreaded disease of *mal das folhas* could be effectively prevented by the use of certain fungicides. Previously, various plantations, such as those of Ford in Fordlandia and Belterra, ended in failure mainly because of this disease (*Carta da Amazônia* 48, November 1976).

While the rubber crop was intended mainly for the home market, cocoa production was to be expanded because the foreign markets offered favourable prospects. The programme which it was hoped to realise during the period 1976–1985 aimed at an expansion of cocoa growing by 150 000 hectares and the renovation of 150 000 hectares of already existing cocoa orchards, so that Brazil would eventually be able to produce 700 000 tons of cocoa, as against 240 000 tons in the 1970s, and increase its share of world production from 15 to 28 %. No less than 160 000 of the 300 000 hectares of new plantations were to be created in the Amazon region, 100 000 of them in Rondônia (CEPLAC 1976, 10).

Brazil was also aiming, in connection with its export trade, at a considerable expansion of its forest exploitation, which was rationally planned and organised on a conservation basis. There were also plans to make use of Japanese capital and know-how to process into cellulose the papyrus reed that grew in large quantities on the island of Marajó (*Amazônia Newsletter* 16, 1976). Similar projects existed in respect of a bamboo forest of about 85 000 square kilometres, which had been discovered in Acre. 70 % of the forest consisted of a species of bamboo with long fibres (*Amazônia Newsletter* 14, 1976). The discovery of extensive kaolin deposits in São Domingos do Capim and the presence of rock salt in the region of the Tapajós (making possible the production of chlorine and soda) was very important in this connection (*Carta da Amazônia* 44, July 1976). These developments meant that the necessary raw materials and additives for the manufacture of paper were available within the Amazon region itself.

Development of mining

During the foregoing years the Brazilian government had invested much energy and resources in research into the possibilities for mining, with the aim of meeting a greater part of the country's needs from its own production, of becoming an exporter instead of an importer for certain minerals (such as copper, aluminium and kaolin) and of further expanding the existing export trade in certain other minerals. The most

113 The largest of these projects was that of the Companhia Agro-Pastoril do Rio Dourado, which covered an area of 170 000 hectares and was to be realised in the valley of the Rio Fresno, a tributary of the Tocantins (Pará) (*Boletim Informativo*, 10th September 1975).

spectacular developments in the short-term were to be expected in the area of iron ore and bauxite production.

Enormous iron ore reserves had already been proven in the Serra dos Carajás in south Pará. A reserve was discovered of 18 000 million tons, with an iron content of at least 66–69 %. It had already been decided to build a railway to Itaqui (near São Luis) for the transport of this ore and, in mid-1976, Brazilian firms were invited to tender for the construction of the first section (from São Luis to Ponta da Madeira). It was planned to start production in 1980. Some of the ore would be exported and some processed in a blast furnace plant at Itaqui, which was eventually planned to produce 16 million tons of steel per annum. The ore would be mined by Amazônia Mineração S.A. in which 51 % of the shares were held by the Brazilian Companhia Vale do Rio Doce and the remainder were in foreign hands (United States Steel). Many foreign firms had already promised to purchase ore.[114]

As soon as the railway was completed it would probably also stimulate other branches of raining, since bauxite had also been discovered in the Serra dos Carajás and important manganese reserves had been proved.[115]

Bauxite reserves had incidentally been proven, not only in the Serra dos Carajás (56 million tons with a mineral content of 40 %), but also in Paragominas, Jarilândia (the concession of the multinational D. K. Ludwig concern) and the Trombetas area (municipality of Oriximina). Rio Tinto Zinc (a multinational with its headquarters in London) had shown an interest in the exploitation of bauxite from the 2000 million ton Paragominas reserves, but technical and organisational difficulties had so far delayed the realisation of the plans. The Brazilian government was concentrating its attention in any event on the Trombetas area, which had reserves of 500 million tons. The exploitation of the bauxite would be undertaken by Minerajção Rio Norte S.A., which would be 51 % Brazilian-owned (principally by the Companhia Vale do Rio Doce). Various infrastructure works would be needed for the transport of the ore, including a port which could accommodate seagoing ships of up to 60 000 tons. The building of this would begin in 1977. So much money had been set aside to make possible the exploitation of the bauxite reserves that the Trombetas project would become the largest in the whole of eastern Amazônia. A large part of the ore would be exported. Its removal had to begin in 1980 and the aim was to export initially 3.5 million tons. Some of the ore would also be processed in Brazil, at Murucupi (municipality of Barcarena, Pará). It would be processed to alumina by ALUNORTE S.A. and, finally, to aluminium by ALBRAS S.A. The latter was planned to begin operation in 1981 and eventually to produce 320 000 tons of aluminium per annum. Japanese capital was being used for the realisation of both factories (*Amazônia Newsletter* 17, 1976; *Carta da Amazônia* 48, 1976).

To ensure that the mining and ore processing industries would have enough electrical power, the government had begun the construction of a large dam across the Tocantins river near Tucurui. The first of the twelve turbines was planned to come into operation in 1982 and all twelve of them, each with a capacity of 330 MW, had to be

114 *Boletim Informativo*, 29 July 1975 and 9 April 1976. According to the Second Development Plan it was planned to mine 54 million tons of ore per annum initially.

115 These are estimated at about 30 million tons, which is comparable with the reserves at Amapá. The richest manganese reserves, however (250 million tons), occur in Rondônia (*Carta da Amazônia* 45 and 47, 1976).

installed by the end of 1984 (*Carta da Amazônia* 45, 1976). The creation of the lake behind the dam would result in the flooding of a 120 kilometre length of the Transamazônica, so that a replacement section of road would have to be constructed. This course of events was characteristic of the lack of integration of the development planning.

The energy supply was also being expanded by the increased exploitation of natural gas and petroleum. The search for these had resulted, for example, in the discovery of oil off the coast of Amapá and of a large gas field in the same area. A production of 2.5 million cubic metres of gas was possible. The total reserves were estimated at about 25 000 million cubic metres, which was as much as all the other known reserves together. Brazil hoped, therefore, to be able to cover all of its gas requirements itself in the near future (*Boletim Informativo*, 3 July 1976; *Carta da Amazônia* 47, 1976). Exploration was being made on Colombian territory for reserves of coking coal, which Brazil could obtain from Colombia in exchange for iron ore (*Boletim Informativo*, 22 June 1976).

The role of large enterprises in the development of the primary sector

The Brazilian government believed that livestock and arable farming and mining could be expanded on a large scale only if the private sector was given an important part to play and large capitalist enterprises (particularly from the Centro-Sul) were given an opportunity. In addition, an appeal would be made to foreign firms. During recent years, therefore, the government had been very active in finding large capitalist undertakings ready and able to begin exploiting the riches of Amazônia within the framework of joint ventures in which the Brazilian partner held a majority interest. As appears from what has already been stated, the choice as far as foreign countries were concerned had fallen mainly upon United States and Japanese enterprises.

In order to provide more opportunity for large-scale initiatives by the private sector, the government had not only decided to continue selling parcels up to a maximum area of 3000 hectares, but had also created the possibility of buying areas of state land of more than 3000 hectares. These purchases had to be conducted by means of application, accompanied by the submission of a properly worked-out exploitation plan. The implementation of the plan had to begin within a few years. The land purchases required the approval of the Senate and the National Security Council. The maximum area that could be acquired for arable or livestock farming was 66 000 hectares and, for forestry, 72 000 hectares. In Roraima, Amapá and Amazonas the government had already set aside 5–6 million hectares for this purpose (*Instrução especial* 12, 1976; *Carta da Amazônia* 41, 1976, and 46, 1976).

The government contribution to the development of the primary sector

The expansion and modernisation of arable and livestock farming, forestry and mining were to be carried out through the agency of private enterprise, with the state trying mainly to create a climate that would encourage action by the private sector. Within the framework of the second development plan the government proposed to create a favourable production climate in a limited number of areas. For this purpose it had defined a total of 15 regions (*polos*) within Amazônia Legal. These were areas which had the most favourable conditions for a rapid expansion of the modern primary sector, because they possessed, for example, relatively good soils, rich timber reserves or large mineral deposits, were favourably located in relation to existing communications or offered possibilities for energy production.

The development programme for these selected areas, known as Programa de Polos Agropecuários e Agrominerais da Amazônia (Polamazônia), had as its main aim the improvement of service facilities in the broad sense of the term. The investment of 4000 million cruzeiros during the period 1975–1979 was directed, accordingly, at the construction of main and secondary roads, expansion of power supplies, improvement of water supplies, sewerage etc. in existing urban centres, development of new urban centres, expansion of educational and health facilities, training of labour and the building of stores and abattoirs. The programme also included the legalisation of titles to property and measures to ensure that land was occupied in an orderly manner. Various other measures were connected with the Polamazônia, such as an extensive credit programme of the Banco da Amazônia (within the framework of which 3700 million cruzeiros had been made available for the period 1976–1980 for the encouragement of cattle farming alone and a programme for further investigation into possibilities for the exploitation of Amazônia (*Carta da Amazônia* 41, 1976).

Figure 9. Program of Agricultural and Mineral Poles in the Amazon Region

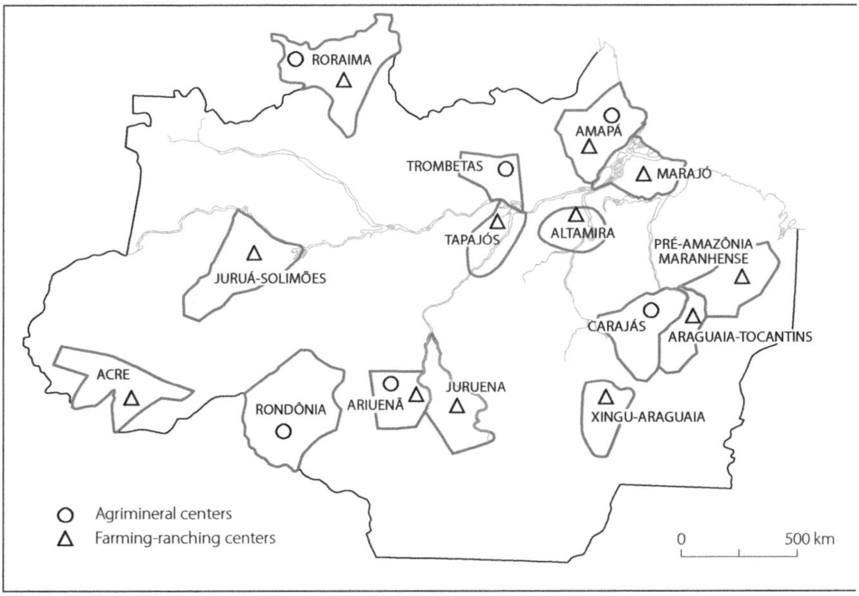

Source: Polamazônia.

The government had developed a similar plan to encourage the large-scale utilisation of the (tree) savannas of western Brazil for modern livestock and arable farming (Programa de Desenvolvimento dos Cerrados, PoLoCENTRo).[116]

116 Several government publications contain detailed descriptions of both programmes (SUDAM 1976).

The revised policy relating to colonisation projects

So far we have not considered the question of what part the Brazilian government had reserved in its development programme for 1975–1979 for integrated colonisation projects involving small farmers. Some thought should be given to this question, however, because there had been a significant change of course since the arrival of President Geisel on the scene in 1974 and the announcement of the new development plan. The encouragement of the settlement of small farmers had been pushed into the background. The government considered that priority should be given to the encouragement of large-scale activities.

The reasons given for the revised policy can be stated briefly to be that, in spite of all the efforts, the planned colonisation projects had done little to increase the gross national and regional products, to further the occupation of Amazônia, to increase production and employment, or to relieve regional difficulties. It had also been acknowledged that the livelihood of the colonists already settled was problematical in several respects. It had even been suggested that the colonisation programmes led to undesirable voluntary migration and that the colonists who were settled on small holdings formed a threat to the ecological balance because of their traditional farming methods. The government had, in fact, concluded that its colonisation policy had failed.[117]

No new integrated programmes were therefore to be embarked upon by the INCRA (which had had to endure severe criticism). It would restrict itself to placing colonists in the already existing projects, without undertaking activities that would greatly encourage the arrival of prospective settlers. It would therefore amount mainly to the INCRA making land grants only to voluntary migrants or fanners who already found a livelihood as *posseiros* in or near the colonisation zones. Besides aiming at a rather more gradual growth of the colonist population, the INCRA was trying to improve the living conditions of the colonists already present.

Another notable change was that the government also wished to give more encouragement to private initiative in the realisation of colonisation projects. Private colonisation companies were being enabled to acquire large areas of land (up to 500 000 ha), provided they submitted a detailed plan showing how the land would be divided into *lotes* of between 100 and 500 hectares and granted out as family holdings, and undertook to give the colonists the necessary support. The role of the INCRA in this was only a supervisory one (*Instrução especial* No. 11, 1976). Up to 1976 the instruction regulating these matters had not led to many schemes being actually realised by private enterprise, although it was known that the Associação dos Impresarios da Amazônia wanted to attempt to colonise 500 000 hectares of land along the Cuiabá–Santarem highway, mainly with farmers from Rio Grande do Sul (*Carta da Amazônia* 48, November 1976). The Companhia Colonizadora Marabá S.A. (COMASA) and the Companhia de Desenvolvimento de Mato Grosso (COD331AT) also seemed to have ambitious colonisation plans for areas near Marabá and the northern Mato Grosso (*Carta da Amazônia* 49, December 1976).

---

117 The new course in relation to colonisation and the arguments supporting it can be found, inter alia, in the INCRA publication "Realizaçoes e Metas" (Ministerio da Agricultura 1975), and in "II Plano de Desenvolvimento da Amazônia" (1975, 17–20). See also Müller *et al.* (1975, Vol. II, 56).

Large cooperatives from the Centro-Sul, with many minifundio owners among their members, were also being allowed to participate in the colonisation of Amazônia. The aim here was to encourage the enlargement of farms with the help of the land released by the emigration of members, thereby improving the agricultural structure in the South Lastly, cooperatives wishing to carry out a colonisation project for their members had to submit a detailed plan to the INCM, which made land available to the cooperative at a low price after it had approved the plan. The cooperative had then to begin the implementation of the project within six months. The price of the land had to be paid off within 20 years, beginning three years after the initiation of the project. The cooperative was responsible for carrying out all the works required within the framework of an integrated colonisation project. It was also expected to create conditions favourable for commercial production. If necessary, credits to finance all this could be obtained from the banks.

The cooperative could obtain land grants of from 100 to 400 hectares, depending upon the kind of farming proposed, the nature of the terrain and the availability of labour in the family. Only half of the project area could be cleared, the rest had to remain *reserva florestal*. With these projects, too, the INCRA kept a watch on the timing and the manner in which they were carried out and intervened where necessary.[118]

The only project that had taken definite form up to 1976 within the framework of these measures was that of COTRIJUI, a cooperative from the district of Ijui in the state of Rio Grande do Sul. This cooperative was planning initially to settle 1000 farmers on holdings of 100–400 hectares along the Transamazônica, 120 km west of Altamira. It was hoped to make a start in 1977 on the basis of the already approved project. The plans of a few other cooperatives were less advanced. The INCRA had reserved a total of no fewer than nine areas for such forms of colonisation, mainly in Rondônia (5) and along the Transamazônica near Altamira (2) (Ministerio da Agricultura 1975, 5–6; "Edição documento sobre o décimo aniversario do estatuto da terra" 1974, 16).

This new course may have meant for the INCRA that it would be able to devote more attention to its current colonisation projects, as well as to an effective and speedy allocation and registration of property titles.

Conclusion

A brief look at the principal developments during the period from 1974 to the present reveals that the interest in colonisation programmes aimed to help simple rural people to find a better living had been pushed into the background. There had been a reassessment, resulting in the abandonment of the ambitious plans of the early 1970s. The new objectives were more modest and private enterprise had been brought in alongside the official institutions in the effort to achieve them. Attention was no longer so much directed on colonisation as upon the rapid and large-scale development of the primary sector, particularly in those areas where success was most certain. The role of the government was mainly to create a favourable climate for enterprise, while the actual expansion of livestock and arable farming, forestry and mining was primarily a matter for the large private concerns.

118 Information derived mainly from *Instrução especial* 13, 1976.

This change of course was undoubtedly partly the result of pressure from the private sector, which, since the early 1960s, had always had mixed feelings about the Brazilian government's colonisation plans. Mention should be made in this connection of the Associação de Empresas Agropecuários da Amazônia. This association had its headquarters in São Paulo and comprised 130 large cattle ranching enterprises, mainly from the Centro-Sul. It had believed for a long time that there were good prospects in the west and north of Brazil for a large-scale expansion of livestock farming and that it was sensible to concentrate the development strategy upon this.

Pressure from the private sector, however, was not the only explanation. Another important reason was the government's desire for a rapid increase in the gross national product and its impression that this did not occur quickly enough through the medium of social colonisation programmes. The chances of achieving a rapid increase were much greater if opportunities are given to large-scale private enterprise.

The government had made the change of course acceptable by stressing the disadvantages and limitations of the colonisation policy pursued previously and pointing at the same time to the advantages of the new course, such as faster economic growth. It had also emphasised that, in a world with much hunger and increasingly scarce raw materials, Brazil could exploit its natural wealth to an increasing degree and had a duty to do so. It appears to us that the time was ripe in about 1974 for such a reorientation. There had been no further droughts in the North East and many people had forgotten the disaster of 1970. It was therefore possible without too much political risk to launch a new "development" policy, based less on social considerations.

The second development plan had still largely to be implemented in 1976 and there was little probability that its aims could be fully realised within the prescribed time, in view of the marked slowing down of economic growth in the past few years. Nevertheless critical comments about the possible consequences of the new policy were almost immediately made in the Brazilian press.

The fact that so much importance was attached to the large-scale development of the primary sector through the agency of large, capital-intensive enterprises gave rise to the fear that employment would again be inadequately expanded in the near future and that the tensions between *posseiros*, small colonists and Indians and the big landowners would continue or even manifest themselves to an increased degree. The past gave little cause for optimism in this regard. It was also to be feared that, again in the future, the economically weak groups would come off worst and that their chances of existence would be further reduced. This would be even more the case if the FUNAl was not more successful in protecting the Indigenous both inside and outside the reserves and if the INCRA was unable to put a stop to the practices of the *grileiros*. Apart from an increasing threat to small farmers, there was a danger of an increase in the malpractices of the *gatos* in their efforts to recruit labour for the big enterprises.

A further fear was that there would be a serious disturbance of the ecological balance, since the increase in agricultural production would not be realised mainly through intensification on the existing area of cultivated land, but through further deforestation. Although the government wished to zone considerable areas as *ecological reserve* and obliged farmers to retain one half of their land under forest, it might be doubted whether it would be able to maintain sufficient control over this and prevent more land than was advisable being cleared. The Brazilian government was still too optimistic about the use potential of Amazônia and underestimated the fact that the region consisted predominantly of poor soils that were rapidly exhausted after being cleared. It was incidentally not only the large enterprises, with their ability to undertake the clearance of vast areas, that were a threat to the Amazon region. The same was true of the small colonists who, for various reasons, had so far been unable to develop farming methods which guarantee the maintenance of the fertility of the soil.

Last, but not least, attention was drawn to the danger of an increasing domination by, and dependence upon, foreign countries, since, with many major projects, use was or would be made of foreign capital and know-how. This applied not only to mining projects (for example, the participation of U.S. Steel in iron ore exploitation and of various multinationals in bauxite mining), but also the livestock ranching, forestry and cash crop farming projects. In spite of restrictive regulations, a lot of land had already fallen into the hands of foreigners. It had already been noted in 1968 that a half of the Amazon region was surrounded by numerous foreign holdings, with a combined area of 20 million hectares. According to estimates, as much as 11 million hectares in Roraima, Pará and Amazonas was already in foreign hands (Martelli 1969, 136). A very important example in this connection was the D. K. Ludwig enterprise, which occupied about 1.5 million hectares along the Rio Jari and Rio Paru and was concerned with modern large-scale rice growing, timber and pulp production, livestock farming and mining (bauxite and kaolin).[119] Would the government's policy lead to more such empire-building?

119 Further details about this multi-national are to be found in Arruda *et al.* (1975, 131 ff.).

Conclusions. Looking back and looking ahead

Retrospect

By mid-1973, the Amazon region had still hardly been colonised. Until then it had never held the interest of the Brazilians for long, because there was still room for colonisation in the more attractive parts of the country. Until shortly before 1973 there was no serious government intervention to stimulate development in the vast Northern region.

In the few years before 1973 a marked change came about in this situation. The government, in particular, was more than ever interested in the integration of the North and took various measures to achieve that end. A free trade zone was created around Manaus, a development body was established, financial incentive measures were declared applicable to Amazônia Legal and spectacular road building projects were started. The universities were also involved through making use of their know-how in the Rondon project. Last but not least, we should mention the colonisation activities begun in 1970.

Up to mid-1973, the results of the various measures were modest, nor could spectacular successes be expected in the short-term from a policy relating to a very extensive and still little developed region. It was therefore still difficult, in fact, to judge whether the development plans were not too ambitious. The future had to show whether Brazil would be able to realise its plan. Volume 2 of this book will give an answer to the question whether it has been successful.

The advantages for the South East

Even if the process of economic development were speeded up during the years after 1973, it was still by no means certain that the population would become more prosperous as a result of the integration. It was not at all unlikely that the mass of the population would not benefit from the economic progress in the North, but that the advantages would go chiefly to entrepreneurs from the Centro-Sul or from other countries. The expansion of economic activity during the past years had been the concern mainly of owners of capital from the more developed South East of Brazil and of foreign firms. It was mainly these categories who had benefitted from the system of *incentivos fiscais* and the other support measures. With the aid of tax monies from the state they had been able to establish capital-intensive enterprises which offered little employment and so produced only limited direct advantages for the community. Some of the enterprises, i.e. those concerned with livestock farming, had taken possession of large areas of land. The profits made in these enterprises flowed largely to the economic heart of Brazil or abroad. This process would probably continue in the future, since the government was still trying to arouse more interest in the North among the business community in the South and South East. In the spring of 1974, the Brazilian Minister of Agriculture declared that the integration of the North would have to be realised, not with small farms, but mainly through large enterprises.

Up to 1975, the business community had shown the greatest interest in the exploitation of natural riches which could be easily utilised and yield good profits in a short time. Mining, forestry and extensive livestock farming were the activities most capable of ensuring rapid economic growth. It was therefore likely that these sectors would continue to play a dominant part in the development process in the future, in which case the North would acquire an increasingly neo-colonial status, both within Brazil and in relation to other countries.

The advantages for the North East

While *Operação Amazônia* had so far brought benefits to the more developed South East, the advantages for the poor North East, on the other hand, had been limited.

When the Programa de Integração Nacional (PIN) was launched in 1970, funds had to be made available quickly for the realisation of this programme. It was then decided that, during the period 1971–1974, 30 % of the tax monies available under the *incentivos fiscais* for investment in the development projects of the SUDAM or SUDENE, or in the sectors of tourism, fishery or reafforestation, should be reserved for the PIN.

In the following year, 1971, the federal government also determined that 20 % of the taxation funds should be set aside for the realisation of the Programa de redistribuição de terras e estímulo à agro-indústria do Norte e do Nordeste (PROTERRA). This was a programme of measures aimed at improving the agricultural sector in the North East and North (Morais *et al.* 1970, 58 f.).

Both measures, which had meanwhile been declared in force until the end of 1976, gave rise to a great deal of criticism in the North East. Although the government immediately emphasised that this other purpose would also be advantageous to the North East and that the funds would be considerably augmented through rising incomes and better tax collection, these arguments by no means convinced all influential *nordestinos*. Many considered the measures to be disadvantageous to the North East. The spectacular road building programmes were also received with less enthusiasm in the North East than in the South East. A joint statement by the bishops of the North East observed that the region still received only a quarter of the money that it could receive within the framework of the original financial incentives. In their view, this was slowing down industrialisation (Câmara *et al.* 1973, 9).

An important question in this connection was to what extent the spectacular road building projects and colonisation activities yielded benefits for the North East. As has appeared from the foregoing, there was unfortunately little benefit until 1975.

Road building was highly mechanised and had consequently provided work for only a few thousand *nordestinos*, while the contractors responsible for the road construction all had their headquarters in the Centro-Sul region. In comparison with the plans from 1970, the colonisation programme had been greatly slowed down, so that migration from the North East to the new colonisation fronts had been on a limited scale during the past few years. In 1973, a total of only 5000 to 5500 colonist families had found a new livelihood in the colonisation projects being realised by the INCRA in Pará and Rondônia. Moreover, by no means all these families originated from the North East. Consequently, the rural and urban problems of the North East had not yet been eased by these colonisation activities and it remained to be seen whether they would be in the following years.

A further point is that advance was only very limited for a great many colonists. Although they now occupied a holding and could look forward to becoming owners in the future, they did not enjoy a reasonably prosperous existence, free of serious worries. In the Altamira I colonisation zone it appeared more as though many had exchanged the poverty and privations of the North East or other regions for those of the North. A continuation of this situation would confirm the view of Ricardo Gontijo that the Transamazônica might equally well be called the "Transmiseriana." It would be no more than a "ligação de terra entre a miséria sôca do Nordeste e a miséria úmida da Amazônia" (Morais *et al.* 1970, 101). If such were the case, there would have been little justification for the extensive and expensive road building programme.

It appeared initially that the primary aim of the road building and colonisation plans was to alleviate the problems of the North East. They were announced immediately after the period of extreme drought at the beginning of 1970, while express reference was made in the publications in which the plans were later explained and elaborated to the problems of the relatively over-populated North East and to the possibilities for settling large numbers of Brazilians in the vast Northern region.[120]

In 1975, several years had passed and it was easier to make an assessment of the motives and success of the Brazilian government's integration policy. On the basis of the developments since 1970, the present writer concluded that a lessening of the social problems of the North East was not the primary motive.[121] The following are some of the arguments in favour of this view:

- The fact that use was made not only of nordestinos, but also of other population groups for the realisation of the road building and colonisation projects. Many local people were also recruited to help in building the Transamazônica and this would again be the case in building the Perimetral Norte. People from all parts of Brazil were settled in the colonisation projects. In the Altamira colonisation zone *nordestinos* even accounted for less than half of the total number of colonists;
- Only in the official Brazilian publications which appeared in 1970 and 1971 was a clear connection made between the colonisation projects in the North and the problems of the North East. In the somewhat more recent publications, however, it

120 See, especially, Andreazza (1970).

121 H. Jon Rosenbaum and William G. Tyler remarked in this connection that it was very improbable that the revolutionary opposition believed that the Brazilian government had started Operação Amazônia in order to weaken the position of the semi-feudal landed proprietors in the North East (1971, 433).

was stated that colonisation had to contribute to the solution of rural problems in those parts of Brazil that were characterised by social tensions;
- Relatively little money per family was invested in the colonisation projects.

It soon became clear that the primary aim of the Brazilian government in setting in train the process of opening up and colonising the Amazon region was to stimulate the country's economic growth, increase the prestige and popularity of the government, secure the occupation of the region and be better able to realise imperialistic ambitions. This means that the problems of the North East, in general, and the consequences of the last extreme drought, in particular, were seized upon only as a pretext for launching the plans for opening up and integrating the territory. They were used in order to ensure the necessary support for the plans and to justify the siphoning of money from special funds.

It should be remembered that the plan for opening up and colonising the Amazon region was, in fact, not new. Eliseu Resende had already referred in 1969 to the desirability of road construction, but he admitted that there was insufficient money to be able to realise the plans in the short term. A special situation had to arise, therefore, that would allow funds to be found as a result of a reordering of priorities.

Naturally, the Brazilian government had first to let the ideas presented in 1969 be further worked out before it could proceed to their realisation. It could have drawn up alternatives, while the cost-benefit analyses of these alternatives could have resulted in a well-considered choice. It could also have prepared detailed colonisation plans. The catastrophic drought, however, which made it possible to justify the integration plans, or at least make them more acceptable, had already arrived in 1970. The government was faced with a choice: either to act somewhat hastily and seize on the disaster of 1970, or wait for the next drought.

The extreme droughts in the North East, however, occurred irregularly. It was therefore by no means impossible that the next *sêca* would not occur until about 1980. Years of waiting had many disadvantages for the Brazilian government, which did not wish to delay its economic growth policy and also needed to increase quickly its prestige and popularity. Obviously, something also had to be done for the drought-stricken North East. Immediate opening-up and colonisation of the Amazon region, therefore, seemed to it to be the most obvious measure.

Yet another possibility is that it had originally been the intention of the Brazilian government to make, in the first place, a contribution towards the reduction of the social and economic problems of the North East by means of the road building and colonisation programme, but that it overestimated the adequacy of its plans and also did not sufficiently recognise the difficulties of realising them. Arguments in support of this proposition include the following:

- Shortly after the launching of the colonisation plans a programme for the agricultural development of the North East and North (PROTERRA) was also announced. Important elements of this programme were land reform, irrigation projects, modernisation of the sugar sector and the colonisation of thinly populated areas within North-East Brazil. This might indicate that the government became aware at an early date that the colonisation projects in the North would not lead to a dras-

tic reduction of the rural problems in the North East, but that these problems required to be tackled chiefly within the North East itself;
- The fact that solution of the social and economic problems of the North East was at first greatly emphasised as an objective, but given much less emphasis in later government publications;
- The fact that the INCRA did not show a preference for some time for colonists from the South and South East of the country with a higher level of general and agricultural education.

We incidentally do not wish to suggest by the above that there were absolutely no social motives underlying the Brazilian government's policy for opening up and integrating the Amazon region. The desirability of solving the problems of the North East and other parts of Brazil and, particularly, of the countryside, was thoroughly recognised. We were only commenting on the impression given in 1970 that social motives were the mainspring of the integration policy announced at that time. In our view, economic, political and imperialistic considerations together weighed heavier than the social motives. This may have been so from the beginning, but it is also possible that a change of emphasis occurred later.

Since 1970 the problems of the North East have been the subject of further studies. The SUDENE concluded in a 1972 publication that it would be possible to provide a living by means of colonisation for 953 000 families on the as yet unregistered lands of the North East during the period 1971–1990 and so achieve a considerable increase in employment in the agricultural sector. 550 000 families would be able to find a living on public lands known to be still available for colonisation, while the other families would have to be settled on other non-registered lands. The authors were thinking here, in particular, of the extensive areas still available for colonisation in Bahia, Maranhão and Piauí (Apote *et al.* 1972, 84–87). Colonisation had already been intensified in Maranhão and it was now better supervised. Among the sources of finance for this were the funds of the World Bank (Tavares *et al.* 1972, 83).

Although ample possibilities had therefore been proved still to exist for further colonisation in the North East and were being increasingly used, the SUDENE concluded in its publication that it would nevertheless be necessary to find a livelihood outside the North East for about 10,500 families annually during the period 1971–1990, in order to combat unemployment and keep abreast of the population growth (Apote *et al.* 1972, 85). The Brazilian government accordingly considered that reasons existed to continue the colonisation activities in the Amazon basin in the future.

Whether the colonisation projects in the North would really lead to a lessening of the social and economic problems depended upon the manner in which the occupation process was realised. Bearing in mind the course of events up to 1975, one is bound to conclude that there was a great danger that colonisation would again provide for the population groups involved an existence characterised by a low level of prosperity.

As far as the *nordestinos* were concerned, many of them had made possible the progress and further colonisation of Brazil through their cheap labour in the past, without having derived much advantage themselves. The advantages had gone mainly to a small group. There was the danger that history would repeat itself. The possibility existed that the colonists from the North East would contribute to a growth of the population of Amazônia Legal, help to ensure its security, raise its agricultural production, expand the exploitation of its forests and intensify its mineral production, while the level of prosperity of the majority would remain low.

Panagides considered it by no means unlikely that large numbers of poor farmers would be living along the new highways in the future, farmers who would be greatly dependent upon the production of simple food crops grown by shifting cultivation. Their activities would contrast sharply with the livestock, forestry and mining enterprises run on modern lines, which had been established or would shortly come into operation with the aid of capital and know-how from the South East and from other countries (Panagides and Vande Lage 1973, 25).

Apart from pointing in these concluding remarks to the danger that the serious social and economic problems would be solved inadequately or not at all through the development strategy of the day, we should refer to two further dangers, i. e. the threat to the natural environment and the further threat to the already decimated Indian population.

The dangers to the natural environment

In various places, including Rondônia, a number of areas had already been deforested by mining to such an extent that erosion and dust storms occurred. If mining were to increase in the future, these unfavourable side-effects might also increase greatly in extent.

Exploitation of the forests near the larger centres had already resulted in valuable species of timber becoming scarce. The SUDAM was aware that this might happen increasingly when the Amazon region was made more accessible. Road building might even lead to exploitation on such a scale that a serious loss of forest might occur. The SUDAM wished to prevent this and pointed out to the timber firms that tropical rain forests could also be unrenewable resources when they were incorrectly exploited. All undertakings which used the forest as raw material or as a source of energy, such as the iron and steel plant at Manaus, were legally obliged to replant. Agricultural and livestock holdings were also bound to leave the forest standing on half of their land. There were various other provisions in Brazil to protect the flora and fauna. A further favourable factor was that reafforestation projects could profit from the *incentivos fiscais*.

The SUDAM had already begun, in cooperation with other bodies, to study more closely various ecological aspects of the Amazon jungle. Foresters were now also being trained. The SUDAM wished to be alert in every way to the dangers threatening the tropical rain forest through incorrect exploitation methods in order to prevent the occurrence of serious disturbance to the ecological balance.[122]

It was still difficult to judge in the 1970s, however, whether the SUDAM would indeed be able in the long run to prevent serious damage to the environment. Reviewing the history of colonisation in Brazil and thinking, for example, of the serious deforestation and erosion which occurred in Paraná and Santa Catarina after 1930, many people were not optimistic about the Amazon region. It had already been noted in any event that the Instituto Brasileiro de Desenvolvimento Florestal still had insufficient

122 A review of a number of measures is to be found in Pandolfo (1972b).

qualified personnel to enforce observance of the protection regulations and to encourage the satisfactory exploitation of the natural resources.

It had also appeared that, up to 1975, the SUDAM had been unable to exercise supervision over the projects it had approved. This applied particularly to those being realised in the still poorly accessible areas. SUDAM officials often had to let themselves be taken there by an aircraft belonging to the firms carrying out the projects, which meant that the latter were already aware beforehand of the arrival of the government officials. Partly because of this, a great deal of timber could be felled undetected and the regulations concerning the *reserva florestal* were not always respected. 300 000 hectares were already being deforested annually in Amazônia, a state of affairs that could lead to catastrophe in the long run (*Relatório à Superintendência...* 1971, 115–116; *Amazônia – integração e marginalização* 1973, vol. 2, 24, and vol. 1, 13).

Destruction of the vegetation was to be feared, not only from the timber firms, but also from the arable farmers. Shifting cultivation was a normal form of arable farming in the Amazon Basin and the colonists who had settled along the new highways were also trying to gain a livelihood in this way.

If the population grew, there was a good chance that, in particular zones, serious disturbances would occur in the natural situation and a similar development would take place to that in the zone of Belém-Bragança. In the latter area, the great population growth, partly stimulated by attempts at sponsored colonisation at the beginning of the century, had already resulted in a continual pushing back of the virgin forest and in an increasing occurrence of *capoeira* and *cerrado*, forms of vegetation which are clear signs of soil deterioration. Some of the land had become virtually unsuitable for arable cultivation and was now fit only for the production of malva, a fibre crop (Sioli 1969a, 314–316). The vegetation along the Belém–Brasília highway had also already become seriously degraded in a number of places and the soil fertility had been reduced.[123] Similar phenomena could also be observed on a rather more modest scale along the road from Cuiabá to Porto Velho.

As far as the new colonisation zones along the Transamazônica were concerned, the reclamations were still of very recent date, but the farming methods were, in fact, the same. In 1975, it was still by no means certain that better exploitation methods would be introduced here in the near future, so that it was also uncertain what would be the ultimate fate of the *reserva florestal*, which had to be retained officially on every colonist's holding. Would it be respected under all circumstances, or would it first be eligible for reclamation when the farmers had succeeded in introducing forms of permanent land use, such as tree and bush crops, on the other fifty hectares of their holding? Or would the government eventually simply be forced to give permission for reclamation of this land in order to give the farmers sufficient room for rotation in the practice of their shifting cultivation?

Incidentally, in the event of shifting cultivation remaining the dominant agricultural method, there did exist possibilities of improving the system. In 1971, Valverde pointed out that the harmful effects of shifting cultivation could be limited by adopting the "taungya forestry system" as employed in various parts of Africa and Asia. Under this system, the valuable trees are felled before the ground is cleared, the plots are then laid out and young trees planted on the fields at the same time. These trees can

123 See, especially, Paula (1971).

then be felled when it is time for the next reclamation, after about 20 years. An important advantage of this system is that it is quite easy to increase the number of specimens of these varieties of timber which are in demand (Valverde 1971a, 5 f.). Its success, however, depends upon the cooperation of the cultivators, the availability of plant material, fairly long rest periods to enable the trees to develop properly and, last but not least, a good market for the timber. In Brazil, no effort had ever been made to introduce the "taungya forestry system," in spite of the widespread occurrence of shifting cultivation in large parts of the country. Large quantities of timber were lost every year as a result of shifting cultivation. It was unfortunately unlikely that there would be a change in this situation in the near future.

A threat to the natural environment was certainly not least to be feared from the practice of livestock farming. In the years before 1975, large areas of land had been taken over for this purpose, resulting in a great reduction in the forest area in the livestock farming zones. This development would undoubtedly continue in the years to come, certainly if the Brazilian government made a serious effort to turn the Amazon region into a great exporter of meat. The floods which occurred in March and April 1974 in the lower part of the Tocantins valley (Marabá-Jatobal district) may be partly connected with the extensive deforestation that had taken place along the lower courses of the Tocantins and Araguaia rivers for the laying down of pasture land.

The increasing economic activity might also create a further threat to the fauna. The hunting of certain species of birds and of animals with valuable furs had already assumed undesirable forms in spite of various prohibitions. Such hunting would only increase as the country became more accessible, unless the government acted firmly to prevent it.

The Brazilian government recognised the problems and the dangers. As it said, serious disturbances of the ecological balance should be avoided as far as possible. There was still no reason for serious alarm in the short term. The various forestry, livestock and colonisation projects, in fact, still occupied only a small part of the Amazon region. There was reason to fear, however, for the more distant future. Forms of exploitation would have to be found in good time which could be harmonised with the natural environment so as to prevent the loss of abundant natural wealth. The future would show whether the organs of the Brazilian government were able to make a major contribution to the realisation of this aim.

The dangers for the Indigenous population

The further threat to the some 120 000–150 000 Indigenous living in Amazônia Legal was certainly not the least of the dangers attached to the integration policy.

The government wanted from the beginning to prevent the building of roads being accompanied by numerous conflicts between the road builders and Indigenous people and so it called in the Fundação Nacional do Indio (FUNAI). The latter created, within the sphere of influence of the Transamazônica, 13 *frentes de atração*, where teams, consisting of *sertanistas*, nurse and interpreter, would be able to make contact with the Indigenous tribes and prepare them for the coming events (*Boletim Informativo* 472, 15 June 1973). By this means it was hoped to prevent the Indigenous being unexpectedly confronted with the road builders and the latter experiencing obstruction from the

Indigenous. During the period of road construction, experts and, sometimes, acculturedIndigenous were present to prevent or sort out difficulties and to ensure the protection of the Indigenous. If necessary, the latter were persuaded to move their settlements. As far as the workers were concerned, they had been instructed, at all costs, not to provoke conflicts with the Indigenous, to avoid contact with them as far as possible and not to behave aggressively, even if the Indigenous should attempt to remove certain objects. According to officials of the FUNAI, contacts had always been particularly friendly as a result of these precautions and no serious problems had arisen.

The FUNAI was also brought in in connection with the construction of lesser roads. Along the road from Cuiabá to Santarém one of its chief tasks was to make contact with the very isolated Kreen-Akarore, living in the Serra do Cachimbo. At the beginning of 1973 contact was indeed made by two experienced *sertanistas,* the Villas Boas brothers (*Boletim Informativo FUNAI,* Ano II, no. 6, p. 36). Such contact was considered necessary, because the road from Cuiabá to Santarém would run across the Serra do Cachimbo.

The government not only took measures to limit conflicts, but also took care to prevent the road builders passing on diseases on a large scale to the Indigenous, who possessed absolutely no resistance to certain forms of infection. One of the measures was the requirement that the employers should sign on only workers in the possession of a *carteira de saude* (a declaration of health) and who had been properly immunised. In order to prevent the Indigenous becoming infected, they had to avoid contact with them as far as possible. The FUNAI also set up a medical *equipe volante* to help the Indigenous.

The same body drew up a support programme in connection with the construction of the Perimetral Norte. 52 tribes lived in the sphere of influence of this highway who still had little contact with civilisation. The total number of Indigenous was estimated at about 20 000 (*Boletim Informativo FUNAI,* Ano II, no. 5, pp. 6–8). In mid-1973, however, it was still uncertain whether the FUNAI would be able to obtain sufficient resources to enable it to realise its programme completely. If not, the FUNAI hoped that the road construction contractors themselves would take supplementary measures, since the prevention of undesirable delay in the construction of the road was very important for these undertakings.

In addition to all this, the FUNAI had already been engaged for several years in demarcating areas for the Indigenous in order to ensure for them permanent possession of certain parts of the Amazon region. It was also studying the creating of two further "Indigenous Parks" to supplement those already existing (*Boletim Informativo* 359, 29 September 1972). The fact that such measures nevertheless by no means fully guaranteed the rights and security of the Indigenous was shown some time ago when the Brazilian government decided to allow the road planned to connect Brasília with Manaus (BR-080) to pass through the Xingu reserve. This would not only create a more direct link between the two cities, but would also enable a number of *fazendeiros* do dispose more rapidly of their livestock products (Filha 1971b, 75).

Although various measures had therefore been taken in the interests of the Indigenous and calamities had so far been avoided during the course of road building, many people nevertheless viewed the future of the Indigenous population with concern.[124] Now that a serious effort was being made to open up the country, the contacts with

124 More information about these problems is to be found, inter alia, in the Dutch *WIZA-bulletin*, a publication of the Werkgroep Indianen Zuid-Amerika (especially issues 12, 16–17 and 20).

farmers, cattlemen, miners and other population groups would unavoidably increase. It was by no means unlikely that these Brazilians would behave aggressively towards the Indigenous and their property as soon as the Indigenous began to be felt as a nuisance. The past had already provided many examples of this. Those who had little confidence in the ability of the FUNAI to prevent this already feared that the end of the Indigenous culture would soon become a fact.

Conclusion

We have tried in the foregoing to give a picture of the attempts up to 1975 to integrate the Amazon region more into the national economy, of the difficulties encountered in these attempts and of the dangers attached to them. Volume Two of this study will give a picture of the development policy pursued from the 1980s up to the present. Has Operação Amazônia been a success economically by contributing to a considerable increase in production in the primary sector and to a significant growth in the national economy? Has it become a success socially through resulting in a sufficient expansion of employment and a sufficient improvement in labour conditions, thus permitting large numbers of people to find a reasonably prosperous existence in the Amazon region? Have the rights of the Indigenous been respected sufficiently? And have the Brazilian authorities tried – as much as they could – to limit deforestation and to propagate sustainable land use?

Up to the mid-1970s it seemed more likely that the policy as pursued in the preceding years would result only in the further geographical extension of the socio-economic structures and processes that had led to the underdevelopment of the more populated part of Brazil, so that they would also become typical of what was once the still largely unoccupied portion of the country. Volume 2 of this book will show what happened in reality.

References

Almeida, Hugo de. 1978. *O desenvolvimento da Amazônia e a política de incentivos fiscais*. Belém: Ministério do Interior, Superintendência do Desenvolvimento da Amazônia.

Alvim, Paulo de Tarso. 1973. "Desafio agrícola da região amazônica." *Geografia e Planejamento* 7. São Paulo: Universidade de São Paulo, Instituto de Geografia.

Amazon Newsletter, Nos. 14–18. 1976 (March/April–November/December). Belém: Banco da Amazônia.

"Amazonas: Porta aberta para o future." 1972. Suplemente do *Manchete* 1059.

"A Amazônia desperta." 1970. *Rodovia* 284: n. p. Orgão de Assessoria de Imprensa e Divulgação do Departamento Nacional de Estradas de Rodagem.

Amazônia – integração e marginalização. 1973. Salvador: Centro de Estudos e Ação Social.

"Amazonien – ein ehrgeiziges Projekt." 1973. *Die Aktuelle JRO Landkarte* 298. München.

Andrade, Frederico Alberto de. 1971. "Política de incentivos fiscais e distribuição espacial das atividades agropecuarias na Amazônia: necessidades de expansão." *Revista Econômica do Basa* 1, no. 2: 47–58.

Andreazza, Mário. 1970. *Transamazônica*. Pronunciamento feito no Câmara dos Deputados em 1° de Julho de 1970. Brasília.

Apote, Vienzo d' *et al*. 1972. *Bases para uma política de reforma agrária e colonização no Nordeste do Brasil*. Relatório preliminar. Recife: Ministério do Interior, Superintendência do Desenvolvimento do Nordeste.

Arruda, Hélio Palma de. 1972. *A colonização no Brasil. Situação atual, projeções e tendências em Rondônia*. Folhete informativo apresentado ao curso superior de guerra naval da escola de guerra naval, em Rondônia, junho de 1972. Brasília: Ministério da Agricultura/Instituto Nacional de Colonização e Reforma Agrária.

Arruda, Helio Palma de. 1973. *Colonizção na Amazônia brasileira*. Informe apresentado a A.D.-j.S sobre colonização na Amazônia brasileira em Cuiabá MT. Brasília: Ministério da Agricultura/Instituto Nacional de Colonização e Reforma Agrária.

Arruda, Marcos, Herbet de Souza, and Carlos Afonso 1975. *Multinationals and Brazil. The impact of multinational corporations in contemporary Brazil*. Toronto: Brazilian Studies, Latin American Research Unit.

Atlas de Rondônia. 1975. Edição em convenio com o governo do territorio federal de Rondônia. Rio de Janeiro: Instituto Brasileiro de Geografía e Estatística.

Banco da Amazônia. 1976. *Carta da Amazônia*, IV-V, 41–49, (April–December). Belém: Banco da Amazônia.

"Bispo ataca marginalização social e os latifúndios de Mato Grosso." 1971. *A Amazônia brasileira em foco* 6 (July-December 1971): 141–148.

Boghossian, Zaven. N. d. *Plano hidroviário nacional.* Conferência de diretor geral do Departamento Nacional de Portos e Vias Navegáveis Comandante Zaven Boghossian. Brasília: Ministério dos Transportes, Departamento Nacional de Portos e Vias Navegáveis.

Boletim Informativo 1971. 1971. Manaus: Ministério do Interior, Superintendência da Zona Franca de Manaus (Suframa).

Boletim Informativo Funai, I-II. (1972–1973). Brasília: Ministério do Interior/Fundação Nacional do Indio (Funai).

Boletim Informativo Embaixada do Brasil, Nos. 1–230, (1 March 1974–31 December 1976). Paris.

Boletim Informativo Embaixada do Brasil, Nos. 241–509, (23 February 1972–6 November 1973). Paris.

Bromley, R. J. 1972. "Agricultural colonisation in the upper Amazon basin. The impact of oil discoveries." *Tijdschrift voor Economische en Sociale Geografie* LXIII/4: 278–294.

Brücher, Wolfgang. 1970. "Rinderhaltung im amazonischen Regenwald. Beiträge zur Geographie der Tropen und Subtropen – Festschrift für H. Wilhelmy." *Tübinger Geographische Studien* 34: 215–227.

Bunyard, Peter. 1974. "Brazil – the way to dusty death." *The Ecologist,* March-April: 89–93.

Câmara, Dom Helder Pessoa *et al.* 1973. *Eu ouvi os clamores de meu povo.* Recife: n. p.

Camargo, José Geraldo da Cunha. 1973. *Urbanismo rural.* Brasília: Ministério da Agricultura/Instituto Nacional de Colonização e Reforma Agrária.

Carneiro, Oziel Rodrigues. 1972. "Aspectos da economia amazônica. Presença do Banco do Brasil." *Boletim Banco do Brasil* VII/4: 3–30.

CEPLAC. 1976. *Relatório de atividades 1975.* Brasília: Commissão Executiva do Plano da Lavoura Cacaueira (CEPLAC).

Chimamovitz, Mário. 1973. "A triste historia da integração indígena." *A Amazônia brasileira em foco* 8 (July 1972–June 1973): 28–48.

Coelho, Ernesto Bandeira. 1971. "Implantação de uma infra-estrutura técnica para o desenvolvimento da indústria turística na Amazônia" (Conference paper). Conferência pronunciada pelo Exmo. Senh. Superintendente da Sudam, por ocasião do I seminário de turismo da Amazônia. Manaus: Ministério do Interior, Superintendência do Desenvolvimento da Amazônia.

Coelho, Ernesto Bandeira. 1972. *Relatório geral, February 1969–August 1972.* Belém: Ministério do Interior, Superintendência do Desenvolvimento da Amazônia.

Condurú, José Maria Pinheiro. 1973. "A agricultura na Amazônia brasileira." Conference Paper, *Man in the Amazon,* Feb. 18–21, 1973, Gainesville, Florida.

Costa, José Marcelino Monteiro da. 1971a. "Concentração industrial planejada; instrumento básico a industrialização de Belém." *Revista Econômica do Basa* 1, No. 3, May–August: 25–77.

Costa, José Marcelino Monteiro da. 1971b. "Pecuária: setor estratégico à ocupação e ao desenvolvimento da Amazônia." *Revista Econômica do Basa* 1, No. 2, January–April: 59–64.

Coutinho, Luiz Paulo and Rubens Barbosa. 1973. "Desamparo, a recompensa ao peão escravo da Amazônia." *A Amazônia brasileira em foco* 8 (July 1972–June 1973): 73–85.

Daemon, Dalton F. 1969. "Le développement amazonien, défi à l'imigination." *Civilisations* 3: 347–358.

Denevan, W. M. 1973. "Development and the imminent demise of the Amazon rain forest." *The Professional Geographer* XXV/2: 130–136.
Denis, Paul-Yves. 1971. "Manaus: un pôle de croissance régional." *Cahiers de Géographie de Québec* 15, No. 35: 380–388.
Dias, Catharina Vergolino. 1972. "Conteúdo e limites de regionalização na Amazônia." *Revista da Universidade Federal do Pará* II, No. 2, Series 1: 271–293.
Diretrizes básicas para ação do Ministério da Agricultura através do INCRA na Transamazônica. 1971. Estudos preliminaries. Brasília.
"Edição documento sobre o décimo aniversario do estatuto da terra." 1974. *Diario de Brasília*, 8 December.
Equipe de recherches amazoniennes. 1977. *Amazonies nouvelles. Organisation de l'espace rural.* Travaux et Mémoires de l'Institut des Hautes Études de l'Amérique latine, 30. Paris: Institut des hautes études de l'Amérique latine.
Falesi, Italo Claudio *et al.* 1972a. *Zoneamento agrícola da Amazônia.* Boletim Técnico do Instituto de Pesquisa Agropecuária do Norte (IPEAN) 54. Belém: Instituto de Pesquisa Agropecuária do Norte.
Falesi, Italo Claudio *et al.* 1972b. *Solos da rodovia Transamazônica.* Boletim Técnico do Instituto de Pesquisa Agropecuária do Norte (IPEAN) 55. Belém: Instituto de Pesquisa Agropecuária do Norte.
Falesi, Italo Claudio. 1973. "Soils of the Brazilian Amazon." Conference Paper, *Man in the Amazon*, Feb. 18–21, 1973, Gainesville, Florida.
FBCN. N. d. *Guia de ação comunitária para a conservação da natureza e dos recursos naturais.* Belém: Fundação brasileira para a conservação da natureza.
Filha, Irene Garrido. 1971a. "A zona franca de Manaus." *A Amazônia brasileira em foco* 5 (January–June): 72–81.
Filha, Irene Garrido. 1971b. "Sôbre a política de ocupação da Amazônia." *A Amazônia brasileira em foco* 6 (July–December): 69–77.
Foland, Frances M. 1971. "A profile of Amazônia. Its possibilities for development." *Journal of Inter-American Studies and World Affairs* XIII, 1971/1: 62–77.
Foucher, Michel. 1974. "La mise en valeur de l'Amazonie brésilienne." *Notes et études documentaires* 4110-4111, *Problèmes d'Amérique Latine*, XXXIII: 71-96.
Foucher, Michel. 1977. "Sudam et l'Etat brésilien, organisateurs de l'Amazonie: les fonctions idéologiques, administratives et économiques de l'État fédéral." In *État, pouvoir et espace dans le tiers monde*, edited by Claude Bataillon, 247–265. Paris: Institut de hautes etudes d' amerique latine.
Foucher, Michel and H. Riviére d'Arc. 1976. "Et L'Amazonie? Quelques remarques sur la géographie, la recherché et le pouvoir." *Région et régionalisation en Amérique latine* edited by Claude Bataillon, 519–527. Paris: n. p.
"Free zone stimulates expansion in Brazil." 1969. *Overseas Trading* 21, No. 12: 270–271.
FUNAI (fundacion nacional do indio). 1972. "O índio brasileiro. A verdade, só a verdade. Saneamento." *Revista técnica e informativa do Departamento Nacional de Obras de Saneamento* 26/45, October–December: 4–31.
Gallo, Jaques. 1972. *Notas sôbre a pesca na Amazônia brasileira.* Caderno de Ciências da Terra, 28. São Paulo: Universidade de São Paulo, Instituto de Geografia.
Glaser, Gisbert. 1971. "Neue Aspekte der Rinderweidewirtschaft in Zentralbrasilien." In *Beiträge zur Geographie Brasiliens*, 19–42. Heidelberg: Selbstverlag Geogr. Institut.

Goodland, R. J. A. and H. S. Irwin. 1975. *Amazon jungle: green hell to red desert? An ecological discussion of the environmental impact of the highway construction program in the Amazon Basin.* Developments in Landscape Management and Urban Planning, 1. Amsterdam: Elsevier Science.

Gourou, Pierre. 1966. *The tropical world. Its social and economic conditions and its future status.* London: Longman.

Grupo Tarefa da Transamazônica. 1973. *Relatório geral – Exercício 1972.* Brasília: Ministério do Trabalho e Previdência Social.

Hegen, Edmund Eduard. 1966. *Highways into the upper Amazon basin. Pioneer lands in southern Colombia, Ecuador and northern Peru.* Latin American monographs, second series, 2. Gainesville: University of Florida Press.

Kearns, Kevin C. 1969. "Amazônia. The emergence of Brasil's northern frontier." *The Journal of Geography* LXVIII: 535–544.

Kirby, J. 1976. "Agricultural Land-Use and the Settlement of Amazônia." *Pacific Viewpoint* 2, 105–133.

Kleinpenning, Johan M. G. 1971a. "Objectives and results of the development policy in North-East Brazil." *Tijdschrift voor Economische en Sociale Geografie* LXII, No. 5: 271–284.

Kleinpenning, Johan, M. G. 1971b. "Road building and agricultural colonisation in the Amazon basin." *Tijdschrift voor Economische en Sociale Geografie* LXII, No. 5: 285–289.

Kleinpenning, Johan M. G. 1972. *Operação Amazônia.* Nijmegen: Katholieke Universiteit Nijmegen.

Kleinpenning, Johan M. G. 1973. *Brazilië.* Panorama van de Wereld series. Roermond: Uitgeverij Romen.

Kleinpenning, Johan M. G. 1975. *The Integration and Colonisation of the Brazilian Portion of the Amazon Basin.* Nijmegen: Geografisch en Planologisch Instituut, Katholieke Universiteit Nijmegen.

Kleinpenning, Johan M. G. 1977. "An Evaluation of the Brazilian Policy for the Integration of the Amazon Region (1964–1974)." *Tijdschrift voor Economische en Sociale Geografie* LXIII, No. 5: 297–311.

Kleinpenning, Johan M. G. 1978. "A Further Evaluation of the Policy for the Integration of the Amazon Region (1974–1976)." *Tijdschrift voor Economische en Sociale Geografie,* LXIV, No. 1–2: 78–85.

Kleinpenning, Johan M. G. 1979. *An Evaluation of the Brazilian Policy for the Integration of the Amazon Basin (1964–1976).* Nijmegen: Vakgroep Sociale Geografie van de Ontwikkelingslanden.

Kleinpenning, Johan M. G. 1981. "La colonisation récente de l'Amazonie brésilienne: le rôle de l'Etat et des entreprises publiques et privées." In *Les Phénomènes de 'Frontière' dans les pays tropicaux,* 239–259. Paris: IHEAL.

Kleinpenning, Johan M. G. 1982. "Het bedreigde bestaan van de arme Braziliaanse boer." *Internationale Spectator* XXXVI, No. 9: 507–516.

Kleinpenning, Johan M. G. 1997. "De kolonisatie van het Braziliaanse Amazonegebied." *Derde Wereld* 16, No. 2: 167–176.

Knowles, O. H. 1971. *Perspectiva das oportunidades de investimentos no desenvolvimento da indústria florestal da Amazônia brasileira.* Belém: Ministério do Interior, Superintendência do Desenvolvimento da Amazônia.

Kohlhepp, Gerd. 1971. "Junge Entwicklungen im Eisenerzbergbau und Eisenerzexport Brasiliens." In *Beiträge zur Geographie Brasiliens*, 59–82. Heidelberg: Selbstverlag Geogr. Institut.

Kohlhepp, Gerd. 1976a. "Planung und heutige Situation staatlicher kleinbauerlichen Kolonisationsprojekte an der Transamazônica." *Geographische Zeitschrift* 64, No. 3: 171–212.

Kohlhepp, Gerd. 1976b. "Stand und Problematik der brasilianischen Entwicklungsplanung in Amazonien." *Amazôniana* VI, No. 1: 87–104.

Kohlhepp, Gerd. 1978. "Erschliessung und wirtschaftliche Inwertsetzung Amazoniens." *Geographische Rundschau* 1: 2–13.

Leahy, E. P. 1973. "Transamazônica. The rain forest route." *The Geographical Magazine* 1: 298–303.

"Lei sobre venda de terras á estrangeiros." 1971. *A Amazônia brasileira em foco* 6, July–December: 110–114.

Lopes, Joaquin Pessôa Igrejas. 1973. *A Amazônia*. Palestra proferida na escola nacional de informações, em Brasília, 21 de fevereiro. Belém: Ministério do Interior, Superintendência do Desenvolvimento da Amazônia.

Machado, Paulo de Almeida. 1973. "The role of education and research in the development of the Amazon." Conference Paper, *Man in the Amazon*, Feb. 18–21, 1973, Gainesville, Florida.

Mahar, Denis J. 1976. "Fiscal incentives for regional development. A case study of the western Amazon Basin." *Journal of Inter-American Studies and World Affairs* 18, No. 3: 357–359.

"The Manaus free zone and western Amazônia." 1969. *Bank of London and South America Review* 3, No. 27: 146–150.

Martelli, Amália. 1969. *Amazônia. Nova dimensão do Brasil*. Petrópolis: Vozes.

Meggers, Betty J. 1973. "Environment and culture in Amazônia." Conference Paper, *Man in the Amazon*, Feb. 18–21, 1973, Gainesville, Florida.

Mendes, Armando Dias. 1971a. *Estradas para o desenvolvimento*. Belém: Instituto do Desenvolvimento Econômico Social do Pará (IDESP).

Mendes, Armando Dias. 1971b. *Viabilidade econômica da Amazônia*. Belém: Universidade Federal do Pará.

Ministério da Agricultura. N. d. *Desenvolvimento rural*. Brasília: Ministério da Agricultura/Instituto Nacional de Colonização e Reforma Agrária.

Ministério da Agricultura. N. d. *Diagnóstico perspectivo para o projeto de colonização ao longo da rodovia Cuiabá-Santarém*. Edição especial de *Agro-Econômico*. Brasília: Ministério da Agricultura, Escritorio de estatística, analises e estudos econômicos.

Ministério da Agricultura. N. d. *Uma nova marcha ao norte/Une nouvelle marche vers le Nord*. Brasília: Ministério da Agricultura/Instituto Nacional de Colonização e Reforma Agrária.

Ministério da Agricultura. N. d. *Proterra*. Brasília: Ministério da Agricultura, Instituto Nacional de Colonização e Reforma Agrária.

Ministério da Agricultura. 1971a. *Metodologia para programação operacional dos projetos de assentamento de agricultores*. 1971. Brasília: Ministério da Agricultura/Instituto Nacional de Colonização e Reforma Agrária.

Ministério da Agricultura. 1971b. *Atividades do INCRA no setor cartográfico*. Brasília: Ministério da Agricultura/Instituto Nacional de Colonização e Reforma Agrária.

Ministério da Agricultura. 1971c. *Projeto de colonização Sidney Girão*. Brasília: Ministério da Agricultura/Instituto Nacional de Colonização e Reforma Agrária.
Ministério da Agricultura. 1972a. *Colonização da Amazônia. Política de integração nacional*. Brasília: Ministério da Agricultura/Instituto Nacional de Colonização e Reforma Agrária.
Ministério da Agricultura. 1972b. *Projeto integrado de colonização – Altamira I*. Brasília: Ministério da Agricultura, Instituto Nacional de Colonização e Reforma Agrária.
Ministério da Agricultura. 1972c. *Altamira-1*. Brasília: Ministério da Agricultura, Instituto Nacional de Colonização e Reforma Agrária.
Ministério da Agricultura. 1973a. *Amazônia. Terra à venda. Normas de alienação de terras públicas na Amazônia Legal*. Brasília: Ministério da Agricultura/Instituto Nacional de Colonização e Reforma Agrária.
Ministério da Agricultura. 1973b. *Relatório anual 1972*. Brasília: Ministério da Agricultura/Companhia Brasileira de Armazenamento (CIBRAZEM).
Ministério da Agricultura. 1975. *Realizações e metas*. Brasília: Ministério da Agricultura, Instituto Nacional de Colonização e Reforma Agrária.
Ministério da Agricultura. 1976. *Instrução especial Nos. 11, 12, 13*. Brasília: Ministério da Agricultura/Instituto Nacional de Colonização e Reforma Agrária.
Ministério da Educação e Cultura. 1971. *Relatório à Superintendência do Desenvolvimento da Amazônia sôbre estudos básicos de engenharia florestal, na Amazônia*. Viçosa: Ministério da Educação e Cultura/Universidade Federal de Viçosa.
Ministerio da defensa/Exercito brasileiro. 1973. *As obras de cooperação da engenharia military*. Brasília: Ministerio da defensa/Exercito brasileiro.
Ministério das Minas e Energia. 1972. *Projeto Radam*. Relatório No. 7. Brasília: Ministério das Minas e Energia, Departamento Nacional da Produção Mineral.
Ministério de Trabálho e Previdência Social. 1973. *Atuação do INPS ao longo das rodovias de integração nacional*. Brasília: Ministério de Trabálho e Previdência Social.
Ministério de Transportes. 1973. *Perimetral Norte*. Rio de Janeiro: Ministério de Transportes, Departamento Nacional de Estradas de Rodagem.
Ministério do Interior. N. d. *Diretrizes e estrategia para ocupação dos cerrados – Polocentro*. Brasília: Ministério do Interior, Superintendência do Desenvolvimento da Região Centro-Oeste.
Ministério do Interior. N. d. *A Sudam e a cultura do dendê na Amazônia*. Ministério do Interior, Superintendência do Desenvolvimento da Amazônia.
Ministério do Interior. 1968. *Operação Amazônia – Discursos*. Belém: Ministério do Interior, Superintendência do Desenvolvimento da Amazônia.
Ministério do Interior. 1969. *A Amazônia*. Coletânea de trabalhos classificados no concurso Paulo Maranhão, 3 volumes. Belém: Ministério do Interior, Superintendência do Desenvolvimento da Amazônia.
Ministério do Interior. 1970a. *Industrialização de madeiras. A grande oportunidade da Amazônia*. Belém: Ministério do Interior, Superintendência do Desenvolvimento da Amazônia.
Ministério do Interior. 1970b. *Sudam, 4° ano*. Belém: Ministério do Interior, Superintendência do Desenvolvimento da Amazônia.
Ministério do Interior. 1970c. *Amazônia – Estatísticas básicas*. Belém: Ministério do Interior/Banco da Amazônia.

Ministério do Interior. 1971a. *Plano de desenvolvimento da Amazônia 1972-1974*. Belém: Ministério do Interior, Superintendência do Desenvolvimento da Amazônia.

Ministério do Interior. 1971b. *Programa especial de crédito rural – Proterra*. Belém: Ministério do Interior/Banco da Amazônia.

Ministério do Interior. 1971c. *Subsídios ao plano regional de desenvolvimento 1972–1974*. Belém: Ministério do Interior, Superintêndencia do Desenvolvimento da Amazônia.

Ministério do Interior. 1972a. *A Amazônia é o novo Brasil, Sudam 6° aniversario*. Belém: Ministério do Interior, Superintendência do Desenvolvimento da Amazônia.

Ministério do Interior. 1972b. *Amazônia Legal – Manual do Investidor*. Belém: Ministério do Interior, Superintendência do Desenvolvimento da Amazônia.

Ministério do Interior. 1972c. *Legislação básica – Projeto Rondon*. Brasília: Ministério do Interior, Projeto Rondon.

Ministério do Interior. 1972d. *Pesquisa mineral no Iriri/Curuá* (Relatório preliminar). Belém: Ministério do Interior, Superintendência do Desenvolvimento da Amazônia.

Ministério do Interior. 1972e. *Pesquisa mineral no Tapajós/Jamanxim* (Relatório preliminar). Belém: Ministério do Interior, Superintendência do Desenvolvimentoda Amazônia.

Ministério do Interior. 1972f. *Sudam, 6° aniversario da Sudam – a Amazônia se prepara para exportar*. Belém: Ministério do Interior, Superintendência do Desenvolvimento da Amazônia.

Ministério do Interior. 1973a. *Amazônia – modelo de integração – Sudam ano 7*. Belém: Ministério do Interior, Superintendência do Desenvolvimento da Amazônia.

Ministério do Interior. 1973b. *Anuário estatístico 1972 – Suframa*. Manaus: Ministério do Interior, Superintendência da Zona Franca de Manaus.

Ministério do Interior. 1973c. *Funai em números 1973. Dados Correspondentes ao exercício de 1972*. Brasília: Ministério do Interior/Fundação Nacional do Indio.

Ministério do Interior. 1973d. *Legislação da zona franca de Manaus*. Manaus: Ministério do Interior/Superintendência da Zona Franca de Manaus (Suframa).

Ministério do Interior. 1973e. *O que é a Funai*. Brasília: Ministério do Interior/Fundação Nacional do Indio.

Ministério do Interior. 1973f. *Projetos aprovados 1968-1973*. Manaus: Ministério do Interior/Superintendência da Zona Franca de Manaus (Suframa).

Ministério do Interior. 1974. *Levantamentos florestais realizados pela missão FAO na Amazônia – 1956/1961*. Belém: Ministério do Interior, Superintendência do Desenvolvimento da Amazônia.

Ministerio do Interior. 1975a. *Anuário estatístico 1974*. Manaus: Ministerio do Interior, Superintendência da Zona Franca de Manaus.

Ministerio do Interior. 1975b. *II Plano de desenvolvimento da Amazônia. Detalhamento do II plano nacional de desenvolvimento 1975–1979*. Belém: Ministério do Interior, Superintêndencia do Desenvolvimento da Amazônia.

Ministerio do Interior. 1975c. *II Plano nacional de desenvolvimento. Programa de ação do governo para a região Centro-Oeste 1975–1979*. 1975. Brasília: Ministério do Interior, Superintendência do Desenvolvimento da Região Centro-Oeste.

Ministerio do Interior. 1975d. *Projetos industrias aprovados 1968-1974*. Manaus: Ministério do Interior, Superintendência da Zona Franca de Manaus.

Ministerio do Interior. 1975e. *Zona franca. Realidade na econômía da Amazônia Occidental*. 1975. Brasília: Ministério do Interior.

Ministerio do Interior. 1976. *II Plano nacional de desenvolvimento – Programa de ação do governo para a Amazônia 1975–1979.* Belém: Ministério do Interior, Superintendência do Desenvolvimento da Amazônia.

Ministério do Planejamento e Coordenação Geral. 1971a. *Metas e bases para a ação do governo.* Brasília: Ministério do Planejamento e Coordenação Geral.

Ministério do Planejamento e Coordenação Geral. 1971b. *Sinopse estatística do Brasil 1971.* Rio de Janeiro: Ministério do Planejamento e Coordenação Geral/Fundação IBGE/ Instituto Brasileiro de Estatística.

Ministério extraordinario para a coordenação dos organismos regionais. 1967. *O ciclo do homem.* Brasília: Ministério extraordinario para a coordenação dos organismos regionais. [Este volume resume o esforço da elaboração de uma nova política desenvolvimento que teve como marco histórico a I Reunião de Incentivo ao Desenvolvimento da Amazônia].

Miranda, Jorge Babot. 1973. "Os empresarios do sul no desenvolvimento econômico da Amazônia." *Revista Econômica do Basa* 2, No. 1 (January–April): 5–8.

Morais, Fernando, Ricardo Gontijo, and Roberto de Oliveira Campos. 1970. *Transamazônica: primeira aventura na estrada.* São Paulo: Editora Brasiliense.

Moran, Emílio F. 1977. "Estratégias de sobrevivência: o uso dos recursos ao longo da rodovia Transmazônica." *Acta Amazonica* 7, No. 3: 363–379.

Müller, Geraldo, Teresa N. S. Vasconcellos, Fernando Enrique Cardoso, and Juarez R. Brandão Lopes. 1975. *Amazônia. Desenvolvimento socio-econômico e políticas de população.* 2 volumes. São Paulo: Centro de Análise e Planejamento.

Nelson, Michael. 1972. *The development of tropical lands: policy issues in Latin America.* Baltimore/London: Rff Press Series.

Oliveira, Roberto Cardoso de. 1973. "Indigenous people and social-cultural change in the Amazon basin." Conference Paper, *Man in the Amazon,* Feb. 18–21, 1973, Gainesville, Florida.

"Os mitos da Amazônia. Porque a grande floresta não pode ser o pulmão do mundo." 1973. *Cacau atualidades* 10, No. 2: 12–18.

Pacheco, Mário Victor de Assis. 1972a. "A chantagem da explosão demográfica." *A Amazônia brasileira em foco* 7, January–June: 81–83.

Pacheco, Mário Victor de Assis 1972b. "O I congresso da associação médica do estado da Guanabara." *A Amazônia brasileira em foco* 7, January–June: 100–109.

Panagides, Stahis S., and Magelhães Vande Lage. 1973. "Amazon economic policy and prospects." Conference Paper, *Man in the Amazon,* Feb. 18–21, 1973, Gainesville, Florida.

Pandolfo, Clara Martins. 1969. *A Amazônia: seu grande potencial de recursos naturais e oportunidades de industrialização.* Belém: Ministério do Interior, Superintendência do Desenvolvimento da Amazônia.

Pandolfo, Clara Martins. 1972a. *A Amazônia e seus problemas.* (Conference paper). Conferencia proferida na escola superior de agricultura da universidade federal de Viçosa, a 10 de julho. Belém: Ministério do Interior, Superintendência do Desenvolvimento da Amazônia.

Pandolfo, Clara Martins. 1972b. *A atuação da Sudam na preservação do patrimônio florestal da Amazônia.* Belém: Ministério do Interior, Superintendência do Desenvolvimento da Amazônia.

"Pastoral da Terra." 1976. *Estudos da CNBB* (Conferência Nacional dos Bispos do Brasil) 11.
Paula, Ruben Descartes de Garcia. 1971. "A rodovia Belém–Brasília e os fazedores de desertos." *A Amazônia brasileira em foco* 6, July–December: 78–95.
Penteado, Antonio Rocha. 1969. "Condições geo-econômicas da Amazônia brasileira." *Revista do Instituto de Estudos Brasileiros* 6: 35–51.
Pereira, Osny Duarte. 1971. *A Transamazônica: pros e contras.* Rio de Janeiro: Civilizacao Brasileira.
Pinto, Clóvis Gabilanes Côrrea. 1971. "Importancia do setor agropecuário na econômia regional." *Revista Econômica do Basa* 1, No. 2: 7–38.
Presidencia de la republica/Minsterio do interior. 1974. *II Plano nacional de desenvolvimento 1975-1979.* Brasília: Presidencia de la republica/Minsterio do interior.
van der Putten, J. 1973. "Weg door de groene hel legt buurlanden voor Brazilië open." *De Tijd*, 26 May.
Ramalho, Sebastião da Silva. 1971. "Perspectivas do mercado da pecuária." *Revista Econômica do Basa* 1, No. 2: 39–46.
Reis, Arthur Cezar Ferreira. 1971. "A Amazônia e as áreas desérticas do Brasil." *A Amazônia brasileira em foco* 7, January–June: 7–16.
Reis, Arthur Cezar Ferreira. 1973. "Economic history of the Brazilian Amazon region." Conference Paper, *Man in the Amazon*, Feb. 18–21, 1973, Gainesville, Florida.
Relatório anual de atividades 1972. 1973. Belém: Associação de crédito e assistencia rural do estado do Pará (ACAR-PA).
Resende, Eliseu. 1971. "O papel das rodovias no desenvolvimento da Amazônia." In *Transamazônica: solução para 2001*, edited by Alberto Tamer, 288-295. Rio de Janeiro: APEC.
"Resumos dos trabalhos relativos a Amazônia brasileira de Harald Sioli." 1971. *Caderno de Ciências da Terra* 16.
Ribeiro, Nelson de Figueiredo. 1972. "Planejamento e utilização de recursos humanos no processo de desenvolvimento da regiao amazónica." *Revista da Universidade Federal do Pará* II, No. 2, Series 1: 41–55.
Rosenbaum, H. John, and William G. Tyler. 1971. "Policy-making for the Brazilian Amazon." *Journal of Inter-American Studies and World Affairs* XIII, No. 3–4: 416–433.
Saunders, John. 1973. "Population changes and characteristics of the Brazilian Amazon." Conference Paper, *Man in the Amazon*, Feb. 18–21, 1973, Gainesville, Florida.
Senna, Milton Camara. 1973. *Os problemas e desafios da Amazônia brasileira.* Conferência preparada para convívio sociedade brasileira de cultura. Belém: Ministério do Interior, Superintendência do Desenvolvimento da Amazônia.
Senna, Orlando. 1975. "Operação Rondônia. Asalto a mão armada." *A Amazônia brasileira em foco* 10, July 1974–June 1975: 67–83.
Silva, Miguel Cruz e. 1966. *Amazônia e Brasil – Comemoração do 1° centenario da abertura dos pôrtos da Amazônia.* Brasília: Biblioteca Nacional.
Sioli, Harald. 1969a. "Entwicklung und Aussichten der Landwirtschaft im brasilianischen Amazonasgebiet." *Die Erde – Zeitschrift der Gesellschaft für Erdkunde zu Berlin* 100, No. 2–4: 307–326.
Sioli, Harald. 1969b. *Ecologia de paisagem e agricultura racional na Amazônia brasileira* (Conference paper). 21-25 January & 28-30 January, Asociación pro biología trop-

ical – II Simposio y Foro de Biología Tropical Amazónica, Florencia (Caquetá) & Leticia (Amazonas), Colombia.
Sioli, Harald. 1973. "Recent human activities in the Brazilian Amazon region and their ecological effects." In *Tropical forest ecosystems in Africa and South America: A comparative review*, editd by Betty Jane Meggers, Edward S. Ayensu, and W. Donald Duckworth, 321–334. Washington, D.C.: Smithsonian Institute Press.
Sioli, Harald. 1975. "Problemas do aproveitamento da Amazônia." *A Amazônia brasileira em foco* 10, July 1974–June 1975: 21–49.
Soares, José Teodoro *et al.* 1973. *Projeto Rondon: uma experiênca vitoriosa*. Brasília: Ministério do Interior.
Soares, Francisco de Assis Jucá. 1971. *Aspectos da comercialização das madeiras amazônicas*. Belém: Ministério do Interior, Superintendência do Desenvolvimento da Amazônia.
Stephanes, Reinhold. 1972. *O programa de integração nacional e a colonização da Amazônia*. Brasília: Ministério da Agricultura/Instituto Nacional de Colonização e Reforma Agrária.
Sternberg, Hilgard O'Reilly. 1971. *A terra e o homen nos tropicos*. São Paulo: Universidade de São Paulo, Instituto de Geografia.
Sternberg, Hilgard O'Reilly. 1975. *The Amazon River of Brazil*. Geographische Zeitschrift – Beihefte/Erdkundliches Wissen 4. Wiesbaden: Franz Steiner.
SUDAM/Banco da Amazônia. 1972. *Isto é a Amazônia*. 1972. Belém: Superintendência do Desenvolvimento da Amazônia/Banco da Amazônia/Superintendência da Zona Franca de Manaus.
SUDAM. 1976. *Programa de Pólos Agropecuários e Agrominerais da Amazônia (POLAMAZÔNIA) – Pólo Altamira*. Belém: SUDAM, Coordenação de Informática, Divisão de Documentação.
"Sudam (or financial incentives in the Amazon region)." 1970. *Brazil Journal* 28, No. 322: 17–19.
Sudam em revista. 1970–1971. Ano 1/2, Nos. 1–12. Belém.
Tambs, Lewis A. 1973. "Geopolitics of the Amazon." Conference Paper, *Man in the Amazon*, Feb. 18–21, 1973, Gainesville, Florida.
Tamer, Alberto. 1971. *Transamazônica: solução para 2001*. Rio de Janeiro: APEC.
Tamer, Alberto. 1972. *Nordeste, os mesmos caminhos. Reforma agrária, afinal?* Rio de Janeiro: APEC.
Tavares, Vania Porto, Cláudio Monteiro Considera, and Maria Theresa L.L. de Castro e Silva. 1972. *Colonização dirigida no Brasil. Suas possibilidades na região amazônica*. Rio de Janeiro: Instituto de Planejamento Econômico e Social, Instituto de Pesquisas.
Thiery, H. 1978. "Les conquêtes de l'Amazonie: 4 siècles de luttes pour le contrôle d'un espace." *Cahiers des Amériques latine* 18: 129–147.
Tocantins, Leandro. 1968. "A integração da Amazônia no complexo cultural brasileiro." *Boletim Sociedade de Geografia de Lisboa* 86, Nos. 4–6 (April–June): 139–157.
Tocantins, Leandro. 1973. "O mundo amazônico." Conference Paper, *Man in the Amazon*, Feb. 18–21, 1973, Gainesville, Florida.
TransAmazônian highways. 1970. A report of the TransAmazônian and the Cuiabá–Santarém highways presented by the Ministry of Transportation of the federative republic of Brazil. VI World Meeting of the International Road Federation, Montreal, Canada.

"Transamazônica acelera o ritmo." 1971. *Rodovia* 291, July–August: 44–50.

Tribuzzi, Bandeira. 1972. "Maranhão também constroí sua Transamazônica." *A Amazônia brasileira em foco* 7, January–June: 93–95.

Valverde, Orlando, and Catherina Vergolino Días. 1967. "A rodovia Belém–Brasília: estudo de geografia regional." Rio de Janeiro: Fundação IBGE/Instituto Brasileiro de Geografia.

Valverde, Orlando. 1968. "A Amazônia brasileira. Alguns aspectos socio-econômicos." *Finisterra* III, No. 6: 240–256.

Valverde, Orlando. 1971a. "Shifting cultivation in Brazil. Ideas on a new land policy." In *Beiträge zur Geographie Brasiliens*, 1-18. Heidelberg: Selbstverlag Geogr. Institut.

Valverde, Orlando. 1971b. *Dos grandes lagos sul-americanos aos grandes eixos rodoviários.* São Paulo: Universidade de São Paulo, Instituto de Geografia.

Valverde, Orlando. 1972. "O drama do trabalhador nordestino na Amazônia atual." *A Amazônia brasileira em foco* 7, January–June: 17–33.

Velho, Otávio Guilherme. 1972. *Frentes de expansão e estrutura agrária: estudo do processo de penetração numa área da Transamazônica.* Rio de Janeiro: Zahar.

Villacrés Moscoso, Jorge. 1970. "La integración económica de la cuenca amazónica. *Journal of Inter-American Studies and World Affairs* XII, No. 1: 84–89.

Wagley, Charles, ed. 1974. *Man in the Amazon* (Proceedings of the 1973 conference). Gainesville: Center for Latin American Studies/University of Florida.

Wesche, Rolf. 1974. "Planned rainforest family farming on Brazil's transamazonic highway." *Revista Geográfica* 81: 105–115.

Wilhelmy, Herbert. 1966. "Tropische Transhumance: Beobachtungen auf einer Amazonasreise mit G. Pfeifer und H. Lehmann." *Heidelberger Studien zur Kulturgeographie: Festgabe zum 65. Geburtstag von G. Pfeifer*, edited by Hans Graul, 198-207. Wiesbaden: Franz Steiner.

Williams, Jerry R. 1971. *Manaus, Amazonas: A Focal Point for Development in Amazônia.* Washington, D.C.: Pan American Institute of Geography and History.

Wozniewicz, Wenceslau Dyminski. 1973. "Some Brazilian experiences in building highways through the jungle." Conference Paper, *Man in the Amazon*, Feb. 18–21, 1973, Gainesville, Florida.

Part 3: Case studies from the early 1980s

Changes in population size and distribution during the 1970s

The development measures after 1960

Although the Superintendência do Plano de Valorização Econômica da Amazônia (SPVEA) was created in 1953 to develop the Amazon region and 3 % of federal revenues were even set aside for the purpose under a provision of the 1946 constitution, through various circumstances no significant results were achieved. During the 1960s and 1970s, however, there was not only a renewed interest in the Amazon region, but this interest also led to a number of specific government measures, some of which may even be characterised as spectacular. Briefly summarised, the following events from these two decades appear to be the most significant:

- In 1960 a road link was completed between Brasília and Belém (see Fig. 10).
- In 1964 Brazil came under a military regime which had as one of its principal aims the encouragement of rapid economic growth and which also intended to let the Amazon region make a substantial contribution to that growth.
- In 1965 a second very important road link was completed, i. e. that between Cuiabá and Porto Velho, thus enabling Rondônia to be reached overland from the south east.
- In 1966, in pursuit of the government policy described under 2, the Superintendência do Desenvolvimento da Amazônia (SUDAM) was established as a successor to the SPVEA and given the task as a regional organisation of stimulating the progress of the Amazon region and coordinating the measures for the purpose to be taken by the various official bodies together with the activities of private entrepreneurs. One of the most important activities of the SUDAM was the encouragement and supervision of private investments facilitated by the various tax concessions in Amazônia.
- In 1967 a free trade zone was created for Manaus and its environs.
- In 1970 it was decided to build the Transamazônica, the first stretch of which (Estreito–Itaituba) was completed in 1972 and a second section (Itaituba–Humaitá) in 1974. This highway linked the southern part of the Amazon region with the North East of Brazil. Partly in response to the extreme droughts which afflicted the North East in 1970 a programme of social colonisation was launched, within the framework of which the government aimed to provide a new livelihood in the Amazon region for at least 100 000 families within five years. The majority of the colonists were to come from the North East. Although these ambitious aims were

Figure 10. Road and General Reference Map of Amazônia Legal (situation in late 1980)

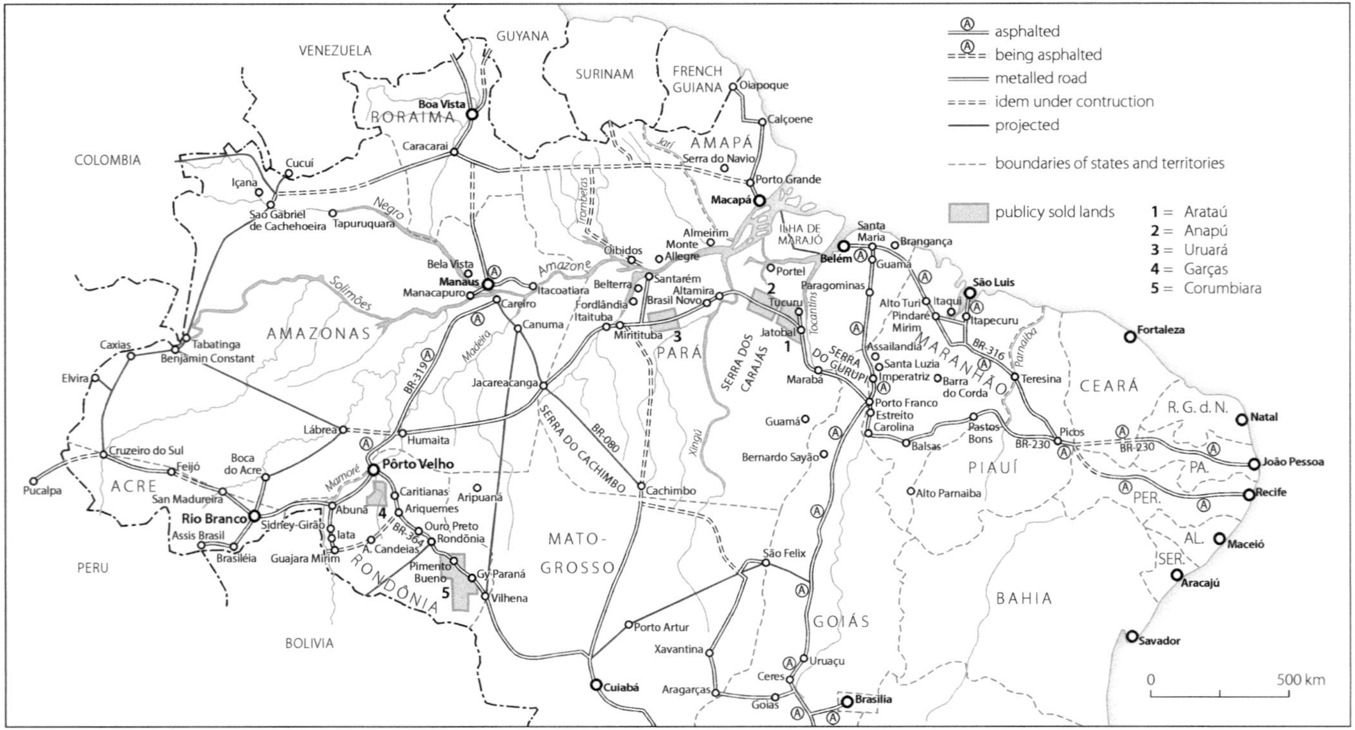

Source: Author's own elaboration.

not realised for various reasons, the completion of the Transamazônica did make possible a considerable stream of spontaneous colonisation. This incidentally also occurred after the completion of other highways (see Fig. 10).

Figure 11. SUDAM-projects in Amazônia Legal

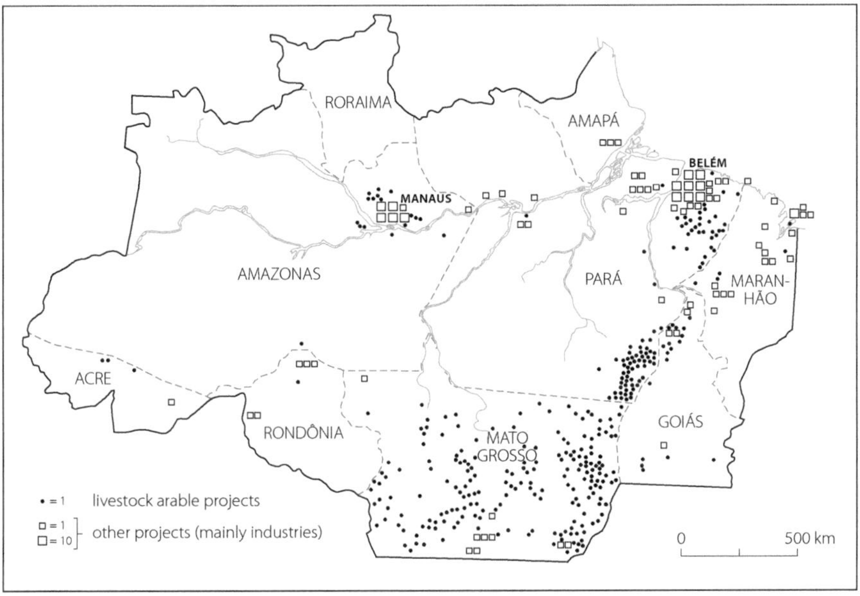

Source: SUDAM/Kleinpenning (1977).

- A number of smaller road links were also completed within the framework of the efforts to achieve further economic development and integration of the Amazon region. These included the roads between Manaus and Boa Vista and Manaus and Porto Velho. Among the larger roads special mention should be made of the link between Cuiabá and Santarém, completed in 1976.
- The policy was modified in the Second Development Plan, covering the period 1975–1979. There had been much criticism of the social colonisation programme for the North East and its rather disappointing results. This led the Brazilian government, which wished to see quick results, to place the emphasis entirely on rapid economic growth and to encourage large-scale cattle farming, arable farming, mining and forestry through the agency of major private entrepreneurs. The government assumed responsibility for the necessary infrastructure, which was concentrated in fifteen polos (Programa de Polos Agropecuários e Agrominerais da Amazônia, Polamazônia). The intention was that private investment should also be concentrated in these *polos*, insofar as it was not concentrated there already (see Fig. 12).
- The Third Development Plan, launched in 1979, aimed essentially at a continuation of the course adopted in 1975.

Figure 12. Programme of agricultural and mineral poles in the Amazon Region (figures indicate the part of the total budget allocated in 1975 to each pole)

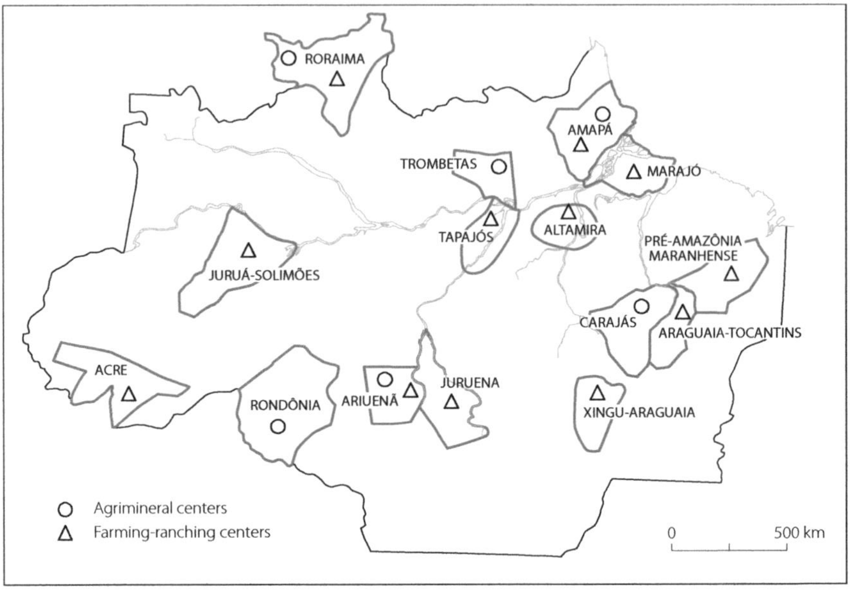

Source: Polamazônia.

Aim and framework of the analysis

It will be clear that this policy for the Amazon region could considerably influence future population trends. The aim of the following sections, therefore, is to examine to what extent this was the case during the period 1970–1980. Not all demographic aspects are considered in the analysis, which is limited mainly to changes in the total population of Amazônia and its sub-regions and to changes in population distribution, including those in rural and urban areas. More specifically, this means that attention is paid to the following questions:

- What changes occurred in the population growth of Amazônia and what consequences did these have for the relative position of this region within Brazil?
- Were there signs of noteworthy shifts in the population distribution within Amazônia under the influence of the development policy being pursued or of its related indirect effects, as a result of which there were changes in the relative position of the sub-regions?
- Were there important shifts in the relationship between urban and rural population?

In answering these questions the analysis will concentrate on the period 1970–1980, because this is the decade during which the most important development measures were taken or in which the effects of earlier measures could manifest themselves most clearly. The most marked demographic changes were therefore to be expected during this period. Where necessary, however, attention is also paid to changes during the years 1960–1970.

The spatial framework to which the analysis relates is almost always formed by Amazônia Legal. Unfortunately, very few statistical data are published for this administrative unit. Various figures relating to population growth and distribution had therefore to be calculated with the aid of data relating to meso-regions, micro-regions and municipalities, at least as far as the sub-regions of Goiás and Maranhão are concerned.

Changes in the relative position of the Amazon region within Brazil

The population of the North increased from 2.602 million in 1960 to 3.651 million in 1970 and 6.029 million in 1980. That of Amazônia Legal was 5.160 million in 1960, 7.150 million in 1970, but had risen to 11.192 million in 1980 (Table 8). This means that the North accommodated only 3.7 % of the Brazilian population in 1960, but that this percentage had risen to 3.9 in 1970 and to as much as 5 % in 1980. The share of Amazônia Legal increased from 7.3 % in 1960 to 7.6 % in 1970 and 9.2 % in 1980.

The population increase of the North was 40.3 % during the period 1960–1970 and as much as 65.1 % for the years 1970–1980. Amazônia Legal experienced an increase of 38.5 % between 1960 and 1970, and of 56.5 % between 1970 and 1980. For Brazil as a whole there was a growth of 33.1 %, during the 1960s and of 28.2 % during the following decade.

It is clear from these figures that the Amazon region was not an area of stagnation, but was even characterised by a rate of growth above the national average. Table 1 shows that this was already the case between 1950 and 1960. From then on, however, the trend intensified, giving rise to a population increase which was even comparable to that experienced during the rubber boom of the years 1890–1920.

It is useful to make a comparison not only with the country as a whole, but also with those regions which had long been known as the most important areas of in-migration within Brazil. This will make it possible to show the relative position of Amazônia as a growth region. In the first place, a comparison is possible with the metropolitan regions of the nine largest cities (i. e. São Paulo, Rio de Janeiro, Belo Horizonte, Recife, Porto Alegre, Salvador, Fortaleza, Curitiba and Belém). The combined population increase of these cities during the period 1960–1970 was 8.5 million, accounting for no less than 36.8 % of the total increase of Brazil. During the period 1970–1980 the increase was 10.71 million, or 41.4 % of the national growth.

Table 6a and b. Population changes in Amazônia Legal and its sub-regions, 1960–1980

Sub-region	Area in sq km[1]	Popu-lation in 1960	Share in 1960 %	Popu-lation in 1970	Share in 1970 %	Increase 1960-1970		Share in regional growth 160-1970
						Absolute	As % of1960	
Amatonas	1 560 327	721 215	14.0	960 934	13.4	239 719	33.2	12-1
Roraima	230 104	29 489	0.6	41 638	0.6	12 149	41.2	0.6
Acre	152 589	60 208	3.1	218 006	3.0	57 798	36.1	2.9
Amapá	139 068	68 889	1.3	116 480	1.6	47 591	69.1	2.4
NW. Am. Leg	2 082 088	979 801	19.0	1 337 058	18.6	357 257	36.5	18.0
W-Maranhão 2	257 451	1 879 959	36.4	2 336 894	32.7	456 935	24.3	23.0
Pará	1 228 870	1 950 935	30.0	2 197 072	30.7	646 137	41.7	32.5
N-Goiás 2	285 793	348 278	6.8	549 050	7.7	200 772	57.6	10.1
Mato Grosso	881 001	330 610	6.4	612 887	8.6	282 277	85.4	14.2
Rondôia	243 044	70 783	1.4	116 620	1.6	45 837	64.7	2.3
SE Am. Leg	2 896 159	4 180 565	91.0	5 812 523	81.3	1 631 958	39.0	82.1
Amazônia Legal	4 978 247	5 160 366	100.0	7 149 581	100.0	1 989 215	38.5	100.0
Brazil	8 511 965	70 992 343	–	94 508 583	–	23 516 240	33.1	–

Sub-region	Popu-lation in 1980	Share in 1980 %	Increase 1970-1980		Share in regional growth 1970-1980	Population density per sq km		
			Absol.	%		1960	1970	1980
Amatonas	1 448 135	12.9	488 201	50.8	12.1	0.5	0.6	0.9
Roraima	82 018	0.7	40 380	97.8	1.0	0.1	0.2	0.4
Acre	306 893	2.7	88 887	40.8	2.2	1.1	1.4	2.0
Amapá	180 078	1.6	63 598	54.6	1.6	0.5	0.8	1.3
NW. Am. Leg	2 018 124	17.9	681 066	50.9	16.9	0.5	0.6	1.0
W-Maranhão 2	3 211 418	28.7	874 524	37.4	21.6	7.3	9.1	12.5
Pará	3 507 312	31.3	1 310 240	59.6	32.4	1.3	1.8	2.9
N-Goiás 2	782 306	7.0	233 256	42.5	5.8	1.2	1.9	2.7
Mato Grosso	1 169 812	10.5	556 925	90.9	13.8	9.4	0.7	1.3
Rondôia	503 125	4.5	386 505	331.5	9.6	0.3	0.5	2.1
SE Am. Leg	9 173 973	82.0	3 361 450	56.8	83.2	1-4	2-0	3.2
Amazônia Legal	11192097	100.0	4 042 516	56.5	100.0	1.0	1.4	2.3
Brazil	121159573	–	26 641 990	28.2	–	8.3	11.1	14.2

Source: Anuario Banco da Amazônia 1971 and Sinopse Preliminar do Censo Demográfico 1970 and 1980.
1. The figures for area were taken from the Anuário BASA 1971. The figures for Maranhão and Goiás relate only to the area lying within the official boundaries of Amazônia Legal. If certain municipalities fell only partly within those limits, only the relevant part of the municipal area was included. Until 1977 the area of Amazônia Legal was somewhat smaller (4.87 million sq km), because only the part of Mato Grosso north of the 16th parallel was included. In 1977 Mato Grosso was split up in two new states: Mato Grosso do Sul and Mato Grosso. At this time the boundaries of Amazônia Legal were modified to include the whole of the new state of Mato Grosso.
2. The population figures relate to whole municipalities even though when only part of the area fell within the limits of Amazônia Legal. Municipalities with more than 25 % of their area outsideAmazônia Legal were not included in the population calculations.

From other figures it may be calculated that the population of these metropolitan areas increased by 55.7% between 1960 and 1970 and by 45% during the following decade. The first percentage was still above the growth figure for the North and for Amazônia Legal, but in the following decade the growth of the North and of Amazônia Legal exceeded that of the metropolitan areas. It will be clear, however, that very different absolute numbers were involved, so that it is understandable that, during the 1960s, the North accounted for only 4.5% of the national population growth and for still no more than 8.9% during the 1970s. Amazônia Legal accounted for 8.5% of national growth during the period 1960–1970 and for 15.2% during the decade 1970–1980.

The population growth of the Amazon region may also be compared with the population increase of the South and the South East combined, these regions forming the economic and demographic heartland of Brazil. During the 1960s the population of the seven states of the South and South East increased from 42.995 million to 57.016 million, and to 71.961 million during the 1970s. This corresponds with a growth of 32.6% between 1960 and 1970, and of 26.2% between 1970 and 1980. The growth rate of the North and of Amazônia Legal was higher than these figures in both decades, but once again the difference in absolute numbers should be borne in mind. Thus the South and the South East accounted for 59.7% of national growth during the decade 1960–1970, and of 56.1% between 1970 and 1980.

It may be concluded that the Amazon region was certainly no longer a demographically stagnant region after 1960. Thanks to an acceleration of the rate of growth, the relative position of the region within the national context was even somewhat strengthened, particularly after 1970. Both absolutely and relatively, however, the contribution of the North and of Amazônia Legal to the national population growth was still a modest one. Consequently, when assessed at the national level, the effects of the development measures so far taken appeared to be limited.

Explanation of the relatively feeble attractiveness of Amazônia Legal

Although the countryside of North East Brazil, because of its extreme droughts, unfavourable ownership and occupation relationships and continuing processes of enlargement of scale, could scarcely offer an acceptable existence to many country-dwellers, and although employment in agriculture continued to fall in the other parts of Brazil, the figures we have just given show that Amazônia did not exercise an exceptional attraction on the rest of the country. Despite the existence of large areas of unused land which were gradually being opened up by road construction, the "surplus" agricultural population was not migrating *en masse* to the North. The share of Amazônia in the national population growth was too modest for that, certainly when it is remembered that a large part of the population growth there was accounted for by natural increase.[125]

125 Detailed and reliable migration data are scarce; in fact, no migration data at all are available for the period 1970–1980, but it may be assumed that the level of natural increase in Amazônia Legal did not differ significantly from that in Brazil as a whole (1960–1970: 33%; 1970–1980: 28%). This means that, during the period 1970–1980, about half of the population increase in Amazônia Legal could be attributed to migration.

It is beyond the scope of this contribution to examine the motives which led Brazilians to migrate to the Amazon region or give preference to seeking a livelihood elsewhere. These motives have been discussed in the great volume of literature about the Amazon region which appeared mainly during the 1970s. They may otherwise be deduced from the discussion of the development processes which occurred up to 1980 in Amazônia Legal. Summarised briefly, the following circumstances, in particular, appear to have exercised a negative effect on the volume of the migration flows to Amazônia Legal:

- The different, humid tropical environment, which required considerable physical adaptation and brought with it dangers to health, as well as imposing very specific demands on the way in which colonists had to make a livelihood. Not for nothing is the Amazon region often described as a "green hell."
- The great unfamiliarity of many people with the potentialities and limitations of the region was not compensated by adequate and intensive information and guidance on the part of the government, even in the official colonisation projects.
- The small-scale colonisation projects realised by the government (more specifically the Instituto Nacional de Colonização Reforma Agrária, INCRA) had little success up to 1980, either quantitatively or qualitatively.
- Spontaneous colonisation consequently formed the only alternative for many people, but because of their unfavourable location in relation to the economic and demographic core areas of the country and their inaccessibility, large areas did not offer much attraction for spontaneous colonisation either. There was scarcely any market for commercial production, so that colonists in such areas could only build up a precarious, more or less self-sufficient existence, especially since all kinds of basic provisions in the fields of education, health care, agricultural advice etc. were lacking.
- Those parts of Amazônia Legal which are favourably located in relation to the South East had become the field of operation of modern, large-scale, capital-intensive agricultural enterprises, which generally made use of taxation facilities offered by the government. Land speculators were also active in these areas. As far as land use is concerned, the emphasis was wholly on extensive cattle ranching, which scarcely provided permanent employment. Added to this is the fact that the majority of spontaneous occupiers were regarded by the large enterprises and the land speculators as undesirable elements, so that a fierce struggle for land arose in many places, ending in most instances to the disadvantage of the spontaneous colonists. These facts were obviously not unknown to many potential migrants and they removed the desire to make the attempt to build up such a risky existence.

The effect of the above was to cause many country people who were struggling to survive to prefer to go elsewhere to find a living, particularly to the big cities, which were consequently growing at an explosive rate.

The consequence for the vast territory of Amazônia Legal was that the population was still modest, both absolutely and relatively. As appears from Table 8, there was a population in 1980 of 11,192 million, 9.2 % of the total Brazilian population. The population densities there were still on the low side and remained well below the national average. The North had an average population density of 1.03 persons per sq km in 1970 and 1.70 in 1980. For Amazônia Legal the densities for 1970 and 1980 were 1.43 and 2.23, respectively. The density for Brazil as a whole was 11.10 in 1970 and 14.23 in 1980.

Population increase per state or territory

The changes in population size have so far been looked at for the North and Amazônia Legal as a whole without separate consideration of the growth figures for the individual territories or states or parts of them. In this section, therefore, we shall make a closer examination of the population changes at the level of the states and territories, paying particular attention to the period 1970–1980, when the population growth was considerably greater than during the preceding decade.

The principal data for this period are summarised in Table 6, which also includes figures for the years 1960–1970, making possible comparisons between the two decades.

The table shows that the population increase of Amazônia Legal during the period 1970–1980 was by no means evenly distributed over the region. Some areas grew considerably more strongly than others, but nowhere was there a decrease.

The population growth of Amazonas, Acre, northern Goiás and the western part of Maranhão between 1970 and 1980 was below the average for the whole of Amazônia Legal. Amapá grew at about the same rate as the regional average, while the growth figures for the other areas were considerably above the regional average of 56.5 %. The most spectacular growth occurred in Rondônia, where the population quadrupled in only ten years.

As a result of the uneven growth there were some shifts in the relative positions of the sub-regions. The share of Amazonas, Acre, northern Goiás and western Maranhão in the total population of Amazônia Legal declined somewhat, while that of Amapá remained the same. The other sub-regions generally strengthened their position. The most remarkable changes were those for Rondônia and Mato Grosso.

Northern Goiás occupies a rather special position in that its share of the total population of Amazônia Legal increased during the 1960s and only decreased after 1970. As far as the three other areas which experienced a weakening of their position between 1970 and 1980 are concerned, this was a development that had already set in during the preceding decade.

Equally, if not more striking, are the figures from Table 8 relating to absolute population increase. 83.2 % of this increase is shown to have occurred in the south-eastern segment, i. e. Rondônia, Mato Grosso, northern Goiás, Pará and western Maranhão, which sub-regions together account for 58.2 % of the surface area of Amazônia Legal. By contrast, the north-western segment, which covers 41.8 % of the surface area and comprises Acre, Amazonas, Roraima and Amapá, experienced only 16.9 % of the absolute increase. The figures in Table 8 show that these striking differences also existed during the period 1960–1970.

The fact that the population growth occurred predominantly in the southern and eastern part of the Amazon region is closely related to the circumstance that these sub-regions had a larger population, so that the natural increase could be much greater than in the states making up the thinly populated north-western segment of Amazônia Legal.

A further factor, however, is the location relative to the economic and demographic heartland of Brazil, i. e. the South and South East. The distance to these core areas is much less for the southern and eastern sub-regions of Amazônia than it is for the northern and western sub-regions, especially since the southern and eastern sub-regions had recently been linked with the "centre" of Brazil by a number of important highways. Consequently, during the 1970s, migration from the South East to the Amazon region had been directed more to the southern and eastern sub-regions.

The highways just referred to had been completed successively since 1960. To be specific, the ones mainly concerned are the link between Belém and Brasília, completed in 1960, which opened up the north of Goiás and the south of Pará, and the link between Cuiabá and Porto Velho, completed in 1965, which provided not only Rondônia but also western Mato Grosso, with a relatively good connection with the South East. In Mato Grosso, moreover, in addition to a section of the road BR-080, a number of small access roads were constructed leading to the north, while the Cuiabá-Santarém link was opened to traffic in 1976. The effect of this latter road, however, should not be overestimated, since the period of four years between when it opened and the census was relatively short and the spontaneous settlement of colonists, land speculators and others along this link appears to be somewhat more controlled than along other roads, because the army – which constructed the road – continued to exercise a certain measure of supervision.

Apart from being stimulated by its favourable location and the building of roads, the greater population increase on the southern and eastern margin of Amazônia Legal was also encouraged by the fact that large investments had been made here or would be made shortly after. Investors from the South East and South of Brazil believed that the southern and eastern areas of Amazônia Legal afforded the most favourable prospects for development because of their relative closeness to the economic "centre" of the country. The hundreds of large-scale cattle ranching projects, which had been or were being realised in the Amazon region, with or without tax concessions, were therefore concentrated predominantly in Mato Grosso, northern Goiás and southern Pará (see Fig. 11). It is also significant in this connection that the southern and eastern margin of Amazônia Legal was much more favourable physically for cattle farming than the more northerly areas, where the tropical forest was denser.

Not only was temporary work created by the cattle farming projects – within the framework of the clearances – after which the temporary workers often remained "hanging about" in the area, but the cattle farming projects, because of their extensive character and the large areas of land they consequently required, led to the construction of numerous secondary and tertiary roads. These were sometimes no more than *picadas* (pinpricks), but they improved accessibility and so encouraged spontaneous colonisation. In the northern sub-regions of the Amazon region all this was much less in evidence, with the exception to some extent of northern Roraima.

The relationship between population growth and communications emerges somewhat more clearly when we consider the point of time at which various roads were completed and when the rapid population growth began. It then appears that the population growth of Rondônia was still relatively "normal" by Brazilian standards during the 1960s (Table 8). The very spectacular increase dates mainly from the end of the 1960s and the 1970s (see Figs. 14–17). The effect of the Cuiabá–Porto Velho road link, completed in 1965, and of the propaganda carried on since then for the development and integration of Rondônia and of the INCRA colonisation projects undertaken within that context, is clearly demonstrable here. There was also an acceleration in the population growth of western Mato Grosso at that time. Northern Goiás experienced quite a strong population growth during the 1960s immediately after the completion of the Belém–Brasília link. During the 1970s the increase remained considerable, but was nevertheless at a reduced rate, because the areas along this road were then partly occupied and other sub-regions within the Amazon region had meanwhile been given better accessibility (see Figs. 14–17).

The Transamazônica, completed during the 1970s, also resulted in a marked increase in the rate of population growth in the areas through which it passes, although in comparison with the north-south links between Belém and Brasília, and Cuiabá and Porto Velho, the influence of the Transamazônica was more modest, because a very small proportion of the population of the North lived in the municipalities which it opened up. This is not only because the highway was completed later, but also because it runs in an east-west direction. In so doing it links the "demographic vacuum" with the North East, which although characterised by serious impoverishment and unfavourable subsistence prospects, so that it might provide many potential colonists, was much less able to do so because of its economic weakness to function as a market and as a provider of capital for development projects. The greater part of the investments in Amazônia Legal originated therefore in the South East and not the North East. Moreover, because of its east-west course, the Transamazônica did not provide a favourable connection with the South and South East of Brazil and, particularly for the western areas along this highway, the distances were very great. A final point is that the official colonisation projects carried out along the Transamazônica had not been very successful. We shall return to the effects of the Transamazônica when we come to examine the population changes within the individual sub-regions. The road was mentioned here only to illustrate the importance of factors such as accessibility and distance from the economic and demographic heartland.

Western Maranhão occupies a somewhat special position. A quite large-scale spontaneous colonisation by simple peasants had already been occurring here for a considerable time. A high proportion of the rural population who could no longer find a possibility of making a living in the North East had migrated to this sub-region. The explanation for this is to be found both in the proximity to the densely populated regions of the North East and the existence of large areas of state land. Another significant factor is that western Maranhão possesses a rather favourable natural environment by comparison with the drought polygon of the North East, while not yet presenting the more extreme characteristics of the humid tropical climate experienced in the more westerly parts of the Amazon region. Until shortly before 1980, large-scale agricultural projects were absent or were so modest in number and extent as not to hinder the chances of the majority of the colonists of making a living. One might speak of an "open" frontier. Only in the late 1970s had this situation changed and, according to newspaper reports from around 1980, there had been an escalation of conflicts over land ownership.

Because western Maranhão already had a considerable population thanks to this spontaneous colonisation during the 1960s, a large part of the absolute natural population increase of Amazônia Legal occurred in this sub-region. Nevertheless, there was a smaller relative and absolute increase during the period 1970–1980 than in the more southerly marginal areas, so that the relative position of Maranhão was somewhat weakened.

Figure 13. Micro-regions of Amazônia Legal[126]

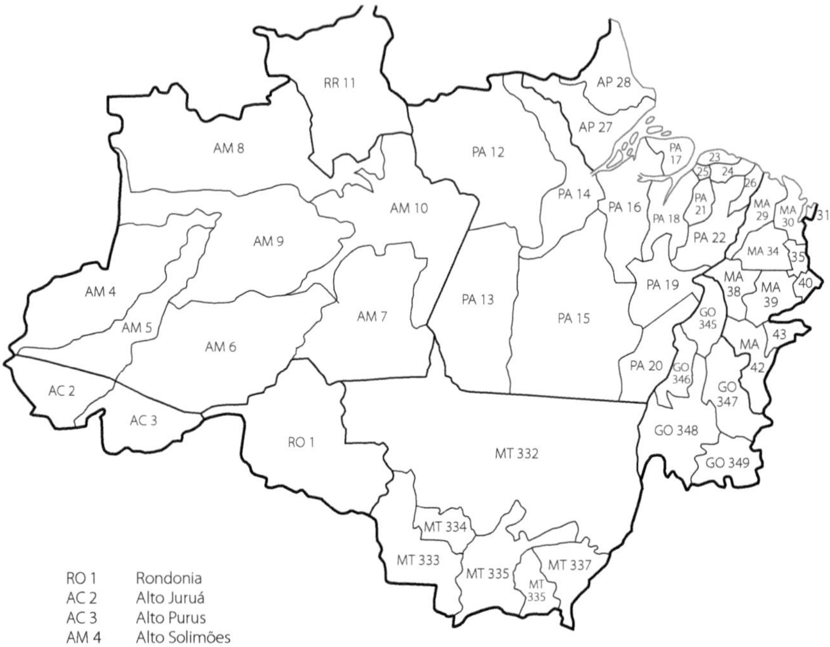

RO 1	Rondonia
AC 2	Alto Juruá
AC 3	Alto Purus
AM 4	Alto Solimões
AM 5	Juruá
AM 6	Purus
AM 7	Madeira
AM 8	Rio Negro
AM 9	Solimões-Japurá
AM 10	Médio Amazonas
RR 11	Roraima
PA 12	Médio Amazonas Paraense
PA 13	Tapajós
PA 14	Baxio Amazonas
pa 15	Xingu
PA 16	Furos
PA 17	Campos de Marajó
PA 18	Baxio Tocantins
PA 19	Marabá
PA 20	Araguaia Paraense
PA 21	Tomé-Açu
PA 22	Cuajarina
PA 23	Salgado
PA 24	Bragantina
PA 25	Belém
PA 26	Viseu
AP 27	Macapá
AP 28	Amapá e Oiapoque

MA 29	Gurupi
MA 30	Baixada Ocidental Maranhese
MA 31	São Luis
MA 34	Pindaré
MA 35	Mearim
MA 38	Imperatriz
MA 39	Alto Mearim e Grajaú
MA 40	Médio Mearim
MA 42	Chapadas do Sul Maranhense
MA 43	Baixo Balsas
MT 332	Norte Mato-grossense
MT 333	Alto Guaporé-Jauru
MT 334	Alto Paraguai
MT 335	Baixada Cuiabana
MT 336	Rondônopolis
MT 337	Garças
GO 345	Extremo Norte Goiano
GO 346	Baixo Araguaia Goiano
GO 347	Tocantina de Pedro Afonso
GO 348	Médio Tocatins-Araguaia
GO 349	Serra Geral de Goiás

126 Source for the following figures: Instituto brasileiro de geografia e estatistica (IBGE).

Population changes at the meso- and micro-regional levels

In the preceding section the effect of location, road building, investment and other development activities was emphasised. The relationship between these variables and the population increase will emerge rather more clearly, however, if we now concentrate on the question of where within the sub-regions of Amazônia Legal the population increase mainly occurred. For this purpose, it is necessary to make an analysis at the level of the meso and micro-regions. Such an analysis will also present an opportunity to identify more precisely the centres of gravity of settlement.
We shall first consider the population of the north western segment.

How incomplete the occupation of northern Amazônia still was appears, for example, from the state of Amazonas, the greater part of which falls within the statistical meso-region of Hileia Amazonense. The latter covers the whole of the state apart from the north-east corner, accounting for no less than 87.1 % of the surface area, but accommodating in 1970 only 38.7 % and, in 1980, only 33.3 % of the population of the state (see Fig. 19).[127] The total population of this meso-region (nearly six times as large as Great Britain) was only 482 924 in 1980, giving an average population density of 0.35 persons per sq km.

Figure 14. Share of each micro-region in the total population growth in Amazônia Legal, 1960–1970

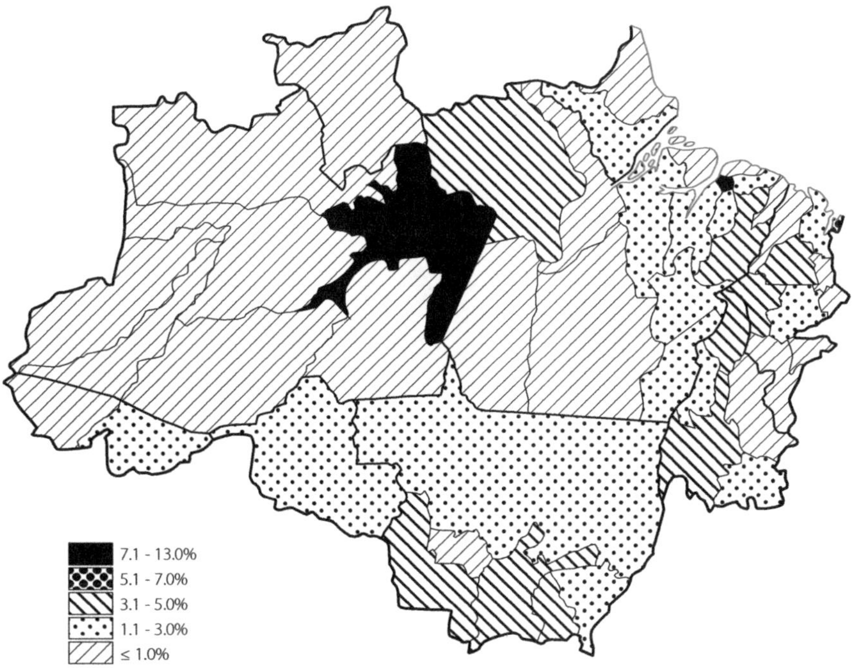

127 This meso-region comprises all the micro-regions of the state of Amazonas with the exception of no. 10 (Médio Amazonas).

Figure 15. Share of each micro-region in the total population growth in Amazônia Legal, 1970–1980

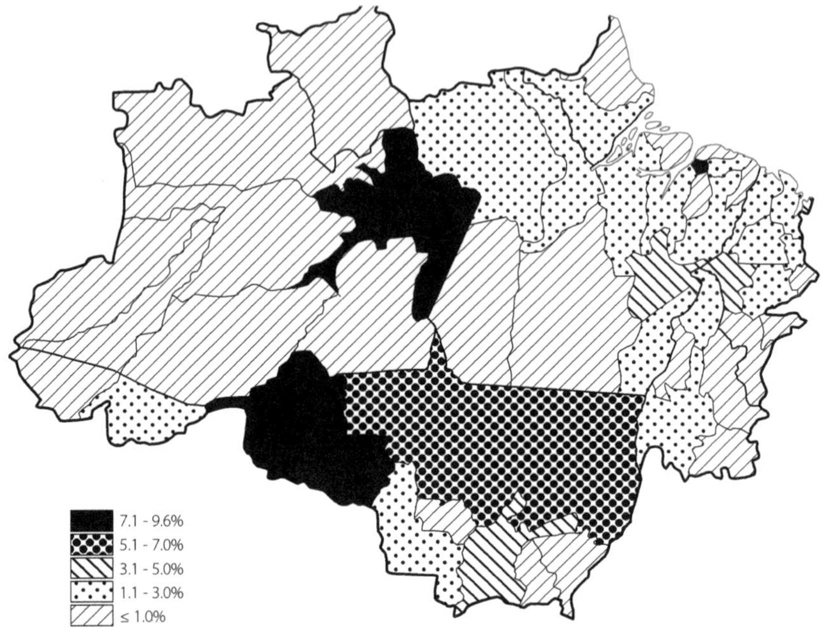

Figure 16. Population growth in each of the micro-regions of Amazônia Legal, 1960–1970 (as % of 1960) (Brazil 33.1 %; Amazônia Legal 39.5 %; none of the micro-regions was characterised by a growth rate within the class of 33.1–38.5 %)

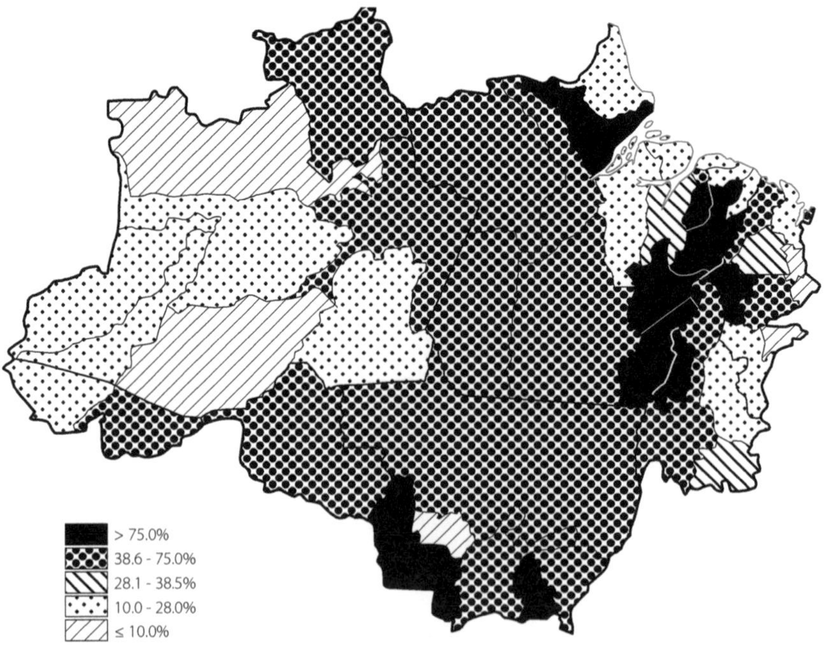

In the meso-region of Manaus, on the other hand, which covers the remaining 12.9 % of the area of the state, 61.3 % of the population of the state lived there in 1970; in 1980 the proportion had risen to as much as 66.7 %.[128]

The Manaus meso-region consists of fourteen municipalities, together covering an area nearly as large as Great Britain, but of which the municipality of Manaus is by far the largest. In 1970 this municipality had 314 197 inhabitants, or 32.7 % of the total population of the state. By 1980 the population had increased to 642 492, bringing it to 44.3 % of the state population.

There was therefore a marked concentration and even a tendency towards further concentration. This development was closely related to the attraction exercised by Manaus as the largest urban centre of western Amazônia on large numbers of migrants, particularly since the establishment of the free trade zone and the other tax facilities had turned it into a concentration point of industry and – more importantly – of all kinds of trading activities. Moreover, various agricultural development projects had been realised in the near vicinity of the city. An influence which undoubtedly cannot be overlooked in this connection is the fact that a number of roads were completed during the 1970s, i. e. the links between Manaus and Boa Vista, and between Manaus and Porto Velho. They encouraged the migration from the country to the city to such an extent that the population growth of the state of Amazonas, excluding Manaus, during the 1970s lay well below the average rate of growth of the whole of Amazônia Legal (24.8 % as against 55.5 %).

Figure 17. Population growth in each of the micro-regions of Amazônia Legal, 1970–1980 (as % of 1970) (Brazil 28.2 %; Amazônia Legal 56.5 %)

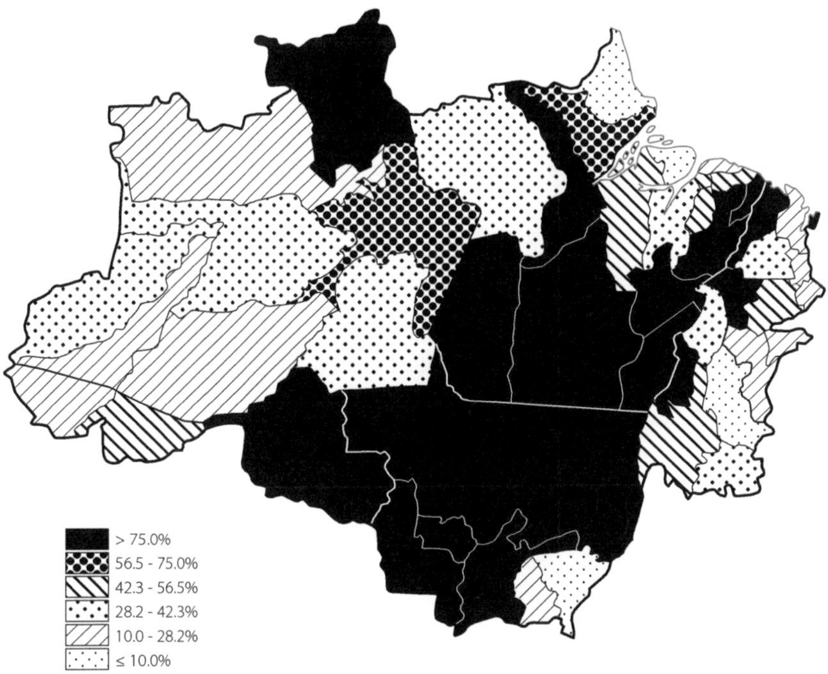

128 This meso-region coincides with the micro-region of Médio Amazonas.

The only development pole of the Polamazônia programme within this state was that of Juruá-Solimões, corresponding with a large part of the micro-region of Solimões-Japurá, which had a population in 1970 of 82 663 and still only 111 728 in 1980. The increase was therefore 35 %, which was not very high by Amazon standards. It should be remembered, however, that this development pole, like others, was not designated until 1975, so that the effect of this status on population growth could be only limited, especially since only 7 % of the total available budget for the programme was allocated to this pole (see Fig. 12).

Roraima is one of the least favourably located areas within Brazil. The northern part of the territory is formed by semi-humid hill country with poor soils, which are largely covered by natural pastures. Cattle farming had already been practised here for some time before 1980, the products of which, until 1975, were almost entirely exported to Venezuela and Guyana, because communications with these countries already existed, while they were still very inadequate with Manaus situated 500 km farther south. Since the mid-1970s, however, with opening of the road from Manaus to Boa Vista, communications had been improved. A further favourable factor was that the northern part of Roraima was designated a development pole in 1975. These changes will have contributed to a relatively high population increase during the 1970s: the population of the territory more or less doubled. In view of the unfavourable location within Brazil, however, and the extensive nature of the cattle ranching, the population in absolute terms was still very small (see Fig. 19). During the 1970s there was not any radical change in the population distribution. 89 % of the population in 1970 lived in the northern part, formed by the municipality of Boa Vista (with an area of 96 501 sq km), while only, about 11 % lived in the municipality of Caracarai, which occupies the southern half of Roraima and covers an area of 133 603 sq km.[129] In 1980 the percentages were 84.9 and 15.1, respectively. There were signs therefore that a slight shift was beginning, which must be related to the increasing use potential of the southern zone, thanks to the better accessibility afforded by the road between Manaus and Boa Vista.

A very uneven occupation also characterised the territory of Amapá, which was largely used for the exploitation of forest products (rubber, timber etc.) and extensive cattle farming, which was practised mainly on the savannahs. In the vicinity of the capital, Macapá, however, mainly along the railway to the port of Porto Santana, there was more cultivation of simple food crops to supply the urban market. The principal activity of Amapá, however, which was directly or indirectly responsible for the relatively high population growth, was the mining of manganese, which began in the 1950s and reached such a magnitude that, in 1978, about 58 %, of Brazilian production was concentrated in Amapá. The fact that one of the 15 *polos* designated in the Second Development Plan was located in Amapá is closely related to this mining potential. The small town of Macapá owed its importance partly to the presence there of the administration of the mining enterprise. In addition, it was the capital of the territory and possessed as such the largest part of the services structure.

---

129 Roraima had not been subdivided into various micro-regions. There was only one micro-region which coincided with de territory and consisted of two municipalities.

Figure 18. Share of each of the micro-regions of Amazônia Legal in the total population, 1960, 1970, 1980

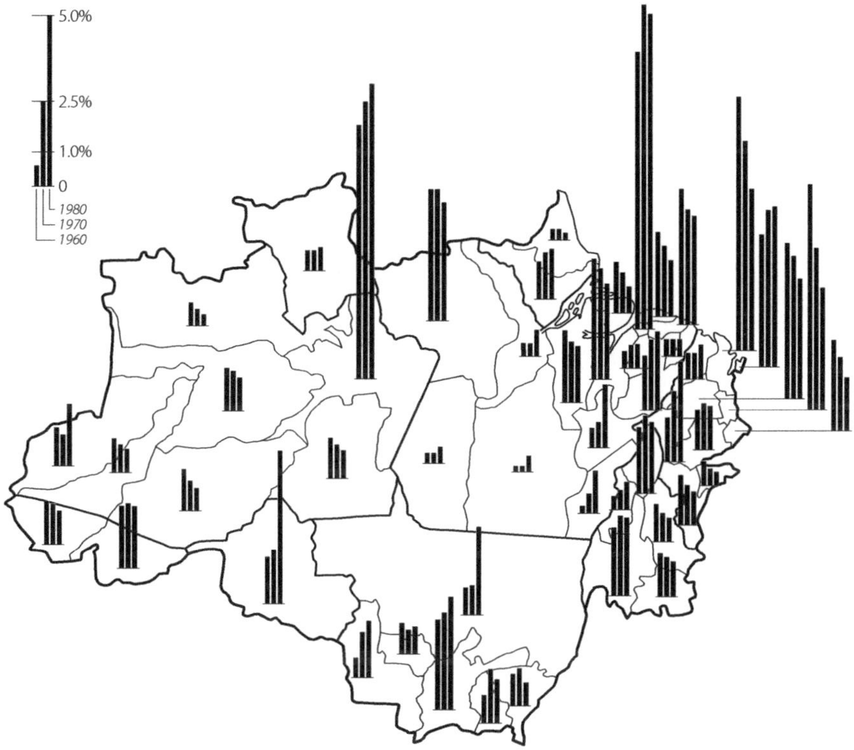

The dynamic effect of the mining activity was mainly responsible for the rather high population growth during the period 1970–1980, although the growth of 54.6 % was not very spectacular by Amazonian standards. In absolute terms, however, the population was still very modest (Table 8). In 1970 no less than 84.4 %, of the population was concentrated in the micro-region of Macapá and, in 1980, 89.8 %. The municipality of Macapá in turn, which occupies only 20 % of the total area of the territory, was the main zone of concentration within the micro-region, accounting for 75.3 % of the population in 1970 and 78.8 % in 1980. A somewhat greater dispersal of population might be expected in later years as a consequence of the completion in the early 1970s of a road link from Macapá northwards towards the frontier with French Guiana (see Fig. 19).

We consider lastly the population distribution in Acre. During the period 1970–1980 the population increase in this state was 40.8 %, which was not exceptionally high when viewed in the regional context. Although there was a road link with Porto Velho, very many migrants from the South East did not make use of it to settle in Acre. They preferred to seek a livelihood in the less distant Rondônia. Acre was therefore less popular, especially since the designation of part of Acre as a development pole (with 6.9 % of the total budget) had until then had relatively little effect.

Figure 19. Population size in each of the micro-regions of Amazônia Legal, 1960, 1970, 1980

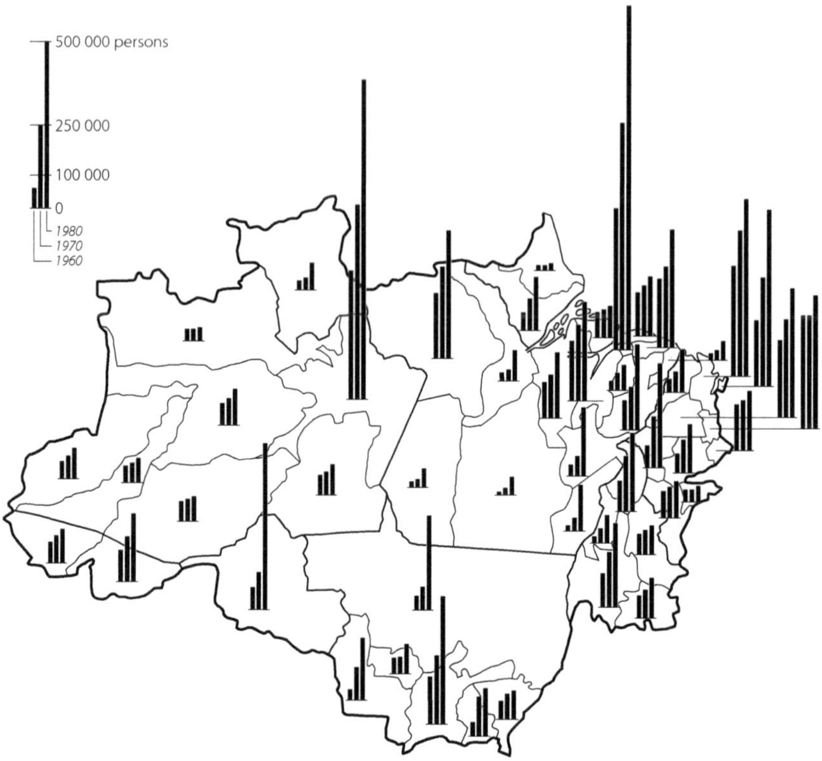

In this state, where the chief economic activities were the gathering of forest products and the practice of shifting cultivation, 61.4 % of the population in 1970 lived in the micro-region of Alto Purus, which covers 52.1 % of the area of the state and occupies its eastern half. 65.1 % of the population lived in this micro-region in 1980, which is indicative of a slight strengthening of its position. Within Alto Purus itself the greatest concentration was to be found in the municipality of Rio Branco, where 32.7 % of the total state population lived in 1970 and 39 % in 1980, although the municipality occupies only 9.4 % of the area of the state.

In conclusion, we may state the following. As was shown earlier, the population of the north-western sub-regions was still very small in 1970, at least with the exception of Amazonas to a certain extent. The population increase during the 1970s was not small in relative terms, but was yet not especially high by Amazonian standards, at least with the exception of Roraima. Consequently, these areas still had a very modest population in 1980, certainly in relation to their area. In 1970 the population was very unevenly distributed. The micro-regions of Alto Purus, Macapá and Médio Amazonas and the municipality of Boa Vista, which emerged as the main concentration areas, occupied only 21.6 % of the total area of the four states or territories. Nevertheless, in 1970, they held 64.2 % of the total population. In 1980, 69.2 % of the population lived there, from which it may be concluded that no important changes had occurred in the population distribution and that the occupation of north-west Amazônia was still very fragmentary. There was even a tendency for the degree of concentration to increase (see Figs. 18 and 19).

The occupation pattern in the part of Pará lying north of the River Amazon also fitted into the picture outlined above. The six municipalities it comprised, making up 22 % of the area of the state, accommodated only 5.7 % of the state population. The municipalities in question are Faro, Oriximiná, Obidos, Alenquer, Monte Alegre and Almeirim, which extend northwards from the Amazon to the frontier with Guyana and Surinam. The population within these municipalities was very much concentrated in the vicinity of the main river; their "hinterland" was practically uninhabited. Northern Pará could therefore equally be included with the "empty" north-west sector of Amazônia, despite the presence of the large-scale Jari project established there by the North American firm of Ludwig in order to provide employment. The centre of gravity of occupation in Pará still lay in the areas situated immediately on or south of the main river.

This observation brings us to a discussion of the growth and distribution pattern of the population in the southern and eastern sub-regions of Amazônia Legal.

Beginning in the western corner, Rondônia first deserves our attention. The particularly spectacular population growth which characterised this area since it was opened up in 1965 occurred mainly in the zones which are most favourably located in relation to the roads linking Cuiabá and Porto Velho, and Porto Velho and Abunã/Rio Branco. The six municipalities making up the north-eastern part of Rondônia (i. e. Porto Velho, Ariquemes, Ji-Paraná, Cacoal, Pimenta Bueno, and Vilhena) accordingly accounted for almost the whole population increase of the territory.[130] Not only was nearly the whole of the spontaneous colonisation concentrated here, but the various, relatively modest, official colonisation projects were also located here. The development pole designated under the Polamazônia programme also included the relatively more accessible parts of the territory, covering as it did the north-western part of Rondônia.

The municipality of Guajará Mirim, which forms the south-western part of Rondônia and occupies 26.3 % of the total area of the territory, is the only municipality not directly served by the roads mentioned above. This municipality accordingly grew little during the period 1970–1980: the population rose from 24 879 to 35 897, which was small in comparison with the population explosion of the territory as a whole.[131] As a result, Guajará Mirim contained only 7.1 % of the population of the territory in 1980. In 1970, however, when the other municipalities were less the scene of large-scale spontaneous colonisation and when various official projects still had to be carried out, the share of Guajará Mirim was as high as 21.4 %.

Striking differences are also to be observed in the new state of Mato Grosso. The micro-region of Norte Mato Grossense, which – as its name shows – covers the northern part of the new Mato Grosso and, as such, occupies no less than 70 % of the total area of the state, accommodated in 1970 only 10.6 % of the population. Communications were improved in the late 1970s, however, with the building of simple access roads and the completion of part of the BR-080 road and of the road from Cuiabá to Santarém. It is therefore not surprising that this micro-region experienced a remarkable increase during the 1970s, such that its share in the total population of the state rose to as much as 24.4 %. In absolute terms there was a growth from 64 878 to 285 168, i. e. more than a quadrupling. This growth was closely related to the further expansion

130 Reference is made here to municipalities because Rondônia had not been subdivided into micro-regions.

131 The limited growth was also related to a small extent to boundary changes.

of cattle farming (and sometimes also of arable farming and mining) and to the creation of two development poles (see Figs. 16–19).

In 1970 nearly 90 % of the total population was concentrated in the southern micro-regions of Alto Guaporé, Alto Paráguai, Baixada Cuiabána, Rondonópolis and Garças, which made possible a large absolute growth, amounting during the period 1970–1980 to 60.5 % of the total population increase of the state. Nevertheless, this demographic predominance began to weaken during the 1970s as a result of the spectacular increase just referred to in the more northerly zone.

The micro-regions situated in the south-west prove to have experienced the strongest absolute and relative growth; the increase in the south-eastern micro-regions, by contrast, was less. This means that the western part, which is served by the road from Cuiabá to Porto Velho, belonged, as far as its growth pattern is concerned, with the area with a strong population increase defined in Rondônia (see Figs. 16 and 17).

The rather narrow and elongated shape of northern Goiás and the fact that this area is completely bisected by the Belém–Brasília highway lead one to suppose that no noteworthy differentiation is to be expected in the population increase within this region. Nevertheless, significant differences are observable when the figures for the micro-regions are compared. The micro-regions of Extremo Norte Goiano, Baixo Araguaia Goiano and Médio Tocantins Araguaia, and the municipality of Araguaçu, which are situated in the west, in the more immediate vicinity of the Belém–Brasília highway, prove to have accounted for 84.3 % of the population growth during the decade 1970–80, and for as much as 84.8 % during the preceding decade, even though they cover only 59.2 % of the surface area of northern Goiás. The two micro-regions of Tocantins de Pedro Afonso and Serra Geral de Goiás, which are situated east of the Tocantins, and are, moreover, not directly bisected by the Belém–Brasília highway, although they are connected to it by a number of secondary roads accounted, on the other hand, for only 15.2 % of the population growth of northern Goiás between 1960 and 1970 (15.7 % in 1970–1980), although they cover 40 % of this sub-region. In 1960 the eastern micro-regions still held 35.6 % of the population of northern Goiás, but the proportion had fallen to 24.4 % in 1980. Because of the drawing power of the western areas, the population growth of the eastern micro-regions even remained below the national average, from which it may be concluded that migration must have had a significant influence on the uneven growth of the preceding two decades (Figs. 16 and 17).

In 1980, Pará – the state with the largest population of Amazônia Legal – still showed a strong concentration in the north-eastern corner, where the occupation process had been mainly concentrated over the past few centuries. The nine micro-regions located here, which include the city of Belém, accommodated 79.6 % of the population of the state in 1970 and still held 73.2% in 1980.[132] 62.4 % of the population growth during the decade 1970–1980 took place in this north-eastern corner, meaning that there were not as yet striking shifts in the distribution pattern. At most there were incipient signs of this, because the area's demographic dominance had decreased somewhat. This incipient loss of position also affected the micro-region of Belém, which held 31 % of the state's population in 1970 and 29.6 % in 1980 (Figs. 16–19).

---

132 The micro-regions in question are Furos (016), Campos de Marajó (017), Baixo Tocantins (018), Tomé-Açu (021), Guajarina (022), Salgado (023), Bragantina (024), Belém (025) and Viseu (026). They cover 18 % of the area of Pará.

Several micro-regions in eastern Pará could attribute their growth partly to the fact that they were situated along or in the vicinity of the road from Belém to Brasília. This applied particularly to the micro-regions of Araguaia Paraense (020) and Guajarina (022), which had a combined population in 1970 of 188 102 and 403 785 in 1980, amounting to an increase of 114.6 %. While the share of the two micro-regions in the total state population was 6.1 % in 1960, by 1980 it had risen to 11.5 %. To what extent accelerations in growth tempo were related only to the road building, however, and to the consequent enhanced possibilities for agricultural exploitation, or were also the consequence of the greater influence of the city of Belém, or of other factors, cannot be determined without further research.

It is somewhat easier to measure the direct consequences of the construction of the Transamazônica. Although the eastern area opened up by this highway also falls generally within the sphere of influence of the Belém–Brasília highway, the more westerly section does not and, in any event, there is no large city (such as Belém) in the vicinity of the Transamazônica that could significantly influence the process of population growth. The effect of the Cuiabá-Santarém link on the population increase can also be discovered relatively easily.

The ten Pará municipalities which, in 1980, were cut through by both of the above highways still contained only 11.1 % of the state population in 1970, but this proportion had risen to 13.9 % in 1980 as a result of the fact that the population increased from 243 412 to 488 598 during the period concerned and thereby more than doubled.[133] The population growth in these municipalities during the period 1970–1980 represented 18.7 % of the growth in the whole of the state of Pará (14.2 % if the municipality of Santarém is excluded). The most striking increase occurred in the municipalities of Marabá, Itupiranga, Jacunda, Altamira, and Itaituba, where the population tripled, or more than tripled, mainly as a result of spontaneous and planned colonisation activities. If these, in themselves impressive, population changes are compared, however, with the effects of the Belém–Brasília link in northern Goiás and southern Pará, one is bound to conclude that the influence of the Transamazônica and the Cuiabá–Santarém link should certainly not be over-estimated. The absolute population growth along both roads in 1970–1980 was only about half that which occurred within the zone of influence of the Belém–Brasília link. The background to this has already been discussed in another connection. Reference has also been made elsewhere to the fact that the part of Pará north of the Amazon still had only a small population.

We may in fact conclude in respect of Pará that, although there had been a somewhat wider dispersion of the population as a result of road construction and related activities in the years preceding 1980, there had not yet been any fundamental changes in the distribution pattern. The designation of a number of *polos* had also had only a small effect at the state level up to then. The long-occupied north-eastern corner was consequently still dominant demographically.

Lastly, reference should be made to western Maranhão. The northern part of this state had long had a denser population than the more southerly interior. This situation did not change fundamentally during the 1970s. The micro-regions of Gurupi (029), Baixada Occidental Maranhense (030), São Luis (031), Pindaré (034) and Mearim (035),

---

133 The municipalities in question are São João do Araguaia, Marabá, Itupiranga, Jacunda, Portel, São José Porfirio, Altamira, Itaituba, Aveiro and Santarém.

plus nine municipalities which together comprise the northern part of western Maranhão, had in 1960 76 %, in 1970 74.1 %, and in 1980 72 %, of the total population resident in the part of the state defined as forming part of the Amazônia Legal. The percentages do show, however, that its position was beginning to weaken. The area which gained from it was the central zone, served by the BR-230 road and comprising the micro-regions of Imperatriz (038), Alto Mearim e Grajaú (039) and Médio Mearim (040) and a few additional municipalities. While only 15.7 % of the population of western Maranhão lived in this central zone in 1960, by 1980 the proportion had risen to 21.9 %. This shift was related not so much to the designation of the area as a development pole, as to the extensive spontaneous colonisation which occurred in this area. The least populated area was the extreme south, the relative position of which was even weakened demographically (Figs. 18 and 19).

In view of the distribution pattern it is not surprising that population growth occurred mainly in the northern part of West Maranhão. It is the area in which São Luis is situated and it had relatively the best communications. The main road from Fortaleza to Teresina and Belém passes through this northern part of the state.

If the distribution pattern of the population within West Maranhão is considered in a wider context, it appears that the more densely populated north links up with the north-eastern part of the bordering state of Pará, where – as has been stated – the largest part of the population of Pará is resident.

In conclusion, the following may be stated with reference to the sub-areas of the south-eastern segment. Because these sub-areas contained a larger population and migration was largely directed towards them, it was here that the population increase mainly occurred. The relatively large population increase, however, does not mean that growth was more or less uniform over the whole of the southern and eastern zone. It actually occurred in a limited number of sub-regions, often the areas which had already been settled for a long time and/or had the best communications. There in fact existed here a very marked fringe of denser population and high growth. This fringe included the municipalities of north-east Rondônia, the micro-regions of southern Mato Grosso, those of North Goiás west of the Tocantins, the adjoining micro-regions of north-eastern Pará and, lastly, the northern micro-regions of western Maranhão (Fig. 19). The zone situated on the "inward" side of this series of important growth regions had a very small population in 1960 and 1970, with the exception to some extent of the long-established population axis in the immediate vicinity of the Amazon. Essentially, there was no radical change in this position despite the fact that certain sub-regions, such as the area lying within the sphere of influence of the Transamazônica, saw quite a marked relative population increase. What it essentially amounts to is that the population increase in southern and eastern Amazônia Legal may be primarily regarded as the result of a process that was occurring in Brazil over a long period, i. e. the advance of the frontier of denser occupation from the South East and the North East. In other words, it was primarily a question of the increasing integration of new areas in southern and eastern Amazônia Legal into the South East, the economic and demographic heartland of Brazil on the one hand, and into the North East, which may be regarded as a demographic core region, on the other. This process was accelerated mainly by the construction of a number of north-south links – the most important east-west link, the Transamazônica, made a much smaller contribution.

Aspects of the urbanisation process

It would be beyond the scope of the present text to consider in detail the process of urbanisation. Instead we must limit ourselves to a few main features of the 1970s, during which period Amazônia Legal experienced its greatest demographic growth. In 1970, 56 % of the Brazilian population was regarded as urban, but in Amazônia Legal no more than about 36 % of the population lived in urban settlements. This lower degree of urbanisation was closely related to the fact that, in the Amazon region, the emphasis was very much on agricultural activities. Considered in itself, however, the degree of urbanisation was not especially low, which is also understandable, since trading and transport activities (related to the gathering economy) were not unimportant there, mining had developed in a number of places, management and administrative functions had to be carried out, the agricultural population required urban services and the cities of Belém and Manaus, in particular, had grown because of a certain measure of industrialisation, based partly on the processing and working up of local raw materials and partly on the manufacture of various consumer goods. For Manaus there was the further factor that the city had experienced an explosive growth of its commercial activities as a free trade centre. Last, but not least, was the fact that many urban centres provided a temporary or more permanent home for workers who were trying to earn a livelihood in forest clearance or other activities related to the process of further opening up and colonisation of territory.

Figure 20. Population density in Amazônia Legal, 1960, by micro-region

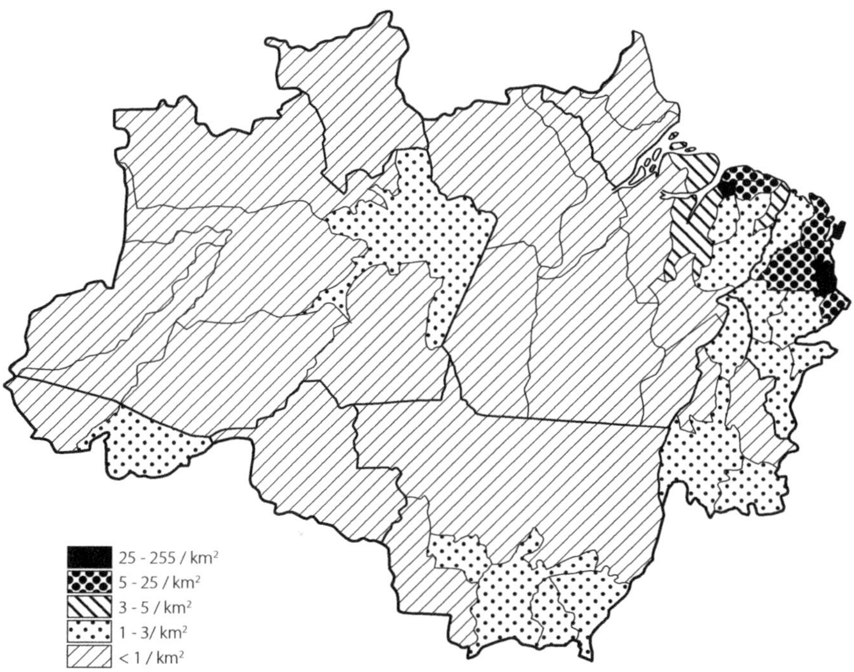

Figure 21. Population density in Amazônia Legal, 1970, by micro-region

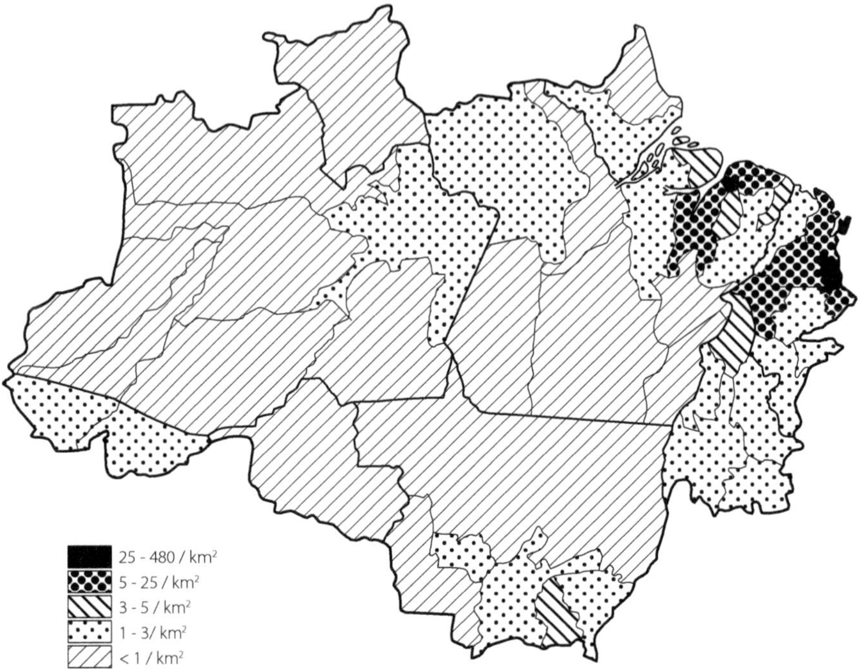

Figure 22. Population density in Amazônia Legal, 1980, by micro-region

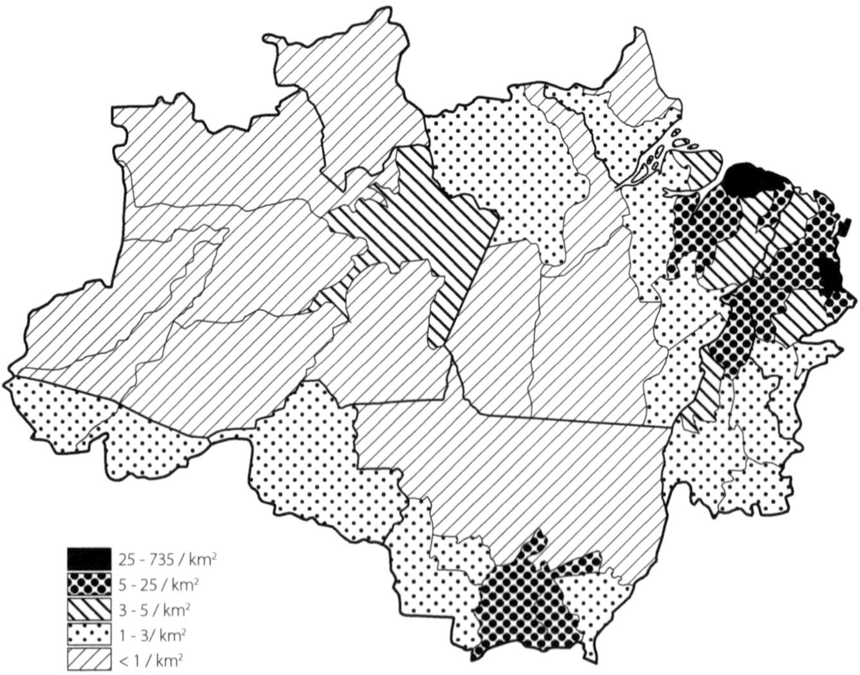

By 1980 the degree of urbanisation for Brazil had risen to 67.7%; in Amazônia Legal it had reached 45.8%. In 1980, therefore, the degree of urbanisation still lay below the national average, which is not surprising in view of the still strongly agricultural character of this region. The as yet relatively modest level of urbanisation appears not only from the proportion of town dwellers, but also from the fact that, of the 198 towns with more than 50 000 inhabitants identified in Brazil in 1980, only eleven were situated within the limits of Amazônia Legal. Four towns (i. e. Castanhal, Rondonópolis, Rio Branco and Macapá) had between 50 000 and 100 000 inhabitants, the remaining seven had more than that. They included Santarém, Porto Velho, Imperatriz, Cuiabá, São Luis, Manaus and Belém. The latter two were by far the largest settlements.

Examination of the level of urbanisation by sub-regions shows that there were not unimportant differences both in 1970 and 1980. The degree of urbanisation was relatively high in the states of Amazonas and Pará, which contain within their boundaries the two largest cities of Amazônia and numerous smaller towns along the main river. This also applied to the relatively small territories of Roraima and Amapá, where – as we have seen – the small population was highly concentrated in or near the metropolitan core with little dispersion beyond that. The latter was incidentally still true of Rondônia in around 1970. The degree of urbanisation was relatively low, on the other hand, in areas like Maranhão, Goiás and Acre, where there was a more dispersed rural occupation, partly by the larger agricultural enterprises, partly by simple small colonists.

Table 7. Size and growth of the urban population of Amazônia Leal, 1970–1980, by sub-region

Sub-region	Urban population 1970		Urban population 1980		Increase 1970-1980	
	Absolute	% of total popu-lation	Absolute	% of total popu-lation	Absolute	%
Amazonas	409 278	42.6	869 020	60.0	459 742	112.3
Roraima	17 929	43.1	49 622	60.5	31 693	177.1
Acre	60 557	37.8	135 754	44.2	75 197	124.2
Amapá	63 785	54.8	106 424	59.1	42 639	66.8
NW. Am. Leg.	551 549	41.3	1 160 820	58.5	609 271	110.5
W-Maranhão	577 288	24.7	997 577	32.8	420 269	72.8
Pará	1 037 340	47.2	1 702 403	48.5	665 063	64.1
N-Goiás	137 262	25,0	312 956	40.0	175 694	128.0
Mato Grosso	239 524	39.1	673 069	57.5	433 645	181.0
Rondôia	60 541	51.9	239 436	47.6	178 895	295.7
SE. Am. Leg.	2 051 955	35.3	3 925 421	43.1	1 873 466	91.3
Amaz. Legal	2 603 504	36.4	5 086 242	45.8	2 482 737	95.4
Brasil	52 904 744	56.0	82 013 375	67.7	29 108 631	55.0

Source: Sinopse Preliminar do Censo Demográfico, 1970, 1980.

Table 8. Population changes in the metropolitan municipalities of Amazônia Legal, 1960–1980

Metropolitan Municipality[1]	Population in		
	1960	1970	1980[2]
Belém (Paraá)	402 170	642 514	949 545
Manaus (Amazonas)	175 343	314 197	642 192
Rio Branco (Acre)	47 882	84 845	119 815
Porto Velho (Rondônia)	51 049	88 856	138 289
Macapá (Amapá)	46 905	87 755	140 624
Boa Vista (Roraima)	26 168	37 062	69 627
São Lluis (Maranhão)	159 628	270 651	460 320
Cuiabaá (Mato Grosso)	57 860	103 427	219 477
All municipalities	967 005	1 629 307	2 740 189

Source: Sinopse Preliminar do Censo Demográfico 1980. 1. The metropolitan municipality of the state of Goiás is situated outside Amazônia Legal. 2. The figure for 1980 is influenced by boundary changes.

A further striking fact is that the urban population almost doubled during the period 1970–1980. This means that the high population growth which characterised Amazônia Legal during this period was not purely an increase of the rural population, but was accompanied by a considerable urbanisation. In fact, the rate of urbanisation in Amazônia Legal during that time lay well above the national growth rate. Examination of the urban increase at the state and territory level reveals that, in some instances, there was an urban growth which was two to three times as great as the growth at the national level. The most spectacular changes occurred in Rondônia, the territory which – as we have seen – was characterised by a very explosive population increase.

The urban growth occurred partly in the larger centres of Amazônia Legal. The population of Manaus doubled during the 1970s, thanks to the free trade activities, increasing industrialisation, various agricultural development projects in the near environs and a greater service function for western Amazônia (related to greater accessibility). The population of the Belém metropolitan region rose from 656 351 in 1970 to 1 000 349 in 1980, a development to which, *inter alia*, a number of industrialisation projects supported by the SUDAM will have contributed. The other metropolitan municipalities also experienced a marked population increase (Table 10). While the population of the eight metropolitan municipalities still accounted for only 18.7% of the total population of Amazônia Legal in 1960, by 1970 the proportion was already 22.8% and, in 1980, 24.7%.[134] The position of the metropolitan municipalities was therefore strengthened rather than weakened. What is striking, however, is not only the growth of the larger urban centres; numerous smaller places also "profited" from the high population increase of Amazônia Legal. This is understandable because the advancing colonisation process created a foundation for more and larger service centres (country towns). Moreover, many migrants settled precisely in these smaller towns either temporarily or more permanently – as a base from which to carry out forest clearance and reclamation, or from which to consider the possibilities of establishing their own holdings. These were partly people who had never had farms of their own, but partly

134 Part of the population of the metropolitan municipalities was classified as rural.

also peasants who had been driven out of the areas of spontaneous colonisation by large landowners, land thieves and speculators. It was particularly in the southern and eastern fringe that the urban settlements grew in number and extent, since that was where the population increase within Amazônia Legal mainly occurred.

Conclusions

The most important conclusions regarding the population growth and population dispersion in Amazônia Legal in the 1960s and 1970s are summarised briefly below.

- In around 1960 the North was still a scarcely colonised region in which the extremely small population was still very unevenly distributed. This was also true of Amazônia Legal, which covers 58.5 % of the surface area of Brazil, but held only 7.3 % of the population.
- From 1960 the Brazilian government introduced a number of measures to bring about the further integration and development of the Amazon region. Since then the population growth of Amazônia Legal lay above the national average, to such an extent that the share of Amazônia Legal in the total Brazilian population had risen to 9.2 % in 1980. The growth was especially marked after 1970. One could certainly no longer refer to the region as one of stagnation.
- Amazônia Legal nevertheless still accounted for only a modest proportion of the national population growth (1960–1970: 8.5 %; 1970–1980: 15.2 %). The increase in the Brazilian population did not occur predominantly in the Amazon region, but in the economic and demographic heartland of the South East and, to a lesser extent, in the North East. Through a series of physical and socio-economic circumstances the Amazon region, despite the implementation of the Government policies, still had a relatively limited attraction for the Brazilian population. Approximately a half of the population growth of Amazônia Legal during the period 1970–1980 was still accounted for by natural increase.
- The population growth occurred in all the states and territories of Amazônia Legal, but during the period 1970–1980, in which the greatest increase occurred, it remained below the regional average in Amazonas, Acre, western Maranhão and North Goiás, so that the share of these areas in the total population of Amazônia Legal fell somewhat. The position of the other sub-regions was strengthened, except for Amapá, where the population share remained the same.
- During the period 1970–1980 no less than 83.2 % of the total population growth of Amazônia Legal occurred in the south-eastern segment, formed by Rondônia, Mato Grosso, North Goiás, Pará and West Maranhão, which together cover 58.2 % of the area of Amazônia Legal. These areas already had a considerably larger population, so that the natural increase could be much greater there. Moreover, migration was directed mainly towards these sub-regions. The explanation for this is to be found mainly in the circumstance that these southern and eastern sub-regions are more favourably located in relation to the economic and demographic heartland (South East Brazil), to which they are linked by a number of major roads, and in the fact that the agricultural development projects were concentrated mainly in these southern and eastern states and territories, partly as a reflection of this

more favourable location and the relatively good communications. The north-western segment, comprising Acre, Amazonas, Roraima and Amapá, consequently accounted for only 16.9 % of the growth.

- Examination of the population distribution and growth at the micro-regional level shows a very uneven pattern in the north-western segment of Amazônia Legal. 64.2 % of the population in 1970 lived in three micro-regions (Alto Purus, Macapá and Médio Amazonas) and one municipality (Boa Vista), which together cover 21.6 % of the states and territories concerned. This concentration even showed a tendency to increase, because the population growth occurred mainly in those same areas, with the result that they contained 69.2 % of the population in 1980. Consequently, the occupation of north-west Amazônia Legal still presented very much a pattern of enclaves in 1980.
- In the south-eastern segment, too, the distribution and growth were uneven. The increase proved to have occurred mainly in the sub-regions which had already been settled for a long time and/or were the most accessible and favourably located. The areas specifically concerned are the municipalities of north-east Rondônia, the micro-regions of southern Mato Grosso, those of North Goiás west of the Tocantins, the adjoining ones of north-east Pará and, lastly, the northern micro-regions of western Maranhão. The area situated on the inner side of this chain of important growth regions had a very small population in 1960 and 1970, with the exception to some extent of the long-existing population axis in the immediate neighbourhood of the River Amazon. There was no radical change in this situation in 1980, despite the fact that certain zones, such as the sphere of influence of the Transamazônica, had experienced a relatively marked population increase.
- What the facts summarised in the last paragraph essentially mean is that the population increase of southern and eastern Amazônia Legal in the period 1960–1980 may be primarily regarded as the result of a process which had already been happening in Brazil over a long period, i. e. the advance from the South East and North East of the frontier of denser occupation. In other words, it was primarily a matter of the increasing integration of new areas of southern and eastern Amazônia Legal into the South East, the economic and demographic heartland of the country, on the one hand, and into the North East, which may be regarded as a demographic core area, on the other.
- The population changes described above were accompanied by what was, by Brazilian standards, a fairly marked urban growth.
- The process of population growth proved to have been accelerated by the construction of a number of north-south links; the most important east-west link (the Transamazônica) made a much smaller contribution. The agricultural and cattle farming projects supported by the SUDAM also proved to have had an influence. These were concentrated mainly in the south-eastern fringe, which was characterised by a rapid and considerable population growth. The establishment of a free trade zone in and around Manaus and various industrial development projects in Belém and Manaus primarily influenced the population growth of these two cities themselves. The influence of the programme of planned colonisation carried out by the government and concentrated along a section of the Transamazônica was relatively small. A similar programme was carried out in Rondônia, but here the possibilities for spontaneous colonisation appear to have played a greater part

in the explosive population growth. The development poles designated within the framework of the Second Development Plan undoubtedly had an influence on the population growth but, because of their recent creation, they could have been of only limited significance, while the lack of adequate information makes it difficult to measure their effects. Moreover; it must be realised that there was generally an interaction at work in the sense that the government capitalised on economic developments already in progress in the area concerned when deciding to designate one or more poles. It is exceptional for the development process to have been set in train by the designations (as in the case of Carajás).

- In the light of the foregoing conclusions, the efforts to let Amazônia Legal have a greater share of the population growth in the years after 1980 would have the most success if the development measures were directed towards the areas which were most favourably located relative to the South East and North East and had good communications with them. In other words, the government would have done well mainly to guide and support the process of the advancing frontier of more intensive occupation. Fewer results could be expected from the measures to develop the still extremely thinly populated regions west and north of the frontier. At best, such measures would create enclaves of development. Viewed in this light, a less hasty opening up of the extreme north of Amazônia Legal by means of the Perimetral Norte would have been only sensible.

Statistical sources employed

Banco da Amazônia. 1970. *Amazônia: Estatísticas Básicas.* Belém: BASA.

Instituto Brasileiro de Geografía e Estatística. 1971. *Sinopse Estatística do Brasil.* Rio de Janeiro: IBGE.

Instituto Brasileiro de Geografía e Estatística. 1971 . *VIII Recenseamento Geral do Brasil. Sinopse Preliminar do Censo Demográfico 1970.* Rio de Janeiro: IBGE.

Instituto Brasileiro de Geografía e Estatística. 1981. *IX Recenseamento Geral do Brasil. Sinopse Preliminar do Censo Demográfico I980.* Rio de Janeiro: IBGE.

References[135]

Kleinpenning, Jan M.G. 1973. *Brazilië.* Roermond: Romen.

Kleinpenning, Jan M.G. 1977. "An Evaluation of the Brazilian Policy for the Integration of the Amazon Region (1964–1974)." *Tijdschrift voor Economische en Sociale Geografie* LXVIII, no. 5: 297–311.

Kleinpenning, Jan M.G. 1978. "A Further Evaluation of the Policy for the Integration of the Amazon Region (1974–1976)." *Tijdschrift voor Economische en Sociale Geografie* LXIX, no, 1–2: 78–86.

Saunders, John. 1974. "The Population of the Brazilian Amazon Today." In *Man in the Amazon*, edited by Charles Wagley, 160–180. Gainesville: University Presses of Florida.

135 Since the present text has been based mainly on an analysis of statistical material, we shall limit ourselves here to mentioning a few publications of a summary kind.

The development of Altamira, before and after the construction of the Transamazônica[1]

Ron Milder

Altamira up to the late 1960s

The town of Altamira, located on the Xingu, a tributary of the Amazon, existed for many years before the national road opening up the territory, the Transamazônica, came to run alongside the river. The foundation must be credited to the Jesuits. After the Portuguese had chased the Dutch from the Amazon region, they were the first to penetrate the tropical rainforest and started colonisation in the period 1625–1750 (Umbuzeiro 1983, 19). They brought the local Indigenous tribes together into communities, instructing them in the Christian faith and using them as labourers. They made a start in farming and set up small trading companies. Altamira was one of such communities.

After the forced departure of the Jesuits from Brazil in 1758 and, therefore, also from the Amazon, the communities fell increasingly into decline, including Altamira. It was not until about 1870 that the settlement was revived when Capuchin Fathers and local Indigenous tribes established a land connection between Altamira and the lower Xingu. This allowed one to penetrate further upstream into the area of the Xingu without being hindered by the "Big Bend" with its numerous rapids.

Around the end of the nineteenth century, the distance was shortened by a new road, more or less corresponding to the current connection between Altamira and Vitória Port.[137] The shortening mainly benefited the traders, who at the time still monopolised the trade in rubber, Brazil nuts and hides from Souzel (farther downstream). As a result, Altamira was able to grow into a trading post of such great importance that, in 1912, it became an independent municipality. The "town" became even more important when rubber mining in the Xingu valley flourished. Local landowner and trader José Porfírio modernised the port of Vitória with a view to the rubber.

136 Based on Milder's master's thesis written in 1985/1986. Fieldwork was carried out in Altamira from August 1984 to February 1985.

137 The construction of this road came about in stages, because the abolition of slavery in 1888 meant that the supply of labour immediately dried up (Umbuzeiro 1983, 20).

Figure 1. General reference map of Altamira and its region

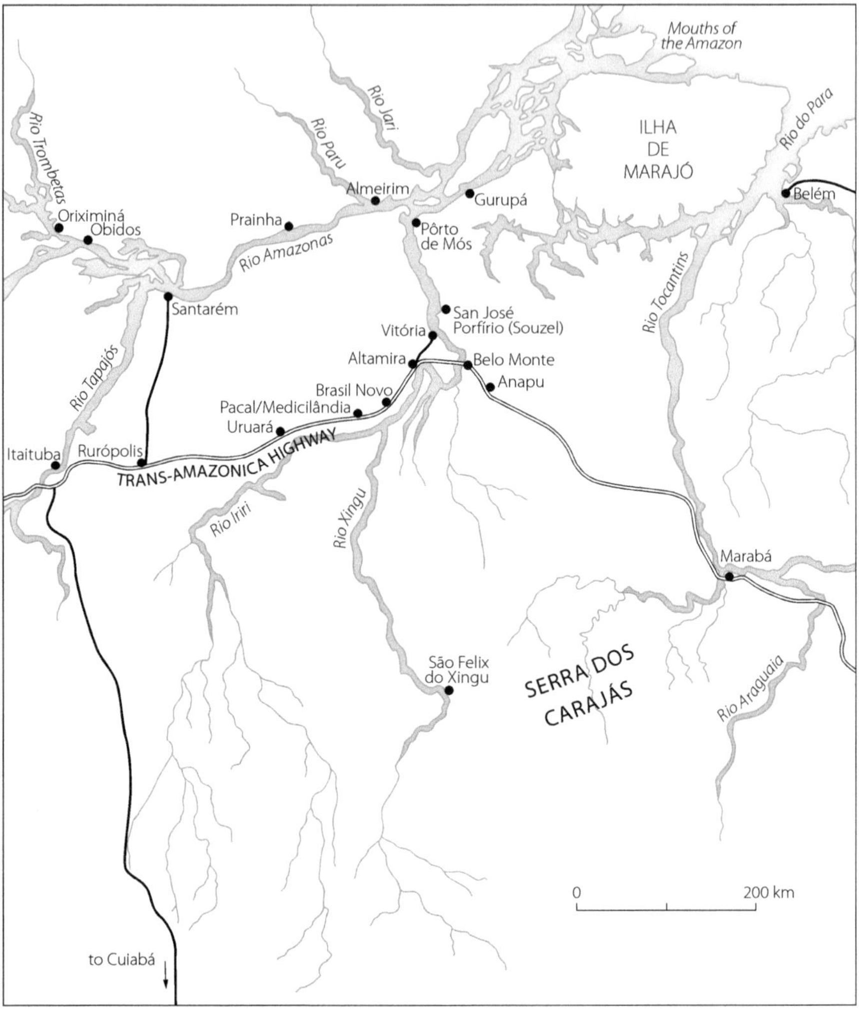

Source: Elaboration by author.

The recession of the 1930s and the crisis in rubber gathering also sent Altamira's economy into crisis. Altamira suffered the fate of so many other Amazonian river towns whose economic development depended on the extra-regional demand for extractive products. High demand led to an influx of labour from elsewhere (mostly *nordestinos*). They earned little. The people who really profited were the local traders and the export firms based in Belém and Manaus who were only interested in favourable transport options (a navigable river and suitable ports). As soon as foreign demand for extractives fell sharply, the entire economy, in the absence of diversity, reverted to the level of local self-sufficiency. The traders stopped buying rubber and moved elsewhere or started something else. And the workers who had been attracted by the boom abandoned rubber collection, moved away or continued to live on the spot and started subsistence farming.

During World War II, when the Allies had an urgent need for rubber, the rubber tap started running again. The government took an active stance and established a special credit bank, the predecessor of the Banco da Amazônia S.A. For Altamira, the revival led to the establishment of a government health post and improvements to the road link with Vitória. This new "rubber boom" was followed in the course of the 1960s by a lively trade in animals and skins. Many rubber tappers then exchanged their work for that of hunter.

In the 1960s, the one-sided character of the rural economy was somewhat broken. The agricultural sector started to grow to meet the growing need for food in the regional capital Belém. In the region with fertile *terra roxa* soils, west of Altamira, arable fields gave way to pastures. This region had become accessible through the expansion of the local road network. The local government began by setting up a modest colonisation project and trying to get a cooperative off the ground – with little success.[138] However, there was no question of a spectacular expansion of agro-pastoral activity. The local market for arable products (not being grains) was too limited and the facilities for sales, almost exclusively aimed at storage and transport, were far from sufficient. Agriculture also remained at a low technical level.

Sales, almost exclusively oriented towards Belém, consisted of rubber, Brazil nuts, hides, rice and wood. Agriculture, which took advantage of the fertile *terra roxa* soils in the area surrounding the town, contributed 94 % of the total value of production in the municipality. The largest branch was extraction, with 34 % of the total production value. In that year, 1968, the trade in animals and skins took off and was estimated to account for three quarters of this. In addition to agriculture, trade played an important role in the economy, especially in Altamira itself (SERFHAU/Ministerio do Interior 1970).

Even before the Transamazônica was built, Altamira was the most important place in the Xingu valley. It was the collection centre of rubber, Brazil nuts and other products collected in the rainforest that were transported via a short and good road connection to the port of Vitória, located at the point where the Xingu River was still navigable. From there they were shipped to Belém, the export port at the mouth of the Amazon. All important administrative functions were concentrated in the town and, from 1948, it was also the seat of the diocese. This explains why there were already a hospital and a secondary school in Altamira.

This diversification of the local economy in the 1960s attracted migrants and accelerated population growth: the rate of growth was above average for the entire state of Pará. In 1960, the municipality of Altamira had 12 100 inhabitants and the urban zone 3210; in 1970 there were 14 000 and 7000 respectively (Matznetter 1981, 114).

138 The cooperative was in debt to the bank and was therefore unable to provide credit to its members.

Altamira in 1970[139]

By 1970, Altamira had a modest secondary sector in terms of both production value (6%) and employment (6.6%).[140] Of the fifteen companies, eight were active in the food sector (including a number of bakeries). There were also three sawmills, two brickyards, one rice huller and one coffee roaster.[141] As far as private initiatives are concerned, the contribution of the diocese should certainly not go unmentioned: Altamira owed this to a sawmill and a printing works. The main problems faced by the industrial sector at the time were the high transport costs for the supply of raw materials and the lack of specialised labour.

Table 1. The labor force aged ten years and older in 1970 and 1980 classified by sector

Sector	1970		1980	
	Abs.	%	Abs.	%
Primary sector	3332	73.7	3797	61.1
Secondary sector	297	6.6	103	17.8
Tertiary sector	890	19.7	1311	21.1
Total	4519	100	6211	100
% of total population	29.4		27.6	

In the tertiary sector, especially commerce, retail sales dominated businesses that usually sold all kinds of goods for daily living. In addition, Altamira had two wholesale stores, one petrol station and a few specialist stores (household appliances). A small number of merchants, who possessed a boat, monopolised the sales market; they arranged the transport farther upstream.

At the time, Altamira had two bank branches. The BASA (Banco da Amazonia S.A.) had established itself to support rubber extraction and the Banco do Brasil opened a branch in 1965 to help develop the fledgling agro-pastoral sector.

In the field of education, Altamira was fortunate to have the presence of a secondary school (*do 2do grau*[4]), founded by the local sisters. However, it was visited only by the children of the elite, for whom it was a springboard to university. For the majority of the local population, admission costs were too high a barrier. The other educational facilities were inadequate. The interior also suffered from a shortage of teachers.

The health care facilities were limited to a post of the Serviço da Saúde de Pará (SESP) and the hospital set up by the diocese (25 beds). A large part of the population drew on their own resources.

Even before the Transamazônica reached Altamira, it already had some infrastructure. In Vitória it had a well-equipped harbour and the town itself had a small harbour without a quay, from which the connections with the interior were maintained. The

139 Data taken from the SERFHAU report on the municipality of Altamira (SERFHAU/Ministério do Interior 1970).

140 Primary sector: 73.7%; tertiary sector: 19.7% (SEPLAN 1980, part 1: Perfil Municipal).

141 A coffee roaster and a rice huller had already been operating in Altamira for several decades; the latter initially had to bring in the rice from elsewhere (Umbuzeiro 1983, 73 f.).

other connections with the outside world were limited to a small airport, a radio station and a telephone exchange.

The water supply network, which had been installed a few years earlier, was not functioning properly. Most residents still had to make do with wells (*poços*). In 1970, the state electricity company CELPA installed an electricity grid and a small "plant" that ran on diesel oil. There was no sewage system. The streets were not paved and most of the houses were built of clay and wood (except those in the centre).

From the social composition of the population it could be concluded that, in around 1970, Altamira did not yet have such a sharp social stratification as it would later on. The independent professionals had the highest status. They owned land and cargo boats and were involved in trade, especially with the interior. At that time it was not yet possible to speak of a powerful group of traders and entrepreneurs or of a large number of officials.

Changes due to the construction of the Transamazônica

The construction of the Transamazônica, in 1971–1972, gave Altamira, hitherto only accessible by river, a direct connection by land with other parts of Brazil and a whole new period of development began. Simultaneously with the construction, the Federal government started a project in the area of Altamira, as well as near Itaituba and Marabá, for the assisted settlement of landless farmers and agricultural workers who no longer had land and work elsewhere in Brazil. This colonisation project was discussed in Part 2 of this book. In the second half of the 1970s, Altamira became one of the development centres of the state of Pará in the Federal government's development strategy. Commercial activity then grew explosively, as did construction activity. The number of government institutions grew significantly and migrants poured in from all parts of Brazil. The emergence of export cultures such as cocoa, pepper and sugar cane and extensive livestock farming led to further expansion and diversification of the commercial and service sectors and the emergence of new industrial sectors. Altamira turned into a "boom town," underwent a major metamorphosis in a short time and became the informal capital of the Transamazônica.

The construction work, not only for the road, but also for the housing for *colonos* and civil servants, caused a boom in the commercial and industrial sector. The industrial sector was enriched with two new brick factories, one in Altamira itself, the other along the Transamazônica (Umbuzeiron 1983, 74). The number of commercial establishments tripled in one year.[142] Traders in building materials and the retail trade, in particular, benefited from the construction boom. A number of traders were attracted by the new market that had now been opened up and from the direct supply channels from the Centro-Sul. They bought a piece of land for a pittance and started to set up wholesale stores in food and building materials. Many made a substantial profit during the construction boom and moved elsewhere after the boom had subsided. A

142 131 in 1971, 337 branches a year later. After the heyday of the construction boom, the commercial sector would also contract somewhat. But in 1975 the municipality of Altamira still numbered 261 businesses with 600 employees (SERFHAU/Ministerio do Interior 1970; IBGE 1976a).

few merchants remained in Altamira from then on and managed to gradually expand their holdings and not just wholesalers.[143]

Photo 15. One of the older roads seen in the direction of the cathedral (1985)[144]

Photo 16. Houses built fort he INCRA staff (1985)

143 They had interests in commercial buildings and apartments, hotels and restaurants; one of them controlled the distribution of oil and petrol.

144 Photos by Ron Milder.

The retail trade expanded significantly. The newly arrived government officials and tradespeople created such a rapidly growing need for daily foodstuffs that the local food supply could not cope and supplies from Belém and São Paulo became necessary.[145] This increased the cost of living, but prices did not reach such exorbitant levels as in the isolated traditional riverine communities, where the local trader ruled. As more business was added in a particular industry, prices even started to fall. The price level for crops from the region itself also fell after canned foods from the Centro-Sul started to flood the market. The collapse of the construction boom after a few years brought the death blow to specialised businesses. However, the *secos e molhados* shops, with their varied assortment, managed to hold their own.[146] These stores sourced their food as much as possible from *colonos*, who bought items from them, whether on credit or not.[147] The owners could keep their heads above water by themselves and also buy on credit and respond to specific needs of the moment.[148]

The companies and institutions established in Altamira not only fulfilled a function for the town, but also had a nurturing function for the area beyond. Altamira's sphere of influence extended from 250 km towards Itaituba to 220 km towards Marabá, taking the Transamazônica as the east-west axis. The region thus defined corresponded more or less to the district of Altamira as covered by the Comissão Executiva do Plano de Recuperação Econônic-Ruralda Lavoura Cacaueira (CEPLAC) and the Empresa de Assistência Técnica e Extensão Rural (EMATER). As for the north-south direction, the sphere of influence extended at least as far as Porto de Mós (northwards) and São Felix do Xingu (southwards), with the Xingu River as the axis, at least as based on the catchment area of the Altamira-based consumer durables stores. However, the borders were less sharp here, because Porto de Mós was also supplied via the Amazon River and because São Felix do Xingu got a direct road connection with the Belém–Brasília road in 1982.

Another notable change was the arrival of a number of Federal (and other) government agencies to deal with regional development. Altamira became the seat of the coordination centre of the Instituto Nacional de Colonização e Reforma Agrária (INCRA) for the colonisation projects along the Transamazônica. A large number of tasks were entrusted to this institution. It had to demarcate and subdivide the public lands; select suitable farmers; build homes for the settlers; distribute seeds and other production supplies. Even the sale of production surpluses would be handled by INCRA. The lending was arranged together with the Banco do Brasil.

The INCRA remained in Altamira until 1976.[149] In that year it was moved to Brasil Novo, located 50 km further west. After the failure of the small-scale colonisation projects, INCRA limited its range of tasks to the demarcation and allotment of Federal

---

145 At the same time, some "luxury" food crops, such as beans, found their way into outlets in the Centro-Sul, where such crops were more expensive, as one city councilor told me.

146 *Secos e molhados* (literally: dry and wet) are mini-grocery-cum-department stores. The information in the main text is taken from interviews with two such shops

147 Buying on credit was essential in this region, given the declining turnover in the rainy months; a number of *travessões* (side roads) then became impassable.

148 An owner of a *secos e molhados*, in 1975, started selling hand tools for prospectors in 1980. At the time it was the best selling part of its range.

149 Since then, this coordination centre has had the official tasks of maintaining and opening new *travessoes*, the administrative administration of the *agrovilas* and Brasil Novo; and the distribution of *lotes* among the newcoming migrants.

lands and the selection of settlers. A case like the transport of the produced food crops was henceforth left to private individuals. The INCRA also divested the sugar cane processing factory along the Transamazônica.

The regional development body for Amazônia, the Superintendência do Desenvolvimento da Amazônia (SUDAM), also had a branch in Altamira.[150] Livestock, arable, commercial timber and mining companies had to strengthen the regional economy with support from SUDAM. Altamira also became a regional focal point of EMATER-Pará.[151] From the beginning, this agency has been concerned with the dissemination of new technical applications, seed varieties and other means of production among the settlers. It also provided technical assistance and acted as an intermediary at the Federal banks for the financial support of certain cultures. EMATER started expanding pepper and coffee production as early as 1972.

The opening up of the region meant that huge areas of virgin land became accessible. That attracted migrants from all over the world to Altamira. As a result, two years after the start of the construction boom, the town had a population twice as large as in 1970: 7000 in 1970 and 12–13 000 in 1972 (Matznetter 1981, 114).

Polamazônia. Large scale and privatisation (1974-1980)

In the mid-1970s, a switch took place in Federal development policy. In the Second National Development Plan, the Amazon region was assigned the role of exporter of meat, cocoa, pepper, sugar cane, timber and minerals and ores. In the plan, a clear choice was made for rational occupation by large and medium-sized capital-intensive companies, both in. the livestock sector and for the production of agricultural crops. Thousands of hectares of land at once were given to Brazilian entrepreneurs and multinationals. In order to attract private investors to these sectors, the public investment needed to modernise the infrastructure was concentrated at a limited number of development poles (Programa Polamazônia). The Altamira/Transamazônica region was also declared a development pole.

Altamira went through a brief period of stagnation in the mid-1970s due to a decline in public investment. Small-scale colonisation projects were given less priority in Federal development policy after 1974 and, moreover, the focus of migration flows shifted to other areas, such as Rondônia, which in 1976 had got a direct connection with the Centro-Sul. At the end of the 1970s, however, the trend turned for the better, as new growth impulses emerged, thanks to Polamazônia.

First of all, the asphalting of the Belém–Brasília road provided a better quality connection with central and southeastern Brazil. In addition, the main ports on the rivers were equipped with more modern facilities, thanks to the government's efforts to stimulate river transport and reduce road transport, which had become more expensive. The port of Vitória was also modernised.

---

150 Closed in 1985 under pressure from spending cuts.

151 EMATER's Altamira district comprised five sites: one in Altamira itself and the others along the Transamazônica; in Anapu (Km 180 east of Altamira), Brasil Novo (Km 54 west), Nova Fronteira (Km 80) and Uruara (Km 180).

Altamira also began to reap the benefits of the promised investments from the Polamazonia programme. There was a new airfield; a more modern water supply network, new barracks, a slaughterhouse and a municipal public market. The main streets were paved.[152] All kinds of government institutions, such as the Federal banks, the electricity company and the state hospital, were given more spacious housing. New institutions such as CEPLAC (serving cocoa cultivation) and the Instituto Brasileiro de Desenvolvimento Florestal (IBDF), which was engaged in forestry and reforestation, were established in Altamira. A department of the Bureau of Statistics (IBGE) and various "clubs" of entrepreneurs (including Lions) were established.

A third growth impulse came from the large timber and mining companies. They formed new markets for retail trade and services (repair). The large companies provided considerable employment for the local population. Tertiary activity benefited from the emerging middle class in the rural and urban environment.

Lastly, general population growth stimulated development. The flow of migrants increased again, this time mainly from the Centro-Sul. According to official figures, Altamira had 19 400 inhabitants in 1978; according to local sources, the number was closer to 25 000, a doubling since 1971.

From the second half of the 1970s, Altamira showed a particular growth in those functional activities linked to the regional economy, especially in the sectors that emerged within the framework of Polamazônia. We discuss successively the Federal institutions and banks, the private service institutions, the suppliers of production supplies, the commercial firms, the private banks and the industrial sector.

The Federal government institutions located in Altamira were faced with new tasks thanks to the changed government policy and the aforementioned developments. This includes the Federal banks. Some examples:

CEPLAC became responsible for expanding commercial cocoa farming and was to supply seed, fertiliser and other production supplies, provide technical guidance and provide agricultural education at subsidised prices.

The Empresa Brasileira de Pesquisa Agropecuária de Pará (EMBRAPA) set up a separate research department in Altamira. By working on seed varieties adapted to local climate conditions, this government agency hoped to increase the productivity of food crops and export cultures.

EMATER started supplying fertilisers to pepper producers and brokered credit applications. In the 1980s the institution began distributing seed and fertiliser for the cultivation of coffee, guaraná and cotton (the latter since 1984).

The tasks of the INCRA decreased as a result of the changed government policy. It was now concerned only with regulating land-ownership relations and no longer with the preparation, implementation and supervision of small-scale colonisation projects.[153]

The Federal banks, Banco de Amazônia S.A.A and Banco do Brasil, received the necessary financial resources from the Federal government and were expected to dis-

152 All the municipalities through which the Transamazônica ran were declared National Security Areas in 1970. This meant, among other things, that the mayor was directly appointed by the governor of the state rather than elected.

153 The sugar cane processing factory in Pacal (92 km west of Altamira) had also passed into private hands during the 1970s.

tribute them among the various economic sectors in accordance with the guidelines set out in from government policy.[154] In practice, this meant that the banks were not given any leeway for additional support measures. This was possible only if they used their own resources for this. The Banco do Brasil, for example, had its own support programme for rubber, mining and local infrastructure since 1984.

Export crops and livestock have benefited most from the credit programme for the region.[155] The Banco do Brasil had opened a separate branch in the centre of the pepper, cocoa and sugar cane production area. Of the sawmills, only the export-oriented companies were supported, because only in these were production stable and sales assured.

The Federal banks were also involved in the marketing and processing of "national" food crops such as rice and maize. They subsidised the use of pre-processing installations, while the alternative energy supply was not neglected either.[156] Production costs had to be kept as low as possible and the quality of the harvest had to be improved.

The majority of government agency and Federal bank personnel had been brought in from elsewhere. They enjoyed certain privileges in Altamira in the areas of housing and health care.[157]

Of the private service institutions, mention should be made of PLANTERRA, an agency established in 1978 that made production plans for individual companies in the livestock sector, pepper, sugar cane and guarana cultivation. The office was located in Altamira and was established because there was an EMATER subsidiary and because of the large number of bids from (potential) clients. PLANTERRA also had a branch in the centre of the cocoa, pepper and sugar cane production area. Another private institution was the engineering company CNEC, which was investigating the technical possibilities of a hydroelectric power station on the Xingu River.

The number of private firms that supplied agricultural means of production only began to increase in the years 1977–1978 after a number of rural cooperatives that previously took care of deliveries, had gone bankrupt.[158] One of the firms was attracted to the flourishing pepper culture and livestock farming. At that time, the pepper producers still used large amounts of fertilisers and pesticides. Later they would switch to natural fertilisers, because the costs of fertilisers were too high.

The three specialist shops for motor cycles/chainsaws, set up by managers from Southern Brazil, met 90 % of the need.[159] Their catchment area stretched for 200 km

154 The Federal government had a 51 % majority stake in Banco do Brasil; the remaining 49 % were the bank's own resources. In 1985 a study was underway to privatise the bank.

155 Animal husbandry was an attractive sector for a policy aimed at rapid occupation. Investing in livestock farming was beneficial for the bank because the investments could be recouped in the short term (on average after four years).

156 With regard to the alternative energy supply, I am referring to the introduction of mini-distillers for alcohol and a gas installation that ran on faeces.

157 Example: the Federal banks had their own houses and recreational facilities; CEPLAC paid part of the health care costs for its employees and had its own loan fund. At some shops one could buy on credit.

158 The information below is based on interviews with two businesses in agricultural inputs and one that dealt in engines and chainsaws.

159 In the southern states (particularly Paraná) the growth prospects had diminished to a minimum due to continued deforestation and sharper competition.

along the Transamazonica.[160] One of the businesses, started in 1977, had also branches in Itaituba, Santarém and in the Serra Pelada, the gold miners' camp. They supplied to logging companies, brickworks, sawmills, furniture makers and gold mining (vessels and machines). The business in question prospered so well that, in the 1980s, the total business area was increased. At that time, the company had a separate repair shop on the outskirts of the city and even owned its own trucks and employed a number of drivers. Although it belonged to one of the most flourishing branches in the commercial sector, this company also had to deal with declining sales during the rainy season. Main and side roads then became impassable, making Altamira difficult to reach for the rural population. Construction and gold mining were virtually at a standstill. Moreover, at around that time the purchasing power of the rural population was at its lowest, as virtually nothing was harvested and sold.

It was easy to deduce from the composition of the goods package of these cases which sectors of the economy were doing well at the time. For the suppliers of agricultural inputs, this included dairy farming and cheese production. For the motorcycle specialist, these were mainly gold mining and alternative energy supplies.[161] The first candidates for machinery in the field of dairy and alternative energy were the producers and *fazendeiros*; the commercial dairy sector was mainly a matter for *fazendeiros*.

The specialist shops visited in agricultural means of production were the organisations EMATER and EMBRAPA engaged in the dissemination of new seed varieties and other innovations.[162]

In the marketing sphere, too, cooperatives made way for private trading firms in the second half of the 1970s. The number started to increase only when both production and price levels of rice and cocoa went up. As far as cocoa is concerned, this was mainly after 1981. In 1984 there were fifteen cocoa and pepper buying firms, of which at least six were registered. The firms also traded in maize, beans and Brazil nuts. As for the food crops rice and maize, they took over part of the market from the government buying body, the Companhia Brasileira de Armazenamento (CIBRAZEM). How much that was always depended on the difference between the officially fixed minimum price and the price on the free market. As a rule, the trading companies that bought grains also had a rice huller; the processed rice was sold on the local market or to traders from other regions. CIBRAZEM supplied to Belém, for the urban food supply there, but also to São Paulo and Rio de Janeiro.[163] The better quality pepper and cocoa found their way to the export companies in Belém. The lower quality cocoa was sold on to domestic industries. One of the largest trading firms in Altamira also planned to purchase and process cotton.

COOPERFRON, a private cooperative founded in 1973, was threatened with the same fate as the other cooperatives in the early 1980s. The cost of selling products was

160 Volbeda regarded this industry as one of the activities of great importance for the opening up of a frontier. In this case, the clearing of the rainforest. As a frontier consolidates, companies in the industry will become more focused on machines (Volbeda 1984, 228 and 238).

161 The specialist shops supplied water pumps and suction systems.

162 In the early stages of a frontier, such specialty stores usually supply inputs for deforestation and construction (roads and commercial buildings). In a consolidated frontier, these matters are involved in the further development of the agricultural economy (Volbeda 1984, 237 f.).

163 Altamira has traditionally been a supplier of rice to other regions.

high due to the lack of local infrastructure, there was a lack of equity capital and the *colonos* with their different social backgrounds were difficult to organise, according to officials from EMATER and the Banco do Brasil. EMATER reorganised the cooperative. In 1985, COOPERFRON again had a number of sales points in villages along the Transamazônica for the sale of foodstuffs and agricultural production supplies at a reduced price.

Of the six private banks that Altamira had in the mid-1980s, four had been added after 1978.[164] They were particularly attracted by the growing urban and agricultural middle class and the expanding urban commercial sector. The Federal banks stimulated the development of infrastructure with their loans and helped to start up new companies. The private banks, on the other hand, limited themselves to subsidising already existing profitable agricultural and commercial enterprises.[165] The bank the author visited (Bradesco) also had a branch in Pacal, in the centre of the sugar cane, cocoa and pepper producing zone, 90 km west of Altamira.

While the rural environment managed to attract a number of regionally-powered mining and logging companies, the industrial firms present in Altamira had mostly gone no further than supplying the local market, which was very small. Another problem was the high cost of energy supply and transport. Large-scale production was therefore difficult to achieve. The majority of industrial firms fell under the "mini" and "small" category.[166] They were not officially registered and therefore paid no tax. A number of important industries grew and fell according to the economic situation in the primary sector and the construction industry.

Good examples of the situation of industry in Altamira were the sawmills/woodworking and furniture factories.[167]

The construction boom of the years 1970–1972 also brought a partial revival of the wood processing with it, but when the boom was over, it took a number of sawmills.[168] As in commerce, most owners were out to get rich as quickly as possible, close the business and start something else. What also often happened was that the owner closed his business at the end of the dry season, fired the workers and then opened a new business after the rainy season.

In the second half of the seventies new sawmills were built. They were set up by successful equity farmers or timber traders from the Southern states, where continued deforestation and increased competition had greatly reduced the prospects for growth. Presumably, the large-scale deforestation that preceded the establishment of livestock farms had opened up new perspectives. Favorable financing options and low interest rates also played a role, for example, in the purchase of land.

164 Of the private banks, I spoke only to the Bradesco branch manager.

165 I was also aware of one bank that dealt in artificial insemination on their own fazendas.

166 The line between "mini" and "small" was based on the number of ORTN (*Obrigações Reajústaveis do Tesouro Nacional*), expressing the annual "faturamento."

167 Although the cabinet-making in the region had a traditional character, it is treated here as industry, according to the statistical sources. The differences between sawmills/woodworkers on the one hand and furniture makers on the other will be accentuated, where relevant. Wood processing was the most important industrial sector in terms of employment (in 1978–1979: 47 % of industrial employment; data from F.I.E.P.A.).

168 Sawmills are usually directly involved in the opening of a frontier. In the Altamira region, however, timber extraction did not reach such a high level, because of the high supply costs.

Most of the local sawmills were small and unregistered.[169] The small businesses ran on a limited amount of their own capital and had a highly variable turnover because they were highly dependent on the construction industry, which almost came to a standstill during the rainy season. In the rainy months, the companies worked below their capacity and also employed fewer people. The entrepreneurs were then forced to live on their wood stocks, as transport was almost impossible. In contrast to the large companies, which produced for export, the small companies did not have good means of transport and or skilled workers. For the banks, their financing entailed too much risk; production and sales were too unstable. Only the large export-oriented companies received loans to finance fixed capital (including machinery), according to the BASA branch manager. The small sawmills tried to keep their heads above water by making a deal with *fazendeiros* or *colonos* for their timber supply.[170,171] In order to reduce production costs, the business owners sought to integrate cabinetmaking and sawmill into one firm. Two of the four carpenters visited already had a sawing installation and the other two were planning to buy one.

The furniture makers (who worked to order) had to depend mainly on certain specialisations, for which a regular customer base could be found among traders, construction companies or *fazendeiros*.[172] This was because they were starting to experience more competition from specialist shops that sold ready-made furniture with the option of paying in instalments.

Other industries visited had to have a specific customer base, partly outside Altamira, or specific fast-growing rural economic activities, such as gold mining and rubber culture. An example of the former was an aluminum ware factory that specialised in aluminum vehicle number plates.

Finally, an example of a company with highly mechanised operations, which had established itself in Altamira with government support, namely a modern coffee roaster opened in 1981, which partly ran on coffee beans supplied from the Centro-Sul. After just a few years, the company was able to expand the number of employees and even employed its own drivers. The modern equipment came from São Paulo. The government granted a guarantee subsidy in case sales declined too much. Altamira was the only sales market. The other coffee roasters suffered a languishing existence.

According to data from the Instituto Brasileiro de Geografía e Estatística (IBGE) and the Federação Industrial do Estado do Pará (FIEPA), the industrial sector showed rapid growth in the second half of the 1970s. The statistics recorded as new industries,

169 There were six sawmills within a radius of 5 km and in Altamira itself (IBDF registered). According to one manager, there were as many as eight, four of which were visited. Along the Transamazônica in the direction of Itaituba there were at least eight sawmills, towards Marabá at least one. In Altamira itself there were eight furniture factories, three of which were visited.

170 Some sawmills even owned a piece of forest, which was cleared by hired workers. The companies had to pay tax for this.

171 *Colonos* used to use the forest reserve that was not allowed to be cut down when agriculture yielded too little income.

172 For example, one of the furniture makers visited had mainly *fazendeiros* as regular customers, because it had specialised in the construction of large stern gates (*cancelbas*) for *fazendas*. In the rainy months, turnover fell sharply due to the poor accessibility of the roads and declining activity.

among others, the manufacturing of building materials, electrical engineering and communications.[173]

The processing of export cultures did not take place in Altamira. At the most, the producers and trading companies provided pre-processing (*prebeneficiamento*) with separate installations or hand tools. The processing of rice did take place in Altamira, in rice hullers.

The rise of large-scale retail and wholesale trade

The strong growth of the population and the emergence of a middle class of civil servants, engineers and professionals with purchasing power changed the retail industry. Supermarkets as well as speciality shops in consumer durables were opened. Three of the five registered speciality stores were added after 1980. The change went along, among other things. with improving supply. The bridges of the Transamazônica were renewed and the Belém–Brasília road was asphalted, allowing goods from Centro-Sul to arrive more quickly in Altamira.

Until 1976–1977 there were only two supermarkets, eight years later there were already eight. Some chain stores had two or three branches. A striking feature was the supermarket that was part of a company that also had businesses in related sectors or supply companies. The two largest firms had their own rice hullers. One also had a *fazenda* and a vegetable farm. Another firm also owned a chicken farm. This was in order to limit high supply costs from elsewhere as much as possible. Cost-cutting and larger-scale sales made the supermarkets cheaper than the small grocers and the *secos e molhados*. Several mini-supermarkets had to deal with increasing competition in the early eighties, which had "broken their necks," according to the entrepreneur of one of the companies.

The supermarkets focused especially on the urban middle class. This was apparent from the sale of prepackaged and purified rice, sugar and vegetables that came all the way from São Paulo or Central Brazil and were therefore also more expensive than the local products.[174] At the beginning of the rainy season, the prices of goods supplied from Centro-Sul skyrocketed.[175] One supermarket followed the other.

As for the supermarkets, the situation also changed for businesses that supplied durable consumer goods. The business owners of the local Volkswagen garage and one out of five furniture and household appliances shops whom I interviewed pointed to the favorable development of purchasing power, not only in Altamira itself but also in the rural area, as a result of the newly emerged export cultures and extensive livestock farming.[176] This was also reflected in the fact that the VW company largely relied on *fazendeiros* and cocoa and pepper producers when it came to customers outside Altamira.

173 Data from FIEPA/IBGE.

174 For example, prepackaged rice from São Paulo cost 1300 to 1500 cruzeiros and rice from the region cost about 900 Cr$. For coffee this was 2800 Cr$ against 1600 Cr$ for a pack from the local roaster.

175 Prices rose on average by 30 to 40 %, for some scarce vegetables they even doubled.

176 Volkswagen had branches in Itaituba, Santarém, Marabá and Imperatriz (on the Belém–Brasília road). The latter was also for trucks. Such companies mainly sought out the already more consolidated urban settlements (Volbeda 1982b, 234).

But *colonos* and urban lower income groups also formed part of the sales market; they could buy on credit. The VW branch even supplied cars to residents of Porto de Mós and São Felix do Xingu. Along the Transamazônica, the catchment area extended to a distance of 200 km.

Employment in this sector developed favourably.[177] The VW department even wanted to start a separate company for Ford in 1985. Businesses in this sector also did not escape declining turnover during the rainy season.

Transport and services

The number of transport companies has steadily increased, thanks to the resurgent commerce, agricultural export cultures and activities in timber extraction and mining.[178] It was essential to improve the connections between Altamira and Centro-Sul during this time. The asphalting of the Belém–Brasília road played a crucial role in this. The largest shipping company opened its gates in Altamira in the same year that the port of Vitória was modernised.[179] In 1980 the company started using trailers (*carretas*) that could be used for both land and water transport, so that intermediate loading and unloading was no longer necessary.[180] The road transport company I visited came to Altamira in 1980 to arrange transport for one of the mining companies.[181] After the contract was terminated, the company established contacts with commercial companies. The airline company VASP opened a separate freight department in Altamira in 1980, which fell directly under the head office in São Paulo.

The shipping companies and road transport companies had permanent contracts with wholesalers, supermarkets and specialist shops in consumer durables. One of the shipping companies was even responsible for transporting production supplies to the sugar cane-producing zone around Pacal. The airline had contracts with some mining companies and with the private engineering firm that carried out preparatory work for the construction of a hydroelectric power station. During the rainy season, shipping companies and airlines took over the task of road transport, because the Transamazonica was usually closed to traffic.

Altamira exported rice, maize, cocoa, pepper, rubber and timber to Belém (across the river) and cocoa to factories elsewhere in Brazil. The export of tin ore and gold had risen sharply since 1980. The trade in Brazil nuts, on the other hand, had fallen sharply.

The imports were made up as follows: foodstuffs and clothing; cars and household appliances, furniture; machines and machine parts and other means of production for the primary and secondary sector (iron, building materials), medicines and, some-

177 The furniture/household appliances shop I visited started in 1982 with two employees and had ten in 1985. The Volkswagen branch had a total of 50 employees.

178 The information below is based on interviews with the two shipping companies, one of the two freight carriers (the largest) and one of the four registered road transport companies.

179 The shipping company also had branches in Santarém and Itaituba.

180 The trailers could be transported by water (on rafts) as well as by land.

181 The company still had a branch in Itaituba and planned to establish itself in Santarém and Marabá. The company had already opened a number of branches in the state of Rondônia in the 1970s.

times, poultry. Fuel for electricity generation was brought in by road from a depot on the Xingu, 70 km east.

Because of the high transport rates and the local employment situation, local road transport a circuit of unregistered transport small businesses had arisen, usually with one or just a few drivers. They formed an active link in the connections between Altamira and various towns along the Transamazônica.

Of the other service activities, repairs stood out in particular as a fast growing industry.[182] The company visited was one of three registered repair shops in the metal industry. It not only repaired tools used for gold mining, but also manufactured them themselves. The owner had come to Altamira when exploration of the area was expanding greatly.[183] Gold mining came to a standstill in the rainy season, during which the company fell back on the repair of small machines and cars for mining companies and government institutions and others. The number of employees remained stable during the rainy months, unlike many local sawmills. Another company, which specialised in turning, had government agencies and mining companies as regular customers. These provided the regular income, leaving room to supply credit to other companies.

With regard to other services, the growing number of lawyers, private doctors and clinics was remarkable. The growth was the result of steadily increasing private land ownership and the expanding urban middle class.

Government policy in the early 1980s

The development strategy set out by the Federal government in the mid-1970s was continued into the 1980s. The big difference was that public investment went to a more limited number of projects. In other areas, the government withdrew in favour of private initiative. That implied that various agencies, which depended on the Federal government for their financial resources, had to make do with less. The POLAMAZONIA and the Programa de Redistribução de Terras (Proterra) programmes have been discontinued.[184] Most tax breaks for extensive livestock farming were also abolished.[185] The agency for federal roads, the Departamento Nacional de Estadas deRodagem (DNER), received less money. And the regional development agency SUDAM also had to lose a lot of financial scope and influence.

---

182 In 1970 there were 26 branches with 70 employees, between 1985 and 1990, 67 (registered) branches with 215 employees (Figures: IBGE 1984a and b).

183 Until 1980 he worked in Itaituba, the "El Dorado" of gold mining in the 1970s. In the early 1980s, the centre of gravity would move inland, south of Itaituba.

184 PROTERRA was a programme initiated in 1971 for the distribution of waste lands of *latifundios* among the small farmers and landless workers in the North and Northeast. Later it became a subsidy pot for the agro-industry, livestock farming and infrastructural projects. (Goodman and Redclift 1981, 145).

185 One of the vets based in Altamira pointed out that a number of ranchers no longer called in a separate doctor. The immediate reason was the implemented salary increase, but in the background were the reversed tax benefits and the stagnation in the regional livestock sector.

Photo 17. Altamira's commercial centre where goods from the South could be bought (1985)

Photo 18. Another part of the commercial centre

Photo 20. Illustration of the construction boom and of the expected rise of incomes, mid-1980s (1985)

Federal banks had to accept a cut in rural lending imposed by the Central Bank. They were forced to limit themselves to those companies and branches of commerce from which a reasonable production volume could be expected and sales were assured, according to an official of the Banco do Brasil.

The Federal government expected all the salvation from a few large-scale mining projects, in which it supplied the energy. The best known project was that of the Grande Carajás adjacent to the dam at Tucurui. Here, too, the gigantic infrastructure had to attract foreign investors.

These changes in Federal government policy did not leave the Altamira/Transamazônica untouched: The local branch of the DNER conducted a selective maintenance programme from 1981. The priorities were at the connection with Vitória and with the regional petrol depot. Also the section of the Transamazônica westwards was in fair condition, because that was where the cocoa, pepper, sugar cane and mahogany came from. The large companies and the fazendas had their own means of transport and took care of the maintenance themselves.

As far as the energy supply was concerned, Altamira had to make do provisionally with a diesel generator for the generation of electricity. A request for a connection to the grid of the future Tucuruí plant, which would be cheaper, was rejected.

It was expected that the open choice of the banks for large companies producing goods for export would also lead to a greater concentration of land ownership along the Transamazônica, a process that had already started with the announcement of the Polamazonia project, and existed even before that.[186]

186 Before that, there was already an extremely skewed distribution of land ownership. The statistical office IDESP stated in its research report on the municipality of Altamira that, in 1970, 42 % of the agricultural area was taken up by only 0.7 % of the number of companies.

It was also expected that the emerging rural middle class of *fazendeiros* and wealthy producers of commercial exports would control an increasing part of the production process and that small farmers would become involved. Their power was based on ownership of the land, the possession of means of transport and of storage facilities and other means of production.

In 1982, the INCRA launched a new colonisation project for small farmers, 120–140 km east of Altamira (4000 *lotes* of 100 ha each), but the *colonos* involved received nowhere near the support they needed. Schools and health posts were lacking, so that the newly arrived *colonos* were forced to rely on Altamira for those. Access to the project area was very poor; the side roads were poorly maintained and barely passable during the rainy season, which made sales very difficult. The boundaries between the project area and the neighboring large *fazendas* were not clearly marked and gave rise to land conflicts. The *colonos* were in danger of losing their land unintentionally.

This did not mean that the Altamira/Transamazônica region had completely disappeared from the attention of the Federal government. The 1980s also brought new potential growth prospects.

Modern extractivism and the alternative energy supply (1980-1984)

In 1982, the Federal government started participating in the programme to increase rubber production called Probor (Programa da Borracha). The programme was intended to boost the productivity of declining rubber production areas and establish new rubber plantations. With this, Brazil hoped to become self-sufficient in rubber again. This programme had already started in 1972 and was initially limited to the Amazon region.[187] The 1982–1987 programme aimed for 250 000 hectares of new rubber plantings across the country. The financial support of the programme by the Federal government was (partly) motivated by the need of the motor tyre industry in São Paulo for cheap raw materials.[188]

The coordinating body for this programme, the Superintendência de Hevea (SUDHEVEA), stimulated the cultivation of new varieties (in collaboration with EMBRAPA), provided technical guidance (in collaboration with EMATER), mediated in the start-up of rubber processing mini-companies and traded the purchased rubber to industries in São Paulo. The Banco do Brasil supported the processing companies by subsidising machines, production supplies and even the supply of the raw material. Only the rubber had to be bought by the grower. The bank even participated in PROBOR with its own financial resources, in the expectation that it would bring more stability to the rural sector, according to the agronomist of the Banco do Brasil.

SUDHEVEA did not come to Altamira until 1982, but rubber tapping in cultivated stocks was initiated by EMATER as early as 1975.[189] Until then, it was still extracted in the traditional way. It was collected by rubber tappers and bought up by traders, who

187 During the years 1972–1982, 140 000 hectares of rubber trees were to be planted in Amazônia.

188 As an illustration: the Banco da Amazônia stimulated the sale of the rubber processed in Altamira to the Firestone motor tyre factory in São Paulo.

189 The working area of the Altamira site extended into the municipalities of Altamira, Prainha, São José Porphirio, São Felix do Xingu and Porto de Mós.

transported the rubber in its unprocessed state to Belém. Some landowners made use of the subsidies provided by PROBOR.[190] They started planting rubber plantations or setting up processing businesses.[191] *Fazendeiros* also signed up for the laying out of rubber plantations.

Nor did the rubber programme escape the pruning of the austerity measures. While the interest rate itself had risen sharply, the adjustment of the interest rate to inflation was increased from 35 % to 80 %. As a result, most *seringalistas* were no longer interested in laying out plantations, which would only yield something after five years.[192] A few switched to the production and marketing of seedlings at their own expense. That was more attractive because the stage of production would then be reached earlier.

Traditional rubber tapping also declined, as many rubber tappers turned to gold mining for their fortune. However, a number of them returned to their old places when the gold business disappointed them.

The rubber processing mini-companies failed to reach their production capacity.[193] They didn't have enough capital to buy sufficient latex. In addition, the landowners preferred to sell the collected rubber to merchants, because it then yielded more for them.

In Altamira itself, a rubber processing company was set up in 1983 by local *seringalistas*. They chose Altamira as their location not only because the raw material was available nearby, but also because SUDHEVEA strongly encouraged location in Altamira. After the company was set up with its own financial means, the bank assisted with the purchase of raw rubber, current expenses and the sale of the processed rubber in São Paulo. Even the maintenance of their own rubber trees was subsidised. They had their own freight boats for transport to Belém. The factory employed about twenty workers who were attracted locally.

Mining also started to expand. The French company Canopus began the production of tin ore in 1983. The Brazilian company Taboca also wanted to start mining gold. Two other companies came to the Xingu to do the same. One of them was partly subsidised as a SUDAM project, partly because the gold mined would be sold to the state.

Gold mining in Amazônia was intensified after the government had decided to pay off part of the foreign debt with the national gold reserves. In order to increase gold production, not only were some gold searchers' camps reopened, but the doors were also opened wide for large-scale exploitation.

Lastly, the Altamira/Transamazônica region was also given a task in providing for the national energy supply. A private engineering firm in Altamira began preliminary research for the construction of a hydroelectric power station, which had to be completed in 1996. Construction was due to start in 1989.

---

190 One of the most important subsidies was that the adjustment of the interest rate to inflation was only made for 35 % instead of 100 %.

191 One of the potential advantages was that the latex itself could serve directly as a raw material for the mini-companies and did not have to be defumed first. This meant that the rubber tapper either had more time for his own food supply or could tap more rubber trees per round. Fewer rubber tappers were then needed.

192 A *seringalista* is a large landowner who also has rubber trees on his land. He hires workers to tap the rubber.

193 In 1984/85 there were three mini-companies in the region. One near Porto de Mós, one near Vitória and one at Km 115, west of Altamira. Each had an average of four employees.

In the philosophy of the state-owned company Eletronorte, the hydroelectric power station was to supply energy (CHECK) to the future metallurgical-industrial industry complex that will process the minerals of Carajás. But the primary concern was to achieve an integrated national electricity grid. If the Centro-Sul rivers reached too low a water level to make a satisfactory contribution to the local energy supply, power stations in the North could be called in to help.

Altamira's altered functional structure (1980-1985)

What did the developments outlined above mean for the functional structure of the town of Altamira?

The hydroelectric power station would almost certainly trigger another construction boom, since, in addition to the work on the dam itself, the road network would have to be adapted and a complete residential area for 50 000 people would have to be built for the employees. The engineering firm already employed no fewer than 120 people, most of whom came from Altamira itself. The construction boom had already been foreshadowed in the early 1980s by the expansion of the number of large warehouses for building materials.[194] Two more were built in 1983 and 1984, commissioned by a wholesaler and *fazendeiros*. Private engineering firms were also attracted by the construction boom.

In the retail sector, the impending construction boom had only accelerated the process of scaling-up. One of the largest retail firms planned to open a supermarket-cum-department store in 1985. The owner of the VW branch had a Ford garage built. He also referred to the construction boom and the residential area as his incentive. He wanted to put more expensive models on the market. The relocation of a sawmill to Altamira should also be mentioned. The owner did this, for one reason, to make it easier to obtain cheaper electricity in the future.[195]

Developments were also underway in the field of agricultural research and the introduction of new crops that would have an impact on the urban functional structure. In 1984–1985, EMATER and EMBRAPA began to introduce the *guaraná* fruit and cotton as commercial cultures in the region. *Guaraná* was an indigenous fruit, for which there was a lot of demand, so that sales seemed assured. Cotton, introduced by producers from the Northeast and South, had the advantage that it also thrived on less fertile soil. One of the large trading firms in Altamira had planned to set up a cotton processing plant and had already bought a piece of land for it.

In 1983, EMATER, in collaboration with smallholders from the South, started to set up commercial vegetable farms in the immediate vicinity of Altamira.[196] In this way they hoped to do something about the very expensive import of vegetables from Centro-Sul. An EMATER official said that, since then, imports had fallen by 10 %. The

---

194 There were four large warehouses in Altamira in early 1985; three of these had been added after 1979.

195 Altamira was also more attractive to him as a business location because of the abundant supply of especially stable workers and because of the direct proximity to workshops for maintenance and repair.

196 At that time (1984) there were 15 nurseries in operation throughout the region, four of which were in the immediate vicinity of Altamira. Each nursery employed two to four people.

nurseries also focused on seeds, because it was the high supply costs of seeds that had hindered the cultivation of vegetables on a large scale. In order to stimulate the commercialisation of vegetables, a municipal market was opened in 1983. A second market hall was under construction at the time (financed by the SUDAM, among others). In this way it was hoped to stimulate the direct sale of food crops (Umbuzeiro 1983, 5).

To conclude

Altamira is one of the oldest urban settlements in the Brazilian Amazon and was therefore a landmark, focal point and operating base in the construction of the *Transamazônica*. After the road reached it, Altamira went through a spectacular development, as a result of which it had undergone a complete metamorphosis within ten years and fulfilled many new functions, almost entirely as a result of the measures of the Federal government aimed at the physical and economic integration of Amazônia. The development was not unique to Altamira. In other places, too, such as Marabá, Itaituba and Santarém, a radical change took place. What has been described for Altamira in this chapter is therefore also illustrative of the changes brought about by the *Transmazônica* and other access routes elsewhere.

References

Coelho de Lima, Sebastião. 1983. *Agricultura da subsistência na região de Altamira (PA)*. Altamira: Banco do Brasil/Agência de Altamira.

Dias, Hiran D. 1984. "Can Small Towns Help Farmers?" In *Equity with Growth? Planning Perspectives for Small Towns in Developing Countries*, edited by Hans Detlef Kammeier, and Peter Swan, 171-193. Bangkok: Asian Institute of Technology.

FIEPA/CEAG. 1982. *Cadastro Industrial do Pará 1980/81*. Belém: Federação Industrial do Estado do Pará/CEAG.

Gazeta do Xingu. 1984. Ano IV, No. 43, 6 November: n. p.

Goodman, D., and M. Redclift. 1981. *From Peasant to Proletarian; Capitalist Development and Agrarian Transitions*. Oxford: Blackwell.

IBGE. 1976a. *Censo Comercial 1975 – Pará*, Vol. 4, No. 6. Rio de Janeiro: IBGE.

IBGE. 1976b. *Censo dos Serviços 1975 – Pará*, Vol. 5, No. 4. Rio de Janeiro: IBGE.

IBGE. 1977. *Geografia do Brasil. Vol. 1: Região Norte*. Rio de Janeiro: Superintendência de Estudos Geográficos e Socio-econômicos, Departamento de Geografia.

IBGE. 1982. *Pesquisa Industrial 1979 – Regiões Norte e Centro-Oeste*, Vol. 7, No. 1. Rio de Janeiro: IBGE.

IBGE. 1983a. *IBGE-Altamira, Monografia Informativa*. Município de Altamira.

IBGE. 1983b. *Censo Demográfico – Pará* (IX Recenseamento Geral do Brasil – 1980, Vol. 1, Tomo 3, No. 4). Rio de Janeiro: IBGE.

IBGE. 1984a. *Censo Comercial – Pará* (IX Recenseamento Geral do Brasil – 1980, Vol. 4, No. 6). Rio de Janeiro: IBGE.

IBGE. 1984b. *Censo dos Serviços – Pará* (IX Recenseamento Geral do Brasil – 1980, Vol. 5, No. 6). Rio de Janeiro: IBGE.

IDESP/SEP. 1977. *Diagnóstico do município de Altamira*. Belém: Instituto Brasileiro de Direito e Politica de Seguranca Publica.

Kammeier, Hans Detlef, and Peter Swan, eds. 1984. *Equity with Growth? Planning Perspectives for Small Towns in Developing Countries*. Bangkok: Asian Institute of Technology.

Matznetter, Josef. 1981. "O sistema urbano no norte e nordeste do Brasil e a influência das novas estradas." *Revista Brasileira de Geografia* 43, No. 1, January/March: 99–121.

Milder, Ron. 1986. *Een nieuwe weg voor Altamira. De ontwikkeling van Altamira en haar regio na de aanleg van de Transamazônica*. Unpublished Master Thesis, Nijmegen.

Moran, Emilio F. 1981. *Developing the Amazon. The Social and Ecological Consequences of Government-directed Colonization along Brazil's Transamazonian Highway*. Bloomington: Indiana University Press.

Prelazia do Xingu. 1984. *Relatório da Prelazia do Xingu, preparação para a Assembleia de outubro de 1984*. Altamira.

SEPLAN. 1980. *Plano Anual de Trabalho – Município de Altamira, Estado do Pará*. Belém: Sistema Estadual de Planejamento.

SERFHAU/Ministério do Interior. 1970. *Município de Altamira, 1970*. Relatório preliminar de desenvolvimento integrado. São Paulo: SERFHAU.

SUDAM. 1976. *Programa de Pólos Agropecuários e Agrominerais da Amazônia (POLAMAZÔNIA) – Pólo Altamira*. Belém: SUDAM, Coordenação de Informática, Divisão de Documentação.

SUDAM. 1980. *Amazônia Legal, hierquia urbana*, Vol. III. Belém: Engerix S.A./SUDAM Departamento DDL.

Umbuzeiro, Ubirajara Marquez. 1983. *Altamira a sua história*. Altamira: Prefeitura Municipal de Altamira.

Volbeda, Sjoukje. 1982a. *Urbanisatie in Amazônia Legal. Een identificatie van pionierssteden*. Nijmegen: Katholieke Universiteit Nijmegen.

Volbeda, Sjoukje. 1982b. "Urbanization in the Frontiers of the Brazilian Amazon and the Expulsion of Pioneers from the Agricultural Sector from 1960 to the Present." *Boletín de Estudios Latinoamericanos y del Caribe* 33: 35–59.

Volbeda, Sjoukje. 1984. *Pioniersteden in het oerwoud. Stedelijke ontwikkelingen aan een agrarisch kolonisatiefront in het Braziliaanse Amazonegebied*. Ph.D. thesis, Nijmeegen.